NO BLEEDING HEART

NO BLEEDING HEART:
Charlotte Whitton
A FEMINIST ON THE RIGHT

P. T. ROOKE
and
R. L. SCHNELL

UNIVERSITY OF BRITISH COLUMBIA PRESS
VANCOUVER 1987

NO BLEEDING HEART: CHARLOTTE WHITTON, A FEMINIST ON THE RIGHT

© The University of British Columbia Press 1987

This book has been published with the help of a Canada Council grant.

Canadian Cataloguing in Publication Data
Rooke, Patricia T.
  No bleeding heart

Includes bibliographical references and index.
ISBN 0-7748-0237-5

1. Whitton, Charlotte, 1896-1975. 2. Mayors-Ontario-Ottawa-Biography. 3. Social workers-Canada-Biography. 4. Feminists-Canada-Biography. I. Schnell, R.L. (Rodolph L.). II. Title.
FC3096.26.W5R6 1987 971.3'84 C86-091569-7
F1059.5.09R6 1987

International Standard Book Number 0-7748-0237-5

Printed in Canada

DEDICATION

*To all those single women who "married"
into their professions thus opening them to
the generations that followed.*

CONTENTS

ILLUSTRATIONS

Photo credits: Plates 1-10, 16, 18, 19, 22-25, 27 and 28 are reproduced courtesy of the Public Archives of Canada. Plates 11 and 21 appear courtesy of the Glenbow Archives. Thanks are due to the Library of Congress for plates 13, 14 and 15. Plate 20 is from the University of Toronto Archives. Plate 26 is reproduced courtesy of *Maclean's* Magazine. The inset of plate 23 appears courtesy of *Saturday Night*. Plate 17 is a photograph of the authors'.

PREFACE

The origins of this book go back to 1978 when we embarked on the research which culminated in a study of child rescue in Canada, *Discarding the Asylum* (1983). The most happy event of that experience was our "discovery" of Charlotte Whitton as a key figure in child welfare history. As immigrants our knowledge of the contemporary political scene was spotty; however as we worked through the Canadian Council on Social Development Papers and began our initial foray into the yet unprocessed Whitton Papers at the Public Archives of Canada, we quickly came to realize that there was far more to the "feisty Mayor Whitton" than the folk heroine.

Charlotte Whitton was the historian's delight—a public figure who had left a mass of correspondence, speeches, and published material which was supported by the records of the most important voluntary social welfare organization in Canadian history. The organizational link was tremendously important because it enabled us to understand what a determined, intelligent and energetic individual could create out of generalized sentiment about children and the advancement of women.

During the next seven years, we came to know Whitton better than most of her closest friends could have. We appreciated her social philosophy—if not her politics, marvelled at her ability to unearth humbug, and grew to admire her feminism and indomitable spirit. At the same time, she disappointed us with her racism, fear of the undeserving poor, and vindictive outbursts. In brief, Charlotte Whitton proved an immensely intriguing and complex personality. Her very humanness, with its strengths and flaws (both of which were always startlingly passionate) shattered all stereotypes about women and about feminism.

The present study is not the full blown biography she deserves. There is far more to be said about her work at the League of Nations, her genius in building up the CWC, her lasting contribution to social work training, and her role in standardizing child welfare practice and policy across the nation. The restraints of publishing in Canada have shaped our work into an intellectual odyssey of a pioneering Canadian professional woman who set high goals for herself in the heady, final days of the female suffrage campaign only to find that vistas apparently opening up to women were largely illusions. If Charlotte Whitton was a complex individual, the world she inherited, struggled with, and partially changed was as flawed and as uncertain as she.

As a collaborative effort we have brought our individual interests, assumptions, and talents to the enterprise. The interaction of ideas and institutions with a feeling for psychological and human motivation contributed to the direction that the study ultimately took. The end product reflects our specific contributions in the two major themes of the book, that of feminism and female networks, and that of political thought and institutional development.

Like the winners of the Academy Awards, historians have more acknowledgements to make than most other scholars. We especially acknowledge all those archivists who have been uniformly helpful in guiding us through a myriad of collections at the Public Archives of Canada, Queen's University, and even the Public Record Office in London. Françoise Houle will long be remembered for her prompt and enthusiastic response to our request to process the Whitton Papers in 1979. Kathleen Whitton Ryan clarified several points regarding her sister's childhood and family. Over the years, Anne Marie Main has cheerfully typed with genuine interest many of our Whitton articles.

Shaun Penfold has been with us through more drafts of the manuscript than any of us wish to recall. Her energy, good humour, and meticulousness were remarkable during those times of frustration and urgency. Her energy has earned our greatest admiration. We owe a special thank you to our friends Dave and Donnie Jenkins who listened to our trials and uncertainties during the period of writing and with whom we enjoyed, over many dinners and much wine, numerous long conversations about "CW." The remarkable Dr. Whitton has shared their lives as well as our own and life will be rather dull without her.

Finally, we cannot overlook Jane Fredeman of the UBC Press who recognized the possibilities of our manuscript and whose ruthless and impartial editing and scrupulous and imaginative efforts helped us to isolate the book's two major themes.

Introduction

WHITTON AS LEGEND

So indigenous to the Ottawa scene is this volatile woman, and so vivid a personal splash in the Canadian mosaic, that sometimes her larger role in the country's history can be neglected.

LOTTA DEMPSEY, 1970.

Charlotte Whitton's 1917 Queen's graduation picture bears the prophetic inscription, "She will brook no tarrying—where she comes the winds will stir." Until her death in 1975, Whitton was in perpetual motion: voted Canada's "Woman of the Year" on six occasions, she had inexhaustible energy and drive, powerful personal ambition, an indomitable passion for service, and a gift for leadership. The "facts" alone of her public life are formidable. After working with the Social Service Council of Canada, Whitton guided the major national child welfare agency—The Canadian Welfare Council—from its infancy to maturity between 1922 and 1941. After she retired from its directorship, Whitton spent nine years lecturing across Canada and the United States, establishing a reputation as a popular publicist and journalist, keeping her social work connections as a commissioner into public welfare, and writing *The Dawn of Ampler Life* (1943), which examined the principles behind social security. During the 1940s, she earned a reputation as an outspoken feminist who both defended "women in gainful occupation" and berated them for political inertia. Finally, in 1950 Whitton embarked on a "second career" in civic politics. Elected first as a controller, Whitton was mayor of Ottawa five times before being defeated in 1964. Afterwards, she served as a city controller again for a further eight years.

Whitton deplored women's complicity in the male dominated socio-economic order and their willingness to cut sandwiches or become well-meaning but politically impotent and mute "auxiliaries." In this, she articulated the restlessness of many women. Her disregard for male privileges and prerogatives, however, estranged many men, and her bluntness was often interpreted as belligerence or highhandedness. Her disdain for fashion, her short bobbed hairstyle, and her disregard for the societal ideas regarding desirable female physical attributes and what was and what is and is not becoming to a "true woman" led to descriptions of her as being "mannish" and "unladylike."

Certainly, Whitton's "adder sharp tongue, keen satirical wit, terrifying memory and tremendous knowledge" are the stuff of legend. Statements such as "Whatever my sex, I'm no lady," made at city hall when an alderman implied that certain discussions would be inappropriate because she was present, kept the capital entertained. And still repeated is her terse comment, "Whatever women do they must do twice as well as men to be thought half as good. Luckily it's not difficult."

The legend, however, is based almost wholly on the final third of Whitton's life. Whitton was much more than a politician and celebrity. A remarkably successful career in child and social welfare placed her in the fore of a first generation of professional women who were dependent upon female support structures in their private and public lives and upon female role models to guide them and inspire them through the perplexities of newly emerging single status career patterns early in this century. Whitton's own friends and role models included such prominent American social welfare reformers as Frances Perkins, Edith and Grace Abbott, and Katharine Lenroot, the British Labour member of parliament, Margaret Bondfield, and distinguished Canadian suffragists and social activists as Emily Murphy (Janey Canuck) of Alberta and Helen R.Y. Reid of Montreal.

Whitton's personality and her two careers may be best summarized in the phrase "Public Figure, Private Woman." Besides drawing attention to the public activities and private experiences that make up a remarkable female life, this description conveys a subtle blending of a thoroughly *personalized* life as seen in its public manifestations. In short, Charlotte Whitton was an amazingly personalized public figure. All those problems that intimately challenged her and any hurt or pain or frustration that shaped or thwarted her sense of purpose, either as an individual or as a professional, became universalized and reified through articulate, critical commentary or crusade. A union between public life and private domain emerged from the immediacy of her particular needs and predicament.

An obvious example of the intimate connection between the private and public woman is seen in the hiatus between her two spectacular careers. That dreary decade between 1941 when she resigned from the Canadian Welfare Council and when she sat in city hall in January, 1951, a period of enforced professional retreat, resulted in the bulk of her social criticism. Those ten years of insecurity and impermanency followed nearly a quarter century of productivity, creativity and vigor. Whitton's departure from the CWC was under duress, and for the next ten, long years, she could neither find an appointment equal to that of director of a national welfare organization nor secure an appropriate government appointment. Career changes in the 1940s, especially for women, were hardly the mid-life transitions of the heady 1970s. Mid-life changes were promotions; a move from one successful career to another and a sign of promise and success. For Whitton, the search for a new career was built on failure. That decade between forty-five and fifty-five was not a time of consolidation and achievement but one of scrambling and anxiety.

Out of this frightening hiatus came a serious sense of personal, professional, and social loss, a deprivation of meaning, and the obsession with failure. How could she explain to herself the failure to find an equal appointment to that of the CWC? How could she rationalize such a promiscuously wasteful frustration of her stewardship? Whitton's explanation was formed in the astute rationale and social critique that was her feminist thought. The "boys" were given the "plush executive jobs" and in turn promoted their own favourites—usually men. The "boys" monopolized the political process and positions of power, co-opted men-identified-women as allies and worked against competent women who sought to invade the "compound."

We cannot even tell whether Whitton's *lived* feminism (for she was always committed to equal opportunity, equal rights, equal pay, and equal political responsibility although she did not always articulate it) would have been so eloquently stated or so theoretically based had she not found herself estranged from the mainstream in the forties. Feminists professed a belief in equal opportunity and rewards for women—that there be no distinctions on grounds of gender—and that had always been the brand of Whitton's feminism. She did not see feminism in terms of sexual liberation and saw no need to modify her conventional views on abortion, divorce, family life, and individual or social ethics. Instead, given her imperatives, she argued forthrightly on grounds of work, achievement, contribution, access, and credibility. Since Whitton generalized her own experience, it is doubtful that had she *succeeded* in the forties, she would have produced such an important corpus of feminist thought.

Even Whitton's choice of politics is a curious anomaly in light of her views on women's political participation. The very area she entered—civic politics— had been the one which she had always claimed was particularly appropriate for the *married* woman because she would not have to leave home. The decision by one of the most vocal of the "secular unmarrieds" (who were fitted for national politics and international service) to enter municipal government, therefore, was a serious step. The nation may have acclaimed her successes in Ottawa politics, but this was not the domain to which she had originally aspired. She had been constrained to choose something less because nothing better had been offered. In short, her feminism and her mayoralties were a painful retreat and constituted a psychological resolution that was, at the same time, socially functional, by simultaneously affirming her identity and her public service.

Similarly, Whitton's views on other matters illustrate this penchant for making public capital out of personal defeat and resentment. Several pungent social analyses arose out of her single status and particular grievances. Baby bonuses were a discriminatory subsidy on the childless and marital taxation exemptions, which were denied partnership families or dual households, represented unequal treatment by government. Her relationship with Margaret Grier made her sensitive to the fact that persons in dual households, with or without blood ties, who looked after each other and supported each other in unemployment and illness, were charged higher insurance and medical premiums and were subject to discriminatory inheritance taxes. There is, moreover, an irony in her feminist "fiscal" argument, which while very familiar now was refreshingly uncommon in the forties. We think of the claims of those who cohabit rather than marry and even the claims of homosexual unions which insist that they be accorded equal recognition before the law with the married. Although Whitton would be among the first to reject these as spurious, the unerring logic of her own argument forces similar conclusions.

Whitton's criticisms of the Anglican church were directly in proportion to her exclusion from its governance and the broader implications of according a higher status to the married and mothers than to the unmarried. It is interesting to speculate whether her feminist critique of that institution would have developed if she had married. Her services, after all, had been used by the Church because she was free in the forties to conduct those surveys that drew her attention to the inequities she deplored. Her vigilance over preferments in government or seats in both houses of Parliament (especially women in the Senate) was also predicated on her own frustrated hopes in these matters.

Finally, we can also see Whitton's last crusade in personal terms: the persistent claim that retirement was the ultimate depreciation of identity, a deprivation of social meaning, and that old people were "discarded" while having much to contribute to society. She argued that they must resist compulsory exclusion from the mainstream through militant action. Recent sociological and psychological studies that examine old age, rest homes, pensions, the poverty of female senior citizens, the increasing numbers of people over sixty-five in proportion to the youth argue for an urgent transformation of social attitudes and priorities. Charlotte Whitton anticipated many of these same questions.

The following biographical treatment explores the origins, nature, and extent of Whitton's national, professional, and intellectual development as a Canadian feminist. Her career in child and social welfare, the nine-year hiatus between her resignation from the Canadian Welfare Council in 1941 and her campaign for public office in 1950, and her years in civic politics are all examined in this context. Finally, some attempt is made to assess her place in the history of feminism in Canada.

1

LOTTIE

Through all the song the accompaniment was heard
Now soft and now crescendo always true;
There in a moment stood our President,
Ah Lottie! Thou whose equals are but few.

LEVANA WOMEN'S SOCIETY, 1918.

No longer even a regular stop on the C.P.R., Renfrew, Ontario, was once the hub of county commerce. Home of important industrialists like M.J. O'Brien, who proudly built an opera house, and a hockey team starring the Patricks, Newsy Lalonde, and Cyclone Taylor, which boasted the name "The Millionaires," by the late 19th Century Renfrew's mills and factories produced a wide variety of manufactured goods. There, Charlotte Elizabeth Hazeltyne Whitton was born on 8 March 1896.

Lottie, as she was then called, was never to reveal the attachments which nurtured her first loves, dreams, and loyalties, for she was in many ways a deeply private person despite her public image. The silence that pervades her comments on her early life is suggestive, especially since she was so extroverted normally. Perhaps her experience was too profound or too painful to articulate. Perhaps she felt it as self-indulgent to make those childhood confessions which would demean the struggles of her parents. Charlotte Whitton never betrayed the intimacies that rightly belong to a family unit.

Her father, John Edward Whitton, was born in Belleville, Ontario, in 1871, the grandson of James and Elizabeth Hazeltyne Whitton, who were of austere Yorkshire Methodist stock. They settled in Ontario in the early 1840s and raised a family of fifteen, seven daughters and eight sons. A large, robust man with a mixture of the taciturn and "mischievous," John Whitton was "forbidden the house" by his family when courting Elizabeth Langin, a Roman Catholic of Galway Irish descent born in Rochester, New York, in 1870. Their love was such that they eloped. Wed according to Anglican rites, they agreed to baptize their children into that faith.

To earn a living, John was forced to work as a merchant and caterer for lumber companies "up north" for up to ten months of the year, leaving his wife to cope on a modest income with a household that was made up eventually of four children plus Grandmother Whitton. Matilda Carr Whitton, true to her forbears, disliked both Elizabeth's faith and her ancestry. Despite this, the two women, Grandmother Whitton, separated from her own husband, and Elizabeth Langin, formed a united front based on loyalty to each other in the face of hardship.

In 1907, unable to endure any longer her "churchlessness," Elizabeth returned to the Catholic Church with the three younger children, John Bartholomeau born in 1899, Kathleen in 1904, and Stephen in 1905. Although both John and Elizabeth had remained outside their original communions for a decade, the depth of their gestures differed radically. To move from Methodism to Anglicanism was not the same as leaving Roman Catholicism. When Elizabeth married outside the Church, she bore the full brunt of its condemnation in two areas; first, by living in what the church considered an illegitimate union; and, second, by baptizing and raising her chidren Anglican. Not only was her own soul in jeopardy, but so were her children's. Her desire to return may have been precipitated by the death of a two-year-old daughter, Mary, in 1903. No doubt her decision to do so was strengthened by the "Ne Temere" decree of 1907, which reaffirmed the Church's stand on mixed marriages and insisted on the instruction of the young in the faith.

Elizabeth's return to "Mary's altars" was a heavy blow to Lottie, an intelligent and sensitive child who understood the implications of the decision. The choice she was required to make would have been daunting for an adult. To choose Catholicism in the Ottawa Valley, where the influential majority were Protestant and often anti-Catholic, meant leaving the mainstream, and separating herself from the Whitton side of her family. At the same time, any contrary decision would provoke the hostility of her mother's family (as it did), and occasion "unmitigated grief, and whose recurrent entreaties send me into open, bitter breaks at their implied criticism of the faith which I find does me fairly well."[1] Whitton knew her choice would pull her and her brothers and sister "apart, instead of together," and deprive them of "sharing the same community and social contacts."[2] Thus, she refused to attend St. Francis Xavier Roman Catholic Church, exerting the first signs of personal will and unwavering commitment to principle that would remain part of her character. While her brothers and sisters became Catholics she was confirmed an Anglican at age thirteen. The crisis also made her aware that she could resist coercion, actively shape her own destiny, and assert an identity distinct from her family, but at a price.

The religious conflict seems to have been, in the end, more easily resolved than that other conflict which was part and parcel of her parents' union. The original ardor of two young lovers seeking consummation without the blessing of their separate families was blighted at its roots, and their eldest child observed these anomalies, assimilated the tensions, and reflected on their meaning. As a mature woman she reflected in "Marriage Out of the Faith" (1950):

> A marriage, to be richly happy, should be grounded in an understanding, deep and warm enough to foster and sustain a complete unit of living, spiritually, mentally, and physically. . . . The man and woman who would marry out of their own faiths must be satisfied that the love, which has swept them, is strong enough to fuse such elements of profoundly opposed beliefs and traditions into a transcending personal unity . . . I wonder.[3]

Her decision to forsake marriage indicates that the domestic tension and marital unhappiness were more bothersome for Whitton than she wanted to admit. Also she had a tendency to romanticize her family background, and even the religious question, in her biographical pieces. She was inclined to suggest that the children were divided up for protestantism and catholicism as part of the original marital compromise, and this version is widely believed. That she was impelled to place such a civilized and rational form on what was obviously a painful reality suggests that her emotions always remained ambivalent.

While family life was, thus, not always peaceful, Whitton generally had happy memories of her Renfrew childhood. One of her earliest recollections was hearing the church and firebells tolling the passing of "the old Queen" and "the mighty Victorian Age" on 22 January 1901 and watching the tarpots burning throughout the night in the streets of Renfrew. Nine months later her love affair with Royalty began, when, dressed in a stiffly starched party dress and a little box jacket, she stood beside her grandmother and waved a Union Jack as the Royal Train, containing the Duke and Duchess of Cornwall and York, made its way west from Ottawa. Little Lottie sobbed with disappointment on this occasion, for Royalty was an ordinary bearded man with an ordinary woman beside him, both clad in "street clothes." She had wanted nothing less than the ermine stoles and diamond tiaras she was eventually to see.[4]

Young Lottie was already part of those past generations of Canadians who were loyal monarchists and whose Anglo-Celtic ancestry evoked great passion for the Crown and fierce pride in the British Empire. Such strong Imperial identifications as are found in the Ottawa Valley even to the present inspired her throughout her life to be both Canadian and a part of the Mother Country. This patriotism was reinforced by the display of the Union Jack at school,

Empire Day celebrations, a robust rendering of God Save The King at all social events, and later in the institutionalized loyalties so predominant at Queen's University where young men joined the Canadian Officers Training Corps (COTC) and professors encouraged them to support Britain's efforts in the Boer and Great Wars. The presence of Canada's Military College in Kingston no doubt added to the mystique.[5]

But she was not usually starched, and she was not considered "a nice little girl," for "only Tomboys" haunted the blacksmith's or the livery stable. Lottie loved these two places where she enjoyed playing among "the spanking horses hitched up and got into trouble for telling that Mr. Dewey was taking Miss Bowditch [the kindergarten teacher, and later Mrs. Dewey] for a drive." If little Lottie was enchanted by the "fine sleek horses" in the Dunbars' stable, she was just as enchanted by "Auntie Ruth," the motherly figure who kept "the children's shop." She responded to life, sparkle, and colour in the row upon row of houses in the old town with its "lilting Irish strain," that gave Renfrew much of its "verve." While the little town abounded with young Reillys, Kellys and Gormans, there were also a large group of Presbyterian Scots who were among the earliest settlers, and Northern Irish along with Nodobneys, Cybulskis and Leskis who came in the Polish migrations of the 1860s and 1870s. And always there was the enduring Ottawa Valley; running through the town, the Bonnechere River was draped with green in spring, frozen in winter, ablaze in fall, its eddies offering coolness during the humid summer months.[6]

One arena in which Lottie's parents were not divided and in which she excelled from the beginning was school. One of the first records that exist is her honours promotion from grade one to grade two. Her own ambition was soon enough of a spur, and with such rewards she appears to have begun early to embrace views of innate merit and virtue, where the world fostered the talented and hard-working, and where the self-made man or woman could attain anything desired. But the atmosphere in which Lottie learned reading, arithmetic, geography, and history, mostly from British texts, was still far from cheerful. Forty to fifty students in rooms heated by wood stoves, outdoor plumbing, and dim lights were the order of the day until 1910, when a new building with the latest amenities such as flush toilets, fire extinguishers, and a coal-fired furnace was erected.

During the first years of the twentieth century, Renfrew's School Board was also working hard to raise the high school's status to that of a collegiate so that it could qualify for higher provincial government grants. With over forty per cent of the students commuting from rural areas or boarding by the week in town and paying only twenty-five cents a month as a fee, it was difficult to persuade ratepayers that higher taxes were needed, but it was done, and by 1911 the Gymnasium was built as well. After she passed her High School Entrance examination, Lottie entered the standard course—Euclid, English Grammar and Literature, History, Physical Geography, French, and Latin.

Whitton lived at a time when the prevailing belief was that schooling did not merely accredit people but represented the idea that "Knowledge was Power."[7] Moreover, Whitton was equally determined that her two brothers, J. B. and Stephen, and her sister Kathleen would achieve economic independence and she encouraged them, indeed bullied them, to aspire to University also, which they did with their sister's financial assistance in full or in part. J. B. went down to Queen's after war service and graduated with a Bachelor of Science in 1924; Kathleen, studying for a B.A. in 1925-26 met her husband Frank Ryan at Queen's, and Stephen postponed his studies in 1929 to return in the mid-1930s at age thirty. It was a remarkable achievement for four children of a relatively modest family to attend University in the first decades of this century.

Lottie's successes at Renfrew Collegiate Institute assured her a University education and provided her with the necessary financial assistance for the next four years. The audience at the Eighth Annual Commencement of the Institute applauded the eighteen year-old graduate as she received several awards, which included a board of education scholarship of $50 "for highest standing in the mid-summer examinations by a pupil intending to take up work for the Faculty of Education," and the generous McLaughlin scholarship worth $225 as well as $200 for the Honour of the Registrar award. The latter came from funds given to Queen's by James Carswell who had interests in the lumbering industry. For his gift he was entitled to nominate one student for admission to Queen's with the scholarship providing tuition fees. In addition she received the $100 Carter Scholarship. These awards were in recognition of an outstanding matriculation year when she was first on a list of six having received first-class honours (over 75%) in Latin, French, English, Mathematics and Modern History and a second class honours (over 65%) in German and Medieval History. She had received honours as well for the faculty of education examination part one and part two. For all of this she was given the T. A. Low medal as that year's "student of distinction."[8]

Whitton's choice to attend Queen's over either McGill or Toronto is not surprising. Apart from a proximity that enabled her to spend vacations, mid-terms, and frequent weekends at home with her family, Queen's Faculty of Education trained many teachers for Ontario's collegiates, and the Renfrew Collegiate Institute itself had been greatly influenced by these Queen's graduates. She had, therefore, immediate role models who encouraged her by their own academic backgrounds to attend the Kingston institution and to study for a diploma in paedogogy after completing her Arts degree. Her interests in education as a field of study, or teaching as a prospective career, were never of the enthusiastic kind, but teaching, being a genteel occupation for university trained women, represented an alternative if other career opportunities failed to arise. A teaching diploma from McGill, would not have served her well for she had no intention of working in Quebec, and her board of education obligations were for Ontario.

It has been noted, too, that Queen's was a relatively unsophisticated milieu when compared with the urban settings of Toronto and Montreal, the kind of comfortable and intimate environment that appealed to academically bright students from "homes of moderate means," in the Kingston area and Ottawa Valley, the children of farmers, small merchants and tradesmen. This atmosphere was reinforced by the fact that Queen's was essentially a teaching institution. Indeed, this fact bothered a later Principal, R.C. Wallace, who observed that while the institution was "able in its undergraduate teaching," it lacked in scholarship and research and might be described as "a glorified high school."[9] Moreover, the comparatively low professorial salaries at Queen's was partially caused by the desire to keep student fees competitive with those at the other universities. For a scholarship girl from modest circumstances this, along with a less expensive standard of living in a quiet provincial city, must have been attractive. During Whitton's years at the university she paid $55 per academic year in the Honours Program; $14 annual registration, $25 class fees, $1 for Levana, $3 Athletic fee and $12 examination fee for the honours program as compared with $10 for the regular program.[10]

When she started her university work in 1914 Lottie was an inexperienced adolescent, who on her own for the first time, found herself in an elitist milieu. Although Queen's attracted the offspring of families "of modest means," only a select few attended Canadian universities and even fewer graduated. A study of the 1910-15 birth cohort indicated that only 2.6 per cent of the females and 3.4 per cent of the males received degrees. On the other hand, women generally had more exposure to post-secondary education.[11] This difference stemmed largely from female participation in post-secondary teaching and nursing programs.

Although Lottie had always been among the most able students at her collegiate, she probably shared in the general anxiety of being in a new setting where she would have to test her abilities against the best students from other schools. In time, of course, she did establish her reputation and convince her fellow students and professors of her abilities. Although the programs were frequently individualized and flexible and the University boasted a co-operative atmosphere, leadership and recognition were not guaranteed by success at one's collegiate. When we examine the friends she sought, their obvious talents and later successes, it becomes clear that she was in an academically and socially competitive environment. Some of Whitton's success was fortuitous as in the case of the presidency of the women's society, Levana. This prestigious position, at her own confession, was gained because she "had been defeated for that office in the spring of 1917 by Catherine Holland [now Mrs. H. Joyce, Montreal] but she had been unable to return in the autumn and as runner up I was 'run in.' "[12] The students, moreover, were generally eager to maintain the reputation of Queen's graduates as leaders across the nation in their various professions. Such leadership rested on their own academic work, the recommendations of their professors, and finally, of course, on their success in the world. As a student in the Honours Program, Whitton was among those Queen's students who might be expected to represent the Queen's spirit nationally.

Whitton was determined to shine in all facets of Queen's life. Nicknamed "Charles" and "Carlos," she excelled in sports, particularly field hockey and basketball, and proved to be a superb debater and a competent poet and writer. In addition, during the 1917-18 session, she was elected the first woman assistant editor of Queen's *Journal*, a prestigious student appointment. She was also president of Levana in 1917-18, and in "Ruth's Poem," the author noted that she was "never outwitted but for crisis ready / a leader born yet with a poet's soul."[13] Levana activities included Bible readings, debates, and papers on literary subjects. However, her election to the Alma Mater Society executive was more controversial. Hilda Neatby, the historian of Queen's, notes that during the war Queen's women successfully asserted their right in practice as in principle to be elected to the previously all male executive of the AMS:

> The arts committee . . . did need the mass Levana vote; it is fair to suggest they may have also appreciated the quality of the women proposed. Whatever the motive, Lottie Whitton and Eva Coon were nominated on the arts slate for the positions of assistant to the secretary and committee member respectively and were duly elected. The future Mayor Whitton of Ottawa, who was to receive an M.A. in the spring in recognition of exceptionally high standing, was launched on her administrative career—although not without some rumblings in the *Journal* on the constitutionality of the operation.[14]

Although the number of male students dwindled and Grant Hall and the new Arts building—taken over by the provincial government—were "soon and terribly" converted into hospital units, Queen's remained relatively sequestered from the chaos and turbulence of conflict.[15] After the declaration of war, the enlistment of Queen's men for overseas service went on rapidly. By spring of 1915, three hundred undergraduates had volunteered. Most joined two Queen's units, the 46th Battery, Royal Canadian Artillery and the Fifth Queen's Stationary Hospital, a unit which preserved its Queen's identity in France. One hundred and seventy-nine Queen's graduates were killed in action. During the war years, John Watson, senior professor and Vice-Principal wrote to the Chancellor that "We are naturally short of men at the University, so many have gone to the front . . . without the girls we might as well shut up the College."[16]

That Whitton attended University during this exceptional period was fortunate for the encouragement given to women at this time was certainly not typical. The gradual change in the status of women at Queen's in the preceding thirty-four years accelerated under the demands of wartime exigencies. For example, not only did women gain executive positions on the *Journal* and the Alma Mater Society executive but some women faculty, such as Wilhelmina Gordon, the daughter of Daniel Miner Gordon, who had retired as principal in 1915, were appointed as a temporary wartime measure. In 1919, the first woman, a war nurse, Miss Edith Rayside, was included on the Board of Trustees.[17] Nevertheless, since the first two women with matriculation had registered at Queen's only in the fall of 1880, the number of women undergraduates remained small. The status of women at Queen's was not appreciatively different from other major Canadian universities. Indeed in 1882, University College, Toronto, refused to accept women. In this instance Queen's was ahead of its larger counterpart.[18]

By the turn of the century, there were still only upwards of twenty women at Queen's, and the *Journal* consistently published articles which contributed to the tedious debate as to whether university education was appropriate for women. Lady Aberdeen's speech in 1894 challenged the popular assumptions that assured universities would remain bastions of male privilege and power in an argument that was not based on intellectual evidences but on the belief that the special characteristics of educated females would not be lost because these women would contribute a reforming element to society.[19] Female students in the next decades were seen as a civilizing influence in a raucous male climate. Whitton was subjected to this ideology of "the lady," but wartime had opened up new opportunities at Queen's. She never lost either the Queen's spirit about service or her gynocentric sympathies. Hilda Neatby observes, "One interesting by-product of the war at Queen's and elsewhere was that, in the absence of so many of the men, women although still a small minority began to take an increasingly prominent part in public campus affairs."[20] "A small minority" refers to the national percentage of women students in comparison to male students and total students including extra-mural students at Queen's. In Whitton's case, she was part of a *significant* minority because her reference group consisted of intra-mural Arts and Education students.

After living in "digs," she moved to the "Hencoop," the women's residence on Earl Street, where her emotions and wits were challenged by similarly capable young female residents. The residence was the project of the Women's Residence Association, organized by a group of alumnae and wives of professors in 1901. The Hencoop accommodated sixteen residents and fourteen boarders. By Whitton's time, an ethos had grown up around the spartan conditions of the residence and the long term head of house, Miss Lillian Mowat, who was reputed to have "a Victorian appreciation of what they used to call 'the fitness of things.' " The Women's Residence Association were able to provide a sense of solidarity and board and room for $5.00 per week. One contemporary of Whitton recalled that although breakfast was "catch as catch can," lunch and dinner were always ceremonies. "The meals were nourishing, substantial and no nonsense. I don't remember seeing a salad or a 'fancy' dessert in the three years I lived at 'the Hencoop' but I have not tasted such good meat before or since."[21]

Whitton flourished in this predominantly non-male environment of the women's residence and in a radically changed Faculty of Arts where "practically everyone who was fit had gone to war and the students . . . were mainly women." In 1914-15, the 244 women in Arts and Education out of a total 669 full-time students represented 36 per cent; however, by 1917-18, the 224 women in a total of 327 students represented 68 per cent of the population.[22] If the social or marital expectations of many women students were blighted by the numerically fewer men at the University and the pre-occupation of the remaining men with the war, this environment proved a boon to Whitton, whose temperament and sensibilities blossomed in a female ethos.

The fact that many male students and faculty were at war reinforced female friendships, and as Whitton noted in an address in 1955 before Levana, she and her friends participated in the "feverish excitement" of debates from which sprang "the romantic idealization of a young country which had known little but peace."[23] The friendships themselves fed on what Margaret MacLachlan, a family friend, had written to Whitton—"the rush and turmoil and sorrow and misery and talk of glorious achievements and also of diabolical ones." In another later recollection Whitton said that she and her friends were keyed "to a high pitch of patriotic fervour and emotional tension."[24] In some ways this might describe the intensity of the friendships which, compounded by the Queen's "spirit" itself, inspired the more adventurous to become involved in social action. The faculty and the traditions of Queen's urged its students into serving the nation, either from the seat of government, in the helping professions, or through reform activities.

The Queen's "spirit," although in some ways distorted by the war and feverish patriotism, had been shaped by the most remarkable and first Canadian-born of Queen's early principals, George Monro Grant. Educated at Glasgow University before his ordination in the Church of Scotland, Grant directed Queen's from 1877 to 1902. The "peculiarly strong bonds among professors, students, and graduates that have come to be known as the Queen's spirit" has been described by Hilda Neatby as a permeation of religion into the nation's affairs. A passionate believer in Christian mission united with social service, Grant urged graduates to serve their country through their professions and to see these as "callings," something apart from an interest in material gain. In the case of women, the Queen's spirit sometimes carried over into missionary work in China or settlement work. Several of Whitton's closest friends worked for a time at Chalmers Settlement House in Montreal, following the example of its first two workers, Dr. May L. Macdonnell and Miss Mary Chown, both Queen's graduates who joined it in 1912. The YWCA also reinforced this spirit of service.

This spirit was so assimilated by Whitton that she could not divorce herself from its moral imperatives, and her life reflected its precepts. Consciously or not, she frequently re-iterated Grant's sentiments in her own addresses while committing herself to a career she viewed as a calling.[25]

In the early part of the century, women and men (even on university campuses where social intercourse between the sexes was less restricted) were segregated, often in classes and certainly in boarding houses. Indeed, in 1912-13, the Queen's senate had ruled that men and women could not lodge in the same houses.[26] Women's dress codes were uniformly strict, and the rules of heterosocial conduct were clearly understood and enforced. Supervision was of such a nature that faculty members were as much concerned with the manners and morals of the student body as with matters of the mind. These conventions reinforced same sex identification for the men as well as for the women. And, naturally, Whitton's friendships were mostly with other women, especially those who belonged to the Levana Society. Meanwhile, a tentative romance she had with an undergraduate named William Whittaker King, who had entered Queen's in 1913 and completed his B.Sc. (Hons) in Civil Engineering in 1917, was interrupted by his departure for military service in France. Only in retrospect does it seem to have been a "romance" at all. He did not figure prominently in her correspondence at the time, and it was only on his return to Canada in 1918 that there are suggestions that King was more than a casual and a remotely affectionate attachment.

Although sleigh rides, snowshoe parties, "town teas" with faculty and wives, "fussing" (necking), dances and formals, and the YWCA kept Whitton busy, she was keenly aware of the new career opportunities for women, and she was attracted to the forms of secular stewardship available in the growing helping professions. How best to "serve" society was eagerly discussed in classes, in public lectures, in chapel, and on the camping expeditions to Island Lake with Professor Wilhelmina Gordon each summer. The intense, long-into-the-night conversations and the "pleasant memories of light days and magical evenings" on these trips remained with Lottie and her friends for many years after.[27] Charlotte and her brother J. B. were the guides for the first of these expeditions, and together they introduced several of her "town" friends to the Canadian wilderness. J. B., only fourteen then, joined the Army a year later.

The Levana women fired each other's zeal by excited talk about their futures, by writing poems to each other, by discussing their "grand pashes" and particular friendships, and by excelling academically. The sorority language imitated male preppiness as they called each other "old top," "sport," "you scallawag," "laddie," "you cad," and, in Whitton's case, "dear old Charles."

Charlotte and her friends lived in a time when women expressed their love for each other eloquently and naturally and when romantic friendship satisfied the emotional needs now given over more completely to relationships with men. They did not fear homoerotic labelling, suspicion, or stereotyping, and they wrote to each other in an artlessly pre-Freudian style sometimes unconsciously amorous and, often, passionately vulnerable. They took such love relationships seriously; they were important in themselves and not merely a form of promiscuous emotional apprenticeship common between young boys or young girls deprived of what are now perceived as sexual expression and identity.

The friendships were cemented under other circumstances too, especially when the female students worked together for the Red Cross. In the 1914-15 session alone, 260 male students had enrolled in the Officer Training Corps while "the remaining students on the campus, reduced to about 600 by 1917-18, all continued their auxiliary efforts."[28] Funds were raised for relief efforts and war parcels, and Whitton worked on such endeavours for the YWCA.

It was not only the ethos of Queen's and the wartime atmosphere that shaped Whitton but also her relationships with her female friends. Interestingly, her closest ties during these formative years were with Levana women who were just as ambitious, intelligent, and forthright.[29] Whitton saw Levana as a source of inspiration and a surrogate family of mutually respectful intimates. Thus the spirit of Queen's was reinforced by the spirit of Levana and the bonds that tied Queen's graduates were strengthened by the bonds of the women's society. They all believed that when women were given the vote, which seemed to be increasingly inevitable throughout the war, all avenues must open up to them. In 1917 the Borden government allowed women with close relatives in the armed services to vote, and in May 1918, the Federal Act permitted all women to vote. Whitton was among the first women to get the franchise because J. B. was in France.

In her 1917 Arts valedictory, Whitton said that the women of Levana "were glad, free girls as well as womanly women. To them play was a virtue and healthy and sheer joy."[30] But, for Whitton, excellence and recognition, status and achievement were never really "play"—they were serious business. In the Queen's *Journal*, which she edited in the 1917-18 year while she studied for her diploma in education, Whitton elevated the source of Levana's inspiration from the shallow soil of play to the lofty heights of Olympus. There she said that the Roman goddess, Levana, "binds us with the wonder women of old days" and that the goddess raising the human infant in her hands "to behold that more wonderful than itself"[31] was a reminder that the body is bound to the mind.

The Levana Society was in some ways an aberration in a university which had rejected the idea of male fraternities because Queen's was "one large fraternity." Because Queen's had a middle class rather than upper class clientele, the "Greeks"—fraternities and sororities that reflected a caste system of social standing and wealth—were absent.[32] The Levana Society was established almost as soon as women were admitted. Clearly women had felt, and presumedly continued to feel given Levana's popularity, besieged in a male-dominated world. While Queen's did not encourage a female cloister, Levana offered a support system the women felt was necessary. Despite its open membership, active membership in Levana involved a small but active body of women students and the society's leadership represented a select cadre.

The cohesion of this small female student body provided Whitton with a close support system under the influence of a much admired mentor, English professor Wilhelmina Gordon, who with May Macdonnell of Classics was one of the first of Queen's women instructors. When she died in 1968, her obituary in the *Queen's Alumnae Review* said that "Min," with her "sloping gait and uncareful dress," had remained faithful to her "unmodernized prejudices, social and literary." Her devotion to ideals of a liberal education and social conservatism did not diminish even as they became increasingly unfashionable. Whitton's own attitudes were much the same, which suggests the attraction between mentor and student was based on a similarity of conservative intellectual philosophies. As the first woman appointed to the academic staff of the university, Gordon's example was critical for Queen's girls. Gordon was a role model for "Carlos," whom she regarded as the most interesting in the group. One friend, whose girlish enthusiasms and unrestrained admiration reflected the general response to Gordon wrote to Whitton:

> Miss Gordon still thrills me. Isn't she wonderful? She asked Dot and I over for tea with Elsie and Nora one afternoon. It was nice, but there were *men*! However, they were nice men![33]

The relationship that grew between Gordon and the earnest young Whitton was not confined to the pedagogical; it developed into a real affection and mutual respect that continued after Whitton's university years. A decade later, however, Gordon still felt that Whitton needed reassurance of her lasting affection and gently chided her that there was "no fear of your place being taken, Carlos; one says little, but you know that."[34]

The world at Queen's which Whitton valued and wanted to preserve was in some ways curiously anaemic and unreal in contrast to the carnage of France. Sometimes it is difficult to understand her immersion in her own world when her brother and many of her male friends were at war. J. B. implied as much when he wrote to Lottie in 1918 and referred to her field hockey and basketball.[35] Perhaps he felt that the battles fought on the hockey field, ice rink and the basketball court under the watchful eyes of Coach Gordon were trivial compared to the great military and political decisions being made on the battlefields of Europe. Another facet of Whitton's temperament emerged in these years—the manner in which she seemed to live only in her own present interests and needs. Even during the war, her aspirations were constrained by this sense of immediacy and its possibilities and opportunities. Whitton was nothing if not consistently egocentric, which ultimately proved limiting.

Yet public statements in the *Journal* suggest that Whitton was moved by the broader concerns. These editorials show Whitton's sense of appropriateness and her ability to reflect the concerns of her time, even if sometimes a little disingenously. Of course, she was concerned about the war and its waste and terror but, as with suffrage, only in an abstract sense. The more pressing concerns had to do with her own ambitions and hopes, her own present and future. In the November 1917 issue, she deplored the self-interest and narcissism that seemed to paralyze the university. Always highminded and quite unaware of any dissonance between her self absorption and her fluid and sometimes florid pen she observed:

> Were Socrates to emerge on the campus today he would be an inmate of the House of Industry in a fortnight and Demosthenes, arrested for vagrancy on the sea-shore. We seem to have lost sight of the ideals which lighten all things and concentrate on mere practicalities. . . . As a result our lives rotate on the axis of self and self advancement. We are pledged to making a living, not making a life. . . . Because we succeed, we are satisfied and happy,—and therefore *circumscribed* by the narrowness of our desires . . . there is stagnation—the stagnation of success.[36]

The editorial emphasized the need for service, and there is no doubt about Whitton's sincerity and conviction or the direction her own life would take. Continuing this crusade into the January and February editorials of 1918, she asked "What Shall I take from Queen's?" She insisted that the college graduate above all others was bound to "a sense of national responsibility" and that what distinguished such a person was the ability "to think and to act independently of social pressure."[37] She tentatively inquired whether the students were "equal to the task."

In the summer of 1918 Charlotte Whitton left Queen's University with a Masters of Arts in English, History, and Philosophy. This degree was not a postgraduate one but an honour awarded to students with outstanding undergraduate records. In the Scots tradition, Queen's gave M.A.'s "for full honours in two subjects and a double first."[38] Whitton included the letters M.A. on all her professional correspondence and biographical data for the rest of her life. This recognition of her intellectual abilities never ceased to be a source of great pride to her. She had graduated with medals in English and History as well as the Governor General's medal in paedagogy, although her last year had been an uninspired one for her. Within a week of leaving the university, she took up an appointment in Toronto with the Social Service Council of Canada where, as she humourously commented, she worked for the next four years as a "sin sleuth."[39]

2

INITIATION INTO PUBLIC LIFE

Never in any land has the need for intelligent
womanhood been so great as in the Dominion of
Canada today. And never has the opportunity for
woman's service been as wide and glorious.

WHITTON, 1919.

When Whitton left Queen's in 1918, she moved from quiet and insular Kingston into the hubbub of Canada's major city, rapidly expanding Toronto. Inspired
by the impassioned talk about peace and reconstruction, she and many other
women were confident that female suffrage would open up public offices that
had hitherto been the domain of men and provide many new opportunities.
There were good reasons why an ambitious young woman would choose social
service over other possible careers.

By 1918 Canadian social service was in transition from the old tradition of
associated charities and friendly visiting with its middle class volunteers to a
concept of professional social work in which trained staff were the heart of the
enterprise. The demand for efficient and scientific management of charitable
resources and the growing belief in environment rather than moral defects as
the cause of dependency led social service advocates to see their task as the
discovery of pressures that disrupted normal family. Although social work
leaders regularly attended American meetings, by 1898 they had their own
Canadian Conference of Charities and Correction that provided congenial
annual meetings for the discussion of national issues.

In 1907 an alliance of church and labour groups, which had secured the
passage of the 1906 Lord's Day Act, came together in the Moral and Social
Reform Council of Canada. Under the joint leadership of J.G. Shearer and T.A.
Moore, social service secretaries of the Presbyterian and Methodist churches
respectively, the council gradually came to promote a broad program of social

reform and community action and spawned a number of provincial councils. When the national organization changed its name to the Social Service Council of Canada in 1913, it signalled a growing interest in social over moral issues.[1]

Its most notable early successes were the Social Service Congress held in Ottawa in early March 1914 and a series of provincial congresses held during the war years. With a functioning national structure, the council developed a program of research, publicity, and lobbying during the years 1918 to 1924. It had standing committees on industrial life, Indian affairs, political purity and the franchise, social hygiene, criminology, the family, child welfare, immigration, and legislation.[2]

Shearer, the general secretary of the Presbyterian Church's department of social service between 1907 and 1915, was appointed to a similar position in the SSCC. Within five years he had resigned from the Presbyterian department because he felt that the dominion agency lacked efficiency, economy, and focus and required full-time leadership. While visiting Queen's to persuade "keen young graduates" to serve their society, Shearer handpicked Whitton as a promising worker for his agency in Toronto. Her experiences with the *Queen's Journal* convinced him that she was right for the position of SSCC assistant secretary and assistant editor of the newly founded *Social Welfare*, one of Canada's earliest and most influential social work journals. Shearer sought recruits of Whitton's calibre not just because they had a strong sense of service, but also because they were capable and intelligent. Shearer's reputation as a stern moralist, a stirring preacher, and a sabbatarian with stormy involvements in the controversies surrounding the Lord's Day Act was legend in Winnipeg. But the young Whitton found "Mr. Greatheart" an amiable man, and they enjoyed mutually respectful collegiality until his death in 1925. A hard taskmaster, she observed that, "He threw work at you. You sank or swam and however it turned out he never complained."[3]

As assistant secretary with the SSCC beginning in July 1918, Whitton dealt with the day-to-day routine of the SSCC office as well as all organizational matters connected with committees and liaison between Toronto's welfare agencies. She earned $100 a month. She handled correspondence and attended charity and child welfare conferences at the municipal and provincial level. Her committee and liaison work was an important means of establishing contacts that would serve her well in the future. On the committees were members of the Juvenile Court, Neighbourhood Workers' Association, Big Sisters, children's and infants' homes, children's aid societies, Christopher Settlement House, churches, and social welfare service divisions of the City Public Health Department. Whitton sat on several of the SSCC standing committees during her four years with the council either as secretary, as a member, or as a delegate for Shearer. As secretary of a sub-committee on "Disintegrating Forces in Family Life," she produced a splendid special issue of *Social Welfare* on "Housing, Poverty and the

Family" in September 1920. This issue included sociological, religious, and political analyses of the relationship between poor housing and poverty. In the same year she busily helped organize a national Child Welfare week and began the preparations for a national conference to be held the following year.

Other committees included those on "Legislation" and on "Political Purity and the Franchise," which condemned the party patronage system and examined the merits of proportional representation. She wrote a report in 1921 to be presented to this particular committee on the minimum wage, syndicalism, and guild socialism. The "Family Life" committee examined issues relating to divorce, the age of consent, bigamy, desertion, alimony, unwed parenthood, and the double moral standard. Her later interests in mothers' pensions and child support started during her work on the Family Life committee just as her concerns about child welfare and child labour were amply demonstrated in the juvenile employment division of the council.[4]

While she was in charge of the committee on "Motion Pictures and Censorship," it became apparent that Whitton's major interest was not in questions about the effect movies had on young children or matters of a narrow morality but in broader social and political issues. Housing and poverty absorbed her more than banning guessing games, raffles, and tobacco sales or making adultery a crime. Although the committees she sat on deplored these as well as the hiring of motorized vehicles "for purposes of illicit sexual intercourse or the practice of acts of indecency," more important matters took up the best of her talents.[5] She was, however, involved in petitioning a national censorship board "because of suggestive and arrested undressing . . . rather than outright nudity in films."[6]

Her most zealous efforts were applied to the Industrial Life and Immigration committee and out of its work she produced a major published report. The views she expressed in it remained unmodified for the next five decades. Her efforts on this committee reflected the same zeal that was also apparent when she attended the National Council of Women (NCW) executive meetings or the IODE immigration committees. In 1921, she convinced the NCW to join the SSCC although some women saw the suggestion as "an affront to include the greater with the lesser as equals," but she expressed grave concern that the NCW had resolved to ask the Dominion Bureau of Statistics to place "Canadian" next to all those born in Canada of naturalized citizens.[7] Whitton insisted that it was prudent to have "the problem of racial origin" remain in census data. Racial origin always remained a "problem" for Whitton.

The duties as assistant secretary to the SSCC helped her become conversant with the nature of charity organization, how to use survey techniques effectively, and how to analyze the gaps between child welfare services and actual legislation. However, her most important involvements during the SSCC years were with the children's bureau crusade and with *Social Welfare*.

In addition to soliciting articles for the journal and proofreading, editing, and making sure the monthly deadlines were met, at regular intervals she wrote her own pieces. Since these are the first public expression of her social attitudes, they reveal much about the background to her social policy.

Her contributions on the standing committees of the SSCC, her writings in *Social Welfare*, and her substantial 1922 report and the monograph "Some Aspects of the Immigration Problem" (1924) which came out of that report have several consistent themes, among them the immigration "problem," unmarried parenthood, child welfare, and the role of enfranchised women in social reconstruction. Her treatment of these four themes explain as much about the older as the young Whitton for none of her views substantially altered in the following decades. Neither did her style of writing. It was uniformly didactic and sometimes pontifical—a fault frequently noted by her critics—although she was certainly not alone in such a style in the 1920s. Even the amusing pieces are written as cautionary tales or morality plays. And they are frequently repetitive, especially on matters about which she was passionate. At times her passions became obsessions, as is most obvious in her writings on immigration. Probably it was this quality of single-minded passion that made her such a consummate public speaker.

Even as she was writing "Child Labour," a generally progressive treatise appealing for tighter child protection laws published in November 1918, she connected mental deficiency with immigration. In this case, she argued that the high percentage of "feebleminded" immigrant girls who went into domestic service probably accounted for the high percentage of illegitimate births among them. This apparently innocuous insertion is, in fact, a fair illustration of a view that was to become more forthright in later reports, confidential memoranda, and addresses.

Neither can these comments on immigrant girls and feebleminded fertility be taken out of the context of the overriding theme of the November issue itself, which included an article on defective children from Dr. Helen MacMurchy quoting Lloyd George, "You cannot have an A1 army on a C3 population" (a quote Whitton frequently repeated herself). In the same issue, Dr. C.M. Hincks, the Assistant Medical Director of the Canadian National Committee for Mental Hygiene, wrote on "Feeblemindedness in Canada: A Serious National Problem." In this article, Hincks used Dr. C.K. Clarke's 1917 research into the consequences of inadequate mental inspection of immigrants and the dubious findings of the Psychiatric Clinic of Toronto General Hospital which connected mental deficiency to immigration. A few years later in the February 1925 issue of *Social Welfare* Hincks himself retracted many of his previous claims.

Whenever she spoke on mental defects, Whitton cited these figures and recycled them well into the twenties. In one address she used during her SSCC days, "Mental Deficiency as a Child Welfare Problem," her connections were far from subtle. Part of the address exploited Clarke's figures:

> There should also be prompt dealing with the degenerate settlements in the back areas of many of the provinces, out of which racial and social poison is pouring into our community life.
>
> There is one grave aspect of the Mental Defect problem that lies beyond even provincial control, and that is the relation of immigration as a direct contributory cause to the volume of mental defect in the country today. Statistics abound to show the alarming policy that sought not quality but quantity has contributed to the social problems of this young country.
>
> Our full strength and resources are bent to the task of keeping this country strong, virile, healthy, and moral and we insist that the blood that enters its veins must be equally pure and free from taint.[8]

Whitton's address reflected the anxiety of a colonial country with only eight million people who, despite the existing "two nations," were afraid that an influx of non-Anglo Saxons might radically alter the composition of Canada's political and racial ties and contribute to demographic disjuncture by increasing the drift to the urban centres.

She pursued the theme in an April 1920 article on "Unmarried Parenthood and the Social Order," in which she stressed that figures, presumedly Clarke's once again, demonstrated higher illegitimate births among British immigrant girls over Canadian born. Arguing that because so many British girls were of subnormal mentality, "We cheerfully paid over hundreds of thousands of dollars in bonuses for the gift of their low mentality, consequent subnormality, and still consequent illegitimate and, in many cases subnormal children." She continued that mental hygienists claimed that "the subnormal individual drifts into a work where low mentality can survive." These opinions reflect her overall beliefs concerning desirable immigrants. Desirable immigrants were Anglo-Saxon agriculturalists, whose passages had been unassisted and who had undergone careful physical and psychiatric examinations to determine their mental and moral calibre, thus reducing the risks of eugenic deficiencies in the pure blood of the Canadian people. Undesirable immigrants were Oriental, Armenian, Jewish, Central European, or from the lower classes of British society. "In many, many cases too, especially in the case of the Chinese immigrant, the foreigner is an inferior type of his own race," she argued in another issue of *Social Welfare*.[9]

So far as such ideas had any legitimacy, this was derived from the general popularity of hereditarian ideas in Canada at the time and the concern over the immigration of children and young people as cheap labour from Britain.[10] The pseudo-science of "eugenics"—that morality, criminality, mental and physical defects could lead to race degeneracy supported Whitton's stance. Eugenics was seriously discussed in the leading industrial nations, which feared racial, social, and urban degeneration. That many educated and conservative citizens supported eugenics is not surprising for it justified their opposition to radical social programs that seemed to favour the "unfit." Nevertheless, Whitton's use of eugenics is surprising. Its emphasis on hereditary over environmental factors, which in turn implied that humans made their environment and were not simply moulded by them flew in the face of all those progressive child welfare ideas to which she was committed. Usually child welfare reformers claimed that environment was the crucial variable in the making of young citizens, and they therefore sought vigilantly to meliorate child labour conditions, legislate a comprehensive body of child protection, and support a wholesome family life with such programs as mothers' allowances (which the SSCC fully endorsed). Whitton worked indefatigably in these areas and expressed confidence in the potential of children given the right external conditions, so the eugenics arguments are oddly at dissonance with both her overall philosophy and her practical work.

The movement to Canada of some 80,000 children which had taken place since the previous century under the auspices of British child savers was a problem the SSCC Immigration Committee studied. Some of the unaccompanied immigrants were orphaned, but most had been given over to rescue societies by desperate families who were unable to support them in the urban slums of England and Scotland. Promised social mobility in a land of opportunity, in fact, they were indentured as cheap farm labour and household drudges and subjected to persecution and discrimination throughout their history in Canada. Whitton, who opposed their importation, recognized that the argument that these young immigrants were potential eugenic risks would be supported by many child welfare workers. The domestics she referred to in "Child Labour" were, by implication, products of the juvenile immigration movement.[11]

Nevertheless, "Child Labour," established Whitton's major social welfare concerns, demonstrating for the first time what would become the bane of her child welfare career—the lack of uniform provincial standards and legislation. Warning against the "narrow provincial spirit" which prevented Canada from becoming a real nation, she used Ancient Greece as an example of its "full hatefulness . . . the ultimate test of nationality cannot be passed by an individual state, or even two or three individual states and Canada too, will know her dark days of Corinth."[12] Her frustration about narrow provincial interests was revealed in her later social surveys and was to embarrass her before the League of Nations between 1926 and 1939.

The relationship between the need for child welfare and unmarried parenthood seems obvious, yet when Whitton wrote her two-part article, the relationship was obscured by her penchant for punitive moralizing. The article sympathized with the economic plight of the mothers while condemning their "offence," just as it sympathized with the situation of the innocent party, the child, while deploring the ease with which the father could escape both his responsibilities and social condemnation. Indeed, she deplored the term "illegitimacy" because it legally denied the child "inheritance from either parent in case of their dying intestate."[13] Moreover, she was appalled that the law left all the economic consequences and the public shame, even to the final proof of paternity, with the woman. She recognized that a great evolution of social attitudes had already occurred between the events of *The Scarlet Letter* and Canada of the 1920s, but she still felt that her country had far to go before it reached the point of the progressive legislation recently passed by the Norwegian Störthing on the subject of unmarried parenthood. As long as "the woman is left to answer alone for a mutual offense," Whitton argued, it perpetuates "the injustice and irresistible resentment at a double standard of morals with all its suppression and deceit" where "maternity alone places the brand on her forehead" while the "notorious man of position," "who may be known to every prostitute of any standing in the city, is welcomed with open arms, and the women of your homes offered a living sacrifice for the honour of bearing his name."

However, at the centre of the article, Whitton connected immigration, domestic service, and mental deficiency. She conceded that a domestic who became an unwed mother was "a higher type on the average," although not necessarily a superior mental type, to the prostitute who operated on an imperative of "paid immorality." Having transgressed society's code, perhaps in a surging of maternal longing, she accepted her condition and anticipated its consequences.[14]

Convinced that unwed mothers were usually of low intelligence and weak morality, rather than vicious and depraved, Whitton feared that their offspring would inherit these traits and contribute to the contamination of the Canadian people whose blood had so recently been thinned by the slaughter of their finest youth in the Great War. Whitton consistently connected intelligence with the virtues of self-control and discipline. To yield to the baser impulses, given the likely consequence of pregnancy, was stupidity. Committed to the belief that rationality, intelligence, and sublimation produced the finest artifacts of society and the greatest achievement of culture, she said:

> The regulation and control of instinct and emotion as the basis of civilization, the training away from untrammelled play of natural impulses to a discriminate use and government of them is the whole principle of education.[15]

She curtly dismissed suggestions that seduction could be the consequence of loneliness, duplicity, infatuation, fear, or even love; strong personalities would not succumb to such emotional or economic coercion.

These views are not just insufferable moral rectitude. They illustrate a moral matrix that guided Whitton's life. She was, in effect, insisting that all women without recourse to licit sexual expression be as strong-willed as she; they must demonstrate the same discipline and self-control. Because her own life showed that natural instincts could be effectively channelled into socially useful and creative work, her moralizing may be seen as psychological projection and displacement.

Whitton was still struggling with conflicts and ambiguities regarding her celibacy and the decisions she had to make for her future. She longed for passionate attachment, and she was certainly no asexual ethereal Edwardian maiden. She loved the good things of life "laughter, joy, companionship, and friendship" too much to turn her back on marriage and motherhood without a struggle. These qualities of temperament, coupled with a fairly sophisticated level of discourse among social workers and members of the SSCC Social Hygiene Committee on such matters as birth control, abortion, venereal disease, soliciting and prostitution, the age of consent, unmarried parenthood, the debasement of family life owing to lack of privacy in poor housing, and the "white slave traffic," guaranteed that she was no innocent. That her moralizing continued in later years was related to her final decision to remain single. If Whitton, through volition, could come out squarely on the side of self-control, discipline, and morality, so too, by God, ought others.

As to her views on women's role in social reconstruction, Whitton's distinctive style of writing, always a rallying cry to women, is best seen in two articles, "On Woman's Thought," in *Social Welfare*, May and June 1919. Writing under the pseudonym, "Kit of the Kitchen," she articulates the gynocentric ideal for the first time. Her belief that women were morally finer, purer, stronger, and more naturally on the side of life and humanitarianism than were men is summarized in her words that "out of the debris [of war] new worlds are to be created, and creation is woman's primal right and power." Women were the progenitors of civilizing and life-giving forces; therefore, their political participation "on the eve of the extension of the franchise" was crucial. The following words were to be repeated in various guises and for numerous articles in the 1940s and 1950s, only updated by women's issues of the day:

> Only representation in the House of Commons and the Senate will afford women direct contact with national action. For this, the women of Canada must stand; for this they must strive, if they desire any other office than that of 'Ladies' Aid.' . . . It therefore becomes the duty of every Canadian woman . . . to prepare herself for worthy citizenship. Never in any land has the need for intelligent womanhood been so great as in the Dominion of Canada today. And never has the opportunity for woman's service been as wide and glorious.[16]

Her thorough-going political conservatism was not evident in her youthful writings. She believed that the "After-the-War" woman had the freshness and vigour to reconstruct society and alleviate those old social ills and injustices which had contributed to world war. Criticizing those who preached reconstruction but really meant "readjustment into the old lines," she denounced the "privileged classes."

> Wealth, political power, monopoly, the more influential press interests, higher education, (almost inclusively) much Church influence, and the higher army interests are identified with the 'old-tried-path-party.'
> Of course, this section does not advocate preservation of the old social order as such, but under pleasing programmes and subtle deliverances on reconstruction, it secretes the lulling pill, that is compounded to soothe an annoyingly restless public.[17]

Her article continued to expand such sentiments, discussing the role of the women's vote, the role of the National Council of Women, and the growth of the Women's Institutes. In conclusion she pointed out that the NCW tended to represent Eastern interests and that the Institutes were "more radical, less diffident in making a decided stand on big questions."

In the following month, "Kit of the Kitchen" articulated an embryonic feminism that she was to develop over the next decades. She argued that women in gainful occupation were entitled to equality of wages "on the basis of occupation and not on the basis of sex" and that such wages must be sufficient to care for dependents. Most women were working like men "to obtain their daily bread." On this particular issue she remained uncompromising, as the following curt dismissal of all objections suggests:

> Now, to urge that they be dismissed, as 'war workers,' is an inhumane course for anyone to suggest. They require the wages, which they are earning, as keenly as the men on the machines next them—their claim to consideration is as great, their right to permanent employment as unassailable. In their defence, the woman voter must use her newly given power.[18]

This particular article included all four of Whitton's major concerns during the Toronto period: a discussion of women's political role; the "peculiar, personal contribution of women to national life," or women's talents for humanitarian, moral and social matters; a discussion of child welfare and women's contribution to this issue; and finally, a discussion of the immigration problem, or rather, a warning about the problems Canada faced in assimilating non-British stocks and those "unfit to play their part in nation building."

If Toronto was the place where Whitton tested herself—a four-year apprenticeship into social work which shaped her professional life—it was also the place where she met companions with whom she would share a large part of her future. During her time in Toronto she weaned herself from former relationships and established new ones.

When she moved to Toronto, Whitton found herself deprived for the first time of strong emotional support structures. She came from a close knit family in a small town of less than 5,000 people, and at university she had a close knit surrogate "family" of intimates, who were also sustained by the tight academic community at Kingston. In Toronto there occurred a gradual withdrawal from her Queen's friends as their lives diverged, and her personal life was replenished by the friendships she made at the Kappa Alpha Theta Society house on the campus of the University of Toronto. The "Kats" provided her with a vigorous social life, a place of residence, and connections with other young women involved in various forms of philanthropic work or social service. At the "Kats" Whitton and her friends lived "a virtually male free life." Although Carolyn June Forsyth's description of the "Kats" house as a "collective" in the contemporary sense is exaggerated, the activities and ideals of the women are not.

> [The] ideal of chastity and the causes of social reform bound together Charlotte and her friends . . . The time was one of relative economic prosperity before the Depression. More women were entering the professions than ever before or since in Canadian history. In the collective were students of social work, teachers, nurses, and the odd female law student. They talked of social needs and their own individual opportunities, energized by high friendship and shared purposes of suffragette reform. They wanted juvenile courts established throughout Canada and money and support for Children's Aid Societies to look after neglected and abandoned children . . . In the Toronto collective there was no distinction between living and working together.[19]

Not only did this professional exchange reinforce the direction her own life was taking, but there she also met Margaret Grier, who worked with the juvenile court as well as with the Big Sisters Association and the Girl Guides. They shared rooms and found themselves to be compatible both professionally and emotionally. In some ways their personalities were perfectly complementary: Whitton, younger by four years, was more active, assertive, and ambitious, and Grier, was quiet and somewhat shy except with close friends. Margaret Grier, however, had the kind of warm and trusting personality that automatically attracted people, and she provided permanence and security while her friend continued to remain mercurial and self-absorbed. She was less intimidating and egotistical than Whitton. Some thirty years later Whitton provided a portrait of Margaret Grier and their friendship:

Two more diverse natures could hardly be found, yet so exquisitely did they complement each other that their lives were enriched in an association of the rarest. Margaret was a complete contrast in appearance and nature to the more aggressive Charlotte. She was fair and quiet, with delicate features and colouring and there was a serenity of spirit and gentleness about this girl, which drew people to her as honey attracts bees.[20]

Rose Margaret Grier had graduated from Bishop Bethune College before commencing her studies in social work at St. Hilda's College, Toronto. Her family were eminent Ontario Anglicans. John Grier, her grandfather, formerly of Edinburgh University and Trinity College, Dublin, became the first missionary and Anglican priest at the "Carrying Place," the Bay of Quinte, having been ordained a deacon in the cathedral of the Holy Trinity, Quebec, in 1824. Margaret was niece of Hanna Grier, the founder of the Sisterhood of St. John the Divine whose religious house was St. John's Convent, Willowdale, Ontario, and Archbishop Owen, former Primate of all Canada, was her cousin. Following in this tradition, Margaret's sister, Dora Lillias Grier, who was eighteen years older than she, became the Superior of the Order. Another relative was "old Rosebud," Miss Rose Elizabeth Grier, the former Principal of Bishop Strachan School who signed the charter of St. Hilda's in 1888. Such genteel and socially important genealogical credentials naturally impressed Whitton.

However, before this friendship assumed its eventual importance, Whitton experienced the normal weaning away processes of the transitional period between the family home and establishing her own household. In several ways, Whitton was discontented with her life in Toronto. She found her work with the SSCC too circumscribed since she was not altogether satisfied acting the "sin sleuth." She was far less interested in public morality than in social reform and wanted to be part of a more financially solvent public forum rather than a quasi-philanthropic agency with obvious religious connections and philosophy. Second, she was groping to discover meaning in her private life. Initially she sought sustenance from her Queen's friends, and it was several years before she was able to create a new network of affections and companionship. While she was yearning for passionate attachment, she was also struggling to resolve her ambivalence regarding marriage and career. Third, while her friends may have envied what they perceived as a relatively autonomous position, Whitton's salary was not sufficient to enable her to establish a household of her own. A young woman in her early twenties desired more than shared digs or boarding. In short, Whitton—whose independent nature balked at constraint—was professionally, domestically, socially, and emotionally restless.

During 1918 and 1919 Wilhelmina Gordon remained important to Whitton's emotional life. Because Gordon's faith and encouragement had inspired Whitton at Queen's, she continued to share with her her dreams of graduate education at Bryn Mawr and Oxford. She hoped to be able to embark on graduate studies within four years of leaving Queen's. First, she would work to save money for the enterprise as well as to put her brother J.B. through University. Gordon's enthusiasm in the matter is better understood in light of her own frustrating experiences. A brilliant student at Oxford who had received a first in "English Schools" under Professor Nichol Smith at the turn of the century, she had not been able to graduate officially because women could not convocate. Soon after she left Queen's, Gordon reminded her protegee of the promises she had made to herself, assuring Whitton that she could obtain invaluable references for graduate scholarships from Vincent Massey. "I would back you against any man or woman in Ontario," Gordon wrote, at the same time warning her against marrying "for the sake of the great god Pan . . . before you have a chance at Oxford." The Dean of the Faculty of Education, H.I.J. Coleman, also encouraged Lottie to continue with her studies. In September, after she had been in Toronto only for two months, she enquired about the possibilities of returning to Queen's. Her distress at being away from her old associations and her uncertainties about SSCC prospects apparently motivated the enquiry. Coleman told her that she should sit for the paedagogy examinations which would come up in February

> and you could quite safely attempt at least one part of the B. Paed. Course; possibly two, if you have enough time for reading. I think you could find an admirable subject for a D. Paedagogy thesis in the field in which you are now working.[21]

Thus Gordon continued to steer Whitton away from marriage during the early Toronto years, and it was Gordon to whom she wrote her ambivalent letters as she struggled with considerations of marriage and its conflicts as she came under increasing pressure from Bill King, with whom she had shared three years as a fellow student and with whom she had corresponded until his return to Canada at the conclusion of the war. During those first years after the war, he worked as an engineer, lost his partnership, and then moved into contracting. Whitton perceived this as aimlessness, which was in marked contrast to her sense of purpose and her successes. In May 1919 Gordon firmly replied to her dear "Charles" about the matter of marriage. "Forbye," she wrote, "it would be as well to be out of Bill's way a bit. Not that you are apt to be passion's slave but juxtaposition and importunity are tremendous forces."[22] There is little evidence that Whitton and Bill spent enough time together for the young woman to be diverted through juxtaposition or importunity. Indeed, she scrupulously avoided any such conflict by conducting her relationship mainly through correspondence, although Bill was able to see her occasionally because he was working in Hamilton. They attended college football games together, and Bill was an attractive escort when she needed to be partnered at social events.

Whitton missed her other Queen's friends too. In particular, her classmate Mo's letters provided her with consolation as she struggled with the emotions Bill aroused and the temptations Bill represented, but unlike Gordon, Mo was reluctant to warn her friend away from marriage. All her foreshadowings of the single life were dismal. In 1919 Mo pondered Whitton's relationship with Bill and agreed that she could never picture her as a "kitchen ornament or a fireside tabby cat," but then she doubted that Bill could either. Perhaps he would be willing to let her pursue her own interests? She added, "You care more for him than you will admit and perhaps you are blinding yourself with needless calculations." The letter concluded with a caution about a lonely middle age.[23]

With Gordon warning her against marrying and Mo warning her against spinsterhood, neither did Whitton find consolation in her mother's presentiments on the matter. A 1920 letter from her mother illustrates that she understood the changes that marriage would force upon her daughter. Her mother was probably not apprehensive about a precipitous union since Lottie was twenty-four and had known Bill for five years, but perhaps she was not happy at the thought of her daughter foresaking a career or perhaps she was disaffected with marriage generally. Her simple message contained a nagging anxiety. "I dreamed one night that you were married in the little English Church and everything was so real I have been thinking about it ever since. I hope when you do, you will think beforehand."[24]

The first years away from Kingston were frequently troubling and unhappy for the whole group of women who had enjoyed such exceptional bonds of camaraderie in their undergraduate years. They were all "homesick" for Queen's and for each other. Nell, who had been described in the 1918 Queen's "Predictions" as living the life of a "Court Jester," generally disliked teaching, even though she and Mo taught together in Picton for a while. And the cheerful Mary MacPhail, who had worked for a brief time at Chalmers Settlement House in Montreal with Nell, was not content with teaching either. All were surprised to find that their friend Lottie, predicted to be a "M.A., Ph.D., D.D., L.L.D., Paed. D. etc., etc." and who had been chosen unanimously for the "Chair of Journalism at Balliol College, Oxford," was similarly unhappy. When compared with them, she had done very well.[25]

While her friends lamented their sense of isolation in 1918 and fretted about futures which mostly seemed destined to be lived out in collegiates, they envied Lottie's relative freedom in Toronto, her comparatively interesting work, her editing opportunities, and last, but certainly by no means least, her trips to Virginia, Atlantic City, and New Orleans representing the SSCC at conferences on charity and child welfare. Lottie's inquiries about teaching and suggestions about switching jobs must have puzzled them. She attempted to convey, in long, turgid letters, that nebulous restlessness and loneliness which haunted her, while at the same time she was unable to resist small and self important boasts about her work.

Much of the correspondence belongs to the literary genre which emerged out of "romantic friendships," which were not uncommon in an era where gender roles were clearly defined and where unsupervised heterosexual inter-action and social intercourse were constrained.[26] While men and women now mix with little inhibition, this is a relatively recent phenomenon, and it has been at the expense of same-sex intimacy. Curiously, it has been women whose former support structures have been most eroded and diminished in accor-dance with the increased amount of time now devoted to male-female relationships. The correspondence between these friends tells as much about the fascination of Whitton's personality since it evoked such strong responses, as it does of the naturalness of these responses in a time of pre-Freudian artlessness.[27]

In "long and charming" letters, Whitton indulged in a form of ardent introspection, a semi-serious amorousness. She and her correspondent played with words coquettishly, as if they were paying court to each other. The letters are imbued with unconscious elements of the erotic. Mo once signed herself "with heaps of love from your prosaic Mo," [28] while another friend, Hilda, wondered why Lottie had bared her soul to her because "to be perfectly candid you think me a dull plodder and I am."[29]

Grace informed her "Charles" in 1919 that she did not think her suited for the "routine of teaching."

> You would certainly succeed but you see I have you on such a pedestal I can hardly want to see you enter my sphere. . . . When you become famous and the world clamours for signatures I may blush to remember I ever wrote this.

In this same letter Grace chastized Whitton for a "Kit of the Kitchen" column, claiming its ascerbic tone belied her friend's warmth and kindness. She continued:

> You know you are a clever girl. But your cleverness has cost you no more than my mediocrity. Much of what makes you great cannot be imitated by others. . . . I have almost a holy respect for knowledge and you have forgotten more than I ever knew. . . . Yet when I am with you I never feel the dwarf.[30]

If Grace felt mediocre beside Whitton, another of her friends did not. Indeed, Elizabeth MacCallum was her equal in every way, and the letters between them reflect strong, intelligent personalities. MacCallum too eventually chose career over marriage, but in her youth she also exuded a strong yearning for passion-ate attachment. Her letters to her "dearest Lottchern" were eloquent appeals from Dawson, where she was teaching, to proceed with her to Bryn Mawr or to Columbia. As with Gordon, MacCallum reminded her friend of her plans. Signing herself "Lisei," she mentioned Professor Skelton's assurances that he would write strong references for them to be admitted into either graduate schools. Suggesting that they could go to one or the other together, she continued somewhat wistfully that "we could have uproarious times in our Adamless Eden if we kept house!"[31]

Like Whitton, MacCallum was uncertain about her future and reaching out for a soul mate to share it. She thoughtfully pondered how she could possibly continue teaching "where I myself have no goal toward which to steer." The major differences between their emotional struggles lay in the painful religious conflict MacCallum wrote of, after which the daughter of missionaries declared, "I am no longer a Christian," a declaration which must have provided some sense of discomfort to her orthodox Anglican friend. MacCallum tried to seduce Whitton to join her in Dawson to earn $2,300 a year with $65 for living costs each month and a single ticket from Vancouver at $95. Whitton, however, was not to be persuaded despite her meagre $100 a month salary. Instead, in 1922, she recommended that MacCallum replace her when she resigned from the SSCC, and MacCallum came to Toronto for a year or so before she took up graduate work at Columbia.

The SSCC's failure to increase its budget significantly or to expand its influence makes Whitton's restlessness easier to understand. She saw the Toronto position as a stepping stone to better things and never as an end in itself. At the "Kats" she met a young woman, Esther, whose ardor approximated her own for a brief time. Whenever Esther went home to Tallendal, her correspondence was warm and supportive. Charlotte found a sympathetic ear and attempted to articulate her frustration. Discussing Coleridge, Whitton declaimed in exasperation:

> Any sensibility of a lurking incompleteness always haunts me, almost to the point of sheer temper, at the lack of a finish—it makes me hate life and Coleridge, both for the same reason but from different motives—life because the power to complete it, lies beyond my grasp (unless you choose to take 'complete' in its old Latin 'to fill')—fill life I can and will, and to the brim . . . Coleridge because the power of completion lay within his giving and he would—perhaps he could not—but he baffles me because I cannot finish for myself, with truth—all that he leaves unsaid.[32]

This off chance comment reflects Whitton's incessant and restless compulsion always to be in the thick of things. In turn, her friends urged her to rest, not to overtire herself, but at the same time they re-inforced her idealistic hopes by praising her energy, her intellect, her sense of order, and her "visions." If Whitton ever had doubts about her ability, such encouragement and confidence served to overcome them. Meanwhile she dabbled with ideas about teaching, office work, and graduate studies.

Writing from Tallendal in 1918, Esther thanked Charlotte for the books she sent and admitted to great loneliness.[33] Soon after, she excitedly invited Charlotte to stay for a few days and begged her not to divide her attention this time between her own family and their friendship. "Let your relatives go hang. We owe each other a day or two of our own company." The temptation to bask in Esther's affections and engage in lively discussion must have been great. Certainly, she thought Esther's letters were the most delightful "ever a girl wrote"—no wonder considering the praise they contained: "I heard from Mrs. MacDougall and she said her mother was much impressed with your cleverness. I wrote to her and gave her a long list of your accomplishments and perfections."

With Elizabeth wrestling with her demons in the cold north and Charlotte pacing the floor with self-doubt in Toronto, Nell was abjectly living out the daily teaching routine in Picton. She was overjoyed to receive Whitton's letters for they had been estranged in the last months of Queen's. The reason for the estrangement is unknown, but the joy of reconciliation is recorded. Nell told her friend in February, 1919, of the many nights when she worried Lottie no longer "cared a darn," and she

> had many a quiet little cry in my own room and went out harder and more controlled to show I did not care a darn either. I cared more than I can confess. . . . I want you for a friend just as badly as you could ever want anyone.[34]

There is something strangely touching in Nell's open letters, showing the inmost being of a sensitive, uncertain young woman.

> Lottie, do you get homesick for the girls and Queen's and the grand old life? Sometimes I could just lay my head on my hands and cry. A great loneliness and a great longing just grips me and a veritable flood of emotions, enough to sink a navy, masters me. . . . Queen's gave me friends, she gave me ideals, she gave me life, real and earnest. I came from Queen's selfish enough but still infinitely more unselfish than I entered her halls.[35]

She wondered, in astonishment, what Charlotte liked in her. And Nell concluded miserably that she guessed she needed someone "to cuddle me just a little to take away the homesick longing for the old '17 and set me strong on both feet again." Such letters moved Whitton. Given her own overwhelming nostalgia for the past, she certainly would have given Nell the cuddle she so desperately craved.

When Nell described her ten weeks at Chalmers Settlement House where she witnessed the depths of human misery, her generosity is apparent. "I can see a world outside my own now, infinitely more important and so vast, so powerful, both for good and evil. My whole soul seems reaching out and longing to touch real life."[36] Her longing was not for "service" or a career but for marriage where she could touch real life in a permanent commitment to another. Nell, Mary, and Esther all chose the path that Whitton struggled to resist. They chose to marry.

Not all of Charlotte's demanding and possessive urgings to write were returned. One friend, Dorothy, apparently did not feel the same need to continue with old friendships and wrote only intermittently. Finding Charlotte's letters either too histrionic or too facile, in May 1919, she wrote a bemused reply to her Toronto correspondent.

> You speak of the 'friendship that once was' and you clothe it in a purple wreath and with due honour and ceremony place it aside. But why bury it, old thing? I never knew that it had died. Next time you must send me 'in memoriam' cards, or the shock will be too great. I knew for a while that it had 'lay sick of a fever' but was it my fault old dear? If so, I never realized it. My emotions are of a sedate nature—you speak of would-be friends I have 'discarded.' You know my nature pretty well and I do like frivolity. . . . I simply can't breathe for long in their attitude. It's too high, for me Lottie. I have come down to the good old earth too frequently to dance and laugh away the time. I wasn't made for the other—that's all.[37]

But if Dorothy was not made for high-mindedness or even indulgent metaphysical romanticism, Esther and Mo gave Whitton the blend of emotional sustenance she sought.

The letters between Mo and "Lots" are tempestuous, even ardent. Sometimes Mo felt too deeply to reply immediately, and she tried to make her letters as delicately structured as Charlotte's before she would send them off. Yet Mo intuitively realized that such intensity was destined to diminish and that she and "Law" could not share their lives because they were so different.

> You must have thought me such a weakling to put such a young question to you as I did that night [about the firmness of friendship]. But when you reach the wrenching moments which come now and then; when you doubt yourself and your whole power of gaining the love you crave, when your soul aches silently for that something which you feel in the glow of the sunset or the lap of the water on the stones, or the cool breeze from the pines, or in the warm kindliness of human sympathy, and then feel the barrier of a nature too reserved and sensitive to realize that thing, it means something to you just to hear someone say they can care for you. Thanks so much Law dear. I just felt that if I could only keep you awhile longer, I

could absorb some of your strength and enthusiasm and I could go ahead. I
think I will always remember you as you went out into the night and half
way down the steps turned and smiled good-bye from those queer Irish
eyes of yours that say a dozen of things all at once.[38]

In many ways this was a "good-bye" letter for none afterwards were quite as
emotionally charged.

Nevertheless, within a year or so of leaving Queen's, the intensity between the
friends and the intimacies that came so naturally to them inevitably diminished.
Even Esther's forthright love and Mo's poignant devotion gradually transformed.
Whitton's self-absorption and restlessness to be elsewhere even when with those
she loved assisted in the diminuition. Esther's pleasure in their friendship
made her "glad but much afraid" because she felt that she was "worthy of no
such devotion." To her "dear bit of Loveliness" she added:

> You can do so much in this world and I think you will, with that same
> determination and strength to conquer that which has always been
> yours . . . suffice it that the love you give fills me with a sense of pride,
> responsibility, and a deep desire to be worthy of it.[39]

Elsewhere she tenderly said that "by night and by day" she would claim
Charlotte as her "rightful possession." After a particularly satisfying visit she
wrote teasingly: "I wish I could have kept you until you knew what it meant to do
anything you like following the line of least resistance."[40]

Esther's last remark was not as guilelessly erotic as it appears. She was merely
observing what Whitton's friends did frequently—that this compulsively active
woman did not stay around long nor engage herself deeply. Whitton was always
plotting what problem to attack next. Every day was full of engagements, and
every next day was full of commitments. The line of "least resistance" merely
meant that she might stay a little longer, relax a little more, work a little less
strenuously, and give a little more of herself. The appeal, however, was futile for
this was not Whitton's nature.

It is in Mo's candid and generous letters that most clearly show the objects of
Whitton's ardor fading into the background of memories about Queen's and
the bonds of Levana. Although they were all to retain close ties for the
remainder of their lives, Whitton, while choosing not to marry, was placing her
hopes and affections more and more in Margaret Grier. The seriousness of the
friendship was recognized by Mo as early as 1920 when the two women met. Mo
good naturedly confessed liking her "rival" very much.

> I fancy she is the sort you can rely on all right. I hope you do not always tease
> her as much as you did at the picnic or you will have her sweet disposition
> ruined.[41]

Margaret and "C.W.," as Grier tended to call her in letters to mutual friends, enjoyed a quietly respectful and often playful relationship with each other. "Margs" or "Mardie" had not only a "sweet disposition" but also a droll sense of humour. In an early letter written in the summer of 1920 while Whitton was away at a camp, Grier described "a nice tea at Doris's and a stupid evening of bridge at Mary Price's" after Charlotte left, "but the note that I found in my bed did help to further the delusion that I had something better than a pillow under my head." With repressed anxiety, she teased:

> Well I seem to have given you a very full account of my doings since your departure. I hope yours will be as harmless as mine but of course with all those nice young curates up there, almost anything might happen. I wonder that Bill allows you to go off like this anyway.[42]

As Bill's relationship with Whitton was mostly conducted by writing, with little of that, it seems that Whitton used his interest to rationalize either her disinterest in men or her lack of male company. What is clearer is that she *wanted* her friends, including Margaret, to see him as a serious admirer. Despite her career plans, she obviously felt besieged by the norms of a society that urges its members into heterosexual coupling.

A year later Mo relinquished all claims on Charlotte's affections. After thanking Charlotte for a gift of a necklace, she said:

> I must admit you are a most diplomatic bigamist and an irresistible hubby. It pleases me to think Marg. has a similar string and that I can wear mine in Toronto without fearing losing eyes or hair. . . . Give my love to Margaret and tell her I esteem her in spite of her usurpation.[43]

The terms "hubby" and "bigamist" do not describe any homosexual activity. They are merely a carry-over of the sorority language used between "particular" friends.

When Mo wrote her last really intimate letter in January 1922 and expressed her concern about Lottie's obvious exhaustion and her full calendar, she referred once more to Margaret:

> I have always loved your eyes, Law; they are so expressive, with their changing lights, their yearning appeal and withal that merry understanding twinkle behind them. They are *you*, Law, and I like them but I don't like to see that tired look there . . . I must say the more I see of my rival and successor the more convinced I am of the wisdom of your selection. Jealousy merges into admiration. Margaret *is* splendid, isn't she? She should be in a home of her own, for she would make it a place worth while.[44]

The home Margaret was to make was with Charlotte, and by all accounts together they did make it "a place worth while."

Perhaps the words of Virginia Woolf's Clarissa Dalloway explains the nature of these friendships. As she recalls her young friendship with Sally Seton, she asks "Had not that, after all, been love?" They had "sat up till all hours of the night talking," absorbed in themselves.

> The strange thing, on looking back, was the purity, the integrity, of her feeling for Sally. It was not like one's feeling for a man. It was completely disinterested, and besides it had a quality which could only exist between women, between women just grown up. It was protective, on her side; sprang from a sense of being in league together, a presentiment of some-thing that was bound to part them (they spoke of marriage always as a catastrophe), which led to this chivalry, this protective feeling which was much more on her side than Sally's . . . But the charm was overpowering, to her at least, so that she could remember standing in her bedroom at the top of the house holding hot water can in her hands and saying aloud, 'She is beneath this roof—She is beneath this roof!'[45]

As the emotional side to her life was being met by Margaret Grier, the professional side of her life was being met by her new associations in the social service milieu in Toronto. These associates, from the "Kats" House or made through SSCC committee work and social welfare agencies across the country, she retained for many decades. By the time she was preparing to leave Toronto Whitton had built an entirely new female support structure—a cohort of mostly single younger women uniformly involved at various levels in social and child welfare. The Levana women had been replaced by what might be loosely described as the "Whitton Connection," with Charlotte Whitton its recognized leader and its most articulate spokesperson. It included Marjorie Moore, Elizabeth King, Ethel Dodds (later to become Mrs. G. Cameron Parker), Nora Lea, Kate Dickson, Laura Holland, Elsie Lawson, Jane Wisdom, and Mary MacPhedran, to name only a few. All of these names would appear on future social welfare survey reports conducted under Whitton's directions, and some would be placed in key positions across the country.

Whitton's former mentors were also replaced by other older women whom she admired and emulated. These women demonstrate the importance role models assumed for the new social work professionals. Two of them, Emily Murphy and Helen R.Y. Reid, had proved themselves as significant social reformers in their own right and as representatives of an earlier generation of philanthropists, volunteer social workers, and social reformers.

In *Beyond Separate Spheres* (1982) Rosalind Rosenberg observes that there have been three dominant patterns to female professional life: private financial support, spousal support, and celibacy.[46] While it was celibacy that was to become the common pattern in the first half of the twentieth century, the other two patterns were common when Emily Murphy and Helen Reid reached the peak of their powers. Murphy, a married woman, was sustained partly through inherited economic means but also through the encouragement and financial status of her husband and family connections; Reid, a woman of independent means, was sustained through family inheritance; and Whitton, a woman of modest income and humble family origins was sustained by a single status that enabled her to earn a living.[47] Reid, Murphy, and Whitton were three historical actors who lobbied for the establishment of a Children's Bureau during the immediate post-war years with Whitton, of course, a relative latecomer in the movement which had begun in 1913 and which came to symbolize child welfare as a "woman's cause."

Whitton deliberately cultivated Helen Reid and Emily Murphy as "contacts." Their public approval and personal promotion inducted her into social reform in a generous and practical manner that legitimated Whitton's aspirations for leadership. Their correspondence to Whitton was teasing, amorous, affectionate, and replete with sound advice.

Emily Murphy was already in her early fifties when she and Whitton worked on various SSCC committees and on the executive of the National Council of Women. In 1901 she had written "Impressions of Janey Canuck Abroad" while in England, and by 1917 she was the first woman judge of the Juvenile Court in Alberta. Within a year Alice Jamieson of Calgary and Helen MacGill of Vancouver became judges also. It was Emily Murphy, who in 1927 was to become the main protagonist of the famous "Persons Case" which was to complete the legal enfranchisement of Canadian women.[48]

Murphy was entrusting National Council of Women (NCW) resolutions and executive work to Whitton because:

> There is no one else I would prefer to discuss these matters with, because of your experience in social service work and because of your quick understanding, clear judgement and sense of balance. You're a fair-minded kid, too: are fearless, and—oh well! because I've loved you this *long, long* while.
>
>   Your old pal,
>   Janey Canuck.

It is not difficult to appreciate how much prestige Whitton gained in having such a mentor. On one occasion Murphy wrote to her "dear youngster" that she would "contend"

> until my tongue wears out—if one can contemplate so dire a contingency—that no House of Legislation should continue to exist in which over half the electorate is unrepresented.[49]

Murphy's criticisms of the Senate system fired Whitton's own suffragism, and the two agreed as much on feminist issues as they did on the need for a Canadian Children's Bureau.

Helen Reid, a woman of intellectual clarity and great significance in the field of social reform and one of the major actors in the founding of the CCCW, is less well known.[50] Born in 1868 of Scots parents, Reid was in the first class of women to enter McGill University. Her father directed the Montreal Sculpture and General Marble and Granite Works, and he was also a sculptor, a liberal, and a unitarian. The libertarian atmosphere in which she was raised encouraged her to follow in her mother's social reforming footsteps. Eliza Reid agitated for public playgrounds and public baths; she urged women to exercise the franchise; and she introduced her daughter to ideas about charity organization. The Reids actively promoted the examination of immigrants, government control of liquor, cremation, private hearings for juvenile delinquents, and better housing for the poor.

Active in the Red Cross and the only female member of the Canadian Patriotic Fund, Reid "brought experience and courage and sacrifice and more besides—a genius for organization and the unmistakable flame of leadership." During the First World War, she received imperial honours and international awards, and afterwards, honorary degrees from Queen's and McGill. She became Chairman of the Graduate School of Nurses and Director of the Social Service Department at McGill. It was her shrewd judgment and practical experience that frequently restrained the more impetuous Whitton while they sat together on SSCC committees and during her leadership of the Canadian Council on Child Welfare.[51]

Helen Reid's work life was organized around a "Prayer Star" which she described as "a gentle device for the daily practice of the presence of God." The star had five points; Life, Work, Health, Love, and Peace. Two verses best summarize the gentle but sturdy Miss Reid:

> Work: Hard work in fruitful ways
>   We pray thee, God, so fill our days,
>   Strained muscle, eager mind
>   To strive together for mankind.

> Love: To know what love has been, to love again,
>   To feel the heart leap up as friends draw near,
>   To share their sorrows, understand their pain,
>   To worship God, throughout his sun and rain—
>   Why! God is here!

One line in Reid's poem "Contemplation" illustrates her straightforward and generous nature. She severely chastises herself with a maxim she tried to adhere to—"harness the prattle of thy loose-hung tongue."[52]

Demonstrating a remarkable talent for gaining instant respect while not tolerating autocratic behaviour, Reid confidently asserted her belief in equality whenever she felt she was receiving highhanded treatment.[53] While she was on the committees for Graduate Nursing and the Social Service Department, her exchanges with eminent Montreal gentlemen, including McGill's principal, Sir Arthur Currie, were terse statements of an impatience towards supercilious assertions of status. A woman of genteel circumstance, she was nevertheless a hard-nose pragmatist, and unlike Whitton, she was rarely swayed by the claims of privilege or meritocracy. She refused to be bullied by authority or to try to ingratiate herself. At the same time, she handled Whitton with a singular patience. Her civility emerges in their correspondence where she urges her younger friend to be less cynical and less impatient.

> Now, dear little girl, don't get too discouraged about social work—a person of your ability and pace meets criticism, envy, and impatience, because others cannot keep up with you or have places that do not fall in with yours. Try to see things from their point of view. Politically dictators are effective in times like these. They may be needed in the social field, but there, they have not the same power! Do you ever wish you were in politics?[54]

The last remark could only have been made by someone who both loved Whitton dearly and fully understood her temperament.

This indulgent correspondence demonstrates the importance of exemplars and mentors in Whitton's early career. Encouragement by Reid and Murphy helped her to assess her abilities as well as transform her ambitions into realizable goals. More relaxed with her deferential protegee than Whitton was with her, Reid signed her letters with "admiration and affectionately." They seemed to fire each other's enthusiasms like sparks on an anvil in the mutual attraction of strong personalities. Reid learned how to handle Whitton's impetuousness: in 1925, when she found herself overwhelmed by Whitton's interminably long and always urgent queries, she gently teased her in one reply, "I suppose I might as well arrange to write you daily! Are we in love? Why! Yes! Why not!"[55] Same sex support structures thus continued to sustain Whitton's professional life and the distinctions of collegiality and friendship, protegee and mentor were peculiarly and even refreshingly blurred just as in her private life the distinctions between the erotic and the platonic, the collegial and the personal were also indistinct.

There was a third older woman, an American, who inspired Whitton during her Toronto years. The first chief of the U.S. Children's Bureau, Julia Lathrop represented for Whitton the possibilities of becoming a Canadian counterpart.

Lathrop attended a SSCC conference in 1920, and she and the much younger Whitton immediately responded to each other. Moreover, this was to be a crucial international contact because Lathrop assisted Whitton some years later in obtaining the position as assessor to the League of Nations. At the time of their introduction, Lathrop was sixty-two, and she introduced Whitton to important child welfare workers such as Grace Abbott, the second chief of the Children's Bureau, and Katharine Lenroot, who followed in this position after Abbott's resignation in 1934.

Born in Illinois in 1858, Lathrop graduated from Vassar in 1880 and then worked in her father's legal firm for ten years before joining Hull House. There she became an intimate of the famous American reformer and progressive, Jane Addams. During her early experiences in settlement work, Lathrop mixed with some of the Republic's distinguished thinkers, writers, and social and political reformers, including George Herbert Mead, John Dewey, Emma Goldman, and Booker T. Washington. She had also entertained Kier Hardie, Sydney and Beatrice Webb, and the Russian anarchist, Prince Kropotkin. This friendship strengthened Whitton's resolve to become something more important to Canada than the Assistant Secretary to the SSCC. Thus her restlessness can be seen to be in proportion to those successful women she met in her early career and for whom she cared on a personal as well as on a professional level.

During her four years with the SSCC, the private and the public facets of Whitton's life gradually came together. Her experiences and friendships gave her strength, encouragement, and even inspiration. The network of associates she made were to be her support and mainstay for the next two decades of work in child welfare. Many of her associates on SSCC committees between 1918 and 1922 show up time and again in her social surveys and reports in later years. In addition to Helen Reid and Emily Murphy, they included Margaret K. Nairn of the YWCA and the Reverend Claude Edwin Silcox, whose association would tarnish Whitton's credibility during the bitter family allowances debates in the 1940s. Others such as Vera Moberley, Dorothy King, Robert E. Mills, Howard Falk, Maude Riley, Marjorie Bradford, Canon Vernon, Brother Barnabus, Percy Paget, Eunice Dyke, Adelaide Plumptre, Dr. Gordon Bates, and D.B. Harkness reappeared often as the child and social welfare crusade gained impetus in the 1920s and 1930s. Those individuals who did not sit on the various SSCC committees were corresponding members of the SSCC and represented such diverse social agencies as the Toronto Children's Aid Society, children's homes, Public Health Departments, Neighbourhood Workers' Associations, family life bureaux, Social Service of Calgary, the Montreal Council of Social Agencies, the national YWCA, the Canadian Social Hygiene Council, the Committee for Women's Immigration and Household Service, Victoria's Social Service League, Winnipeg social agencies, the Edmonton Board of Social Welfare, and all the main line protestant churches.

In her last months with the SSCC, during the last week of March 1922, Whitton's triumphal return to Renfrew as one of the town's "most distinguished and scholarly young ladies" took place just as the community was discussing a new Collegiate Institute. At the invitation of the Ladies Aid of the Methodist Church, Whitton spoke on child welfare, challenging her audience by unfavourably comparing Renfrew's infant mortality figures with those of New York and London. She discussed child labour, school attendance laws, the children's aid societies, the plight of the illegitimate child, and the problem of the feebleminded. The last topic was certain to draw a sympathetic and anxious response.

> Many homes . . . from which they had to take children should never have been founded. It was criminal to allow children to be born into the world when one knew that the chances were strong that they would be idiots. The old theory that parents used to have when they had married Daft Mary to Simple Bob they had done a good job would have to be rooted out. We have got to grapple courageously with the feebleminded problem.[56]

In keeping with her position in *Social Welfare*, she deplored the double standard of morality with regard to the illegitimate child by rejecting the notion that without strict laws enforcing paternal support until the child was sixteen, any man "worth calling a man" would accept such responsibilities. She cited figures demonstrating that this was far from the case while she berated lax marriage licence laws and insisted that it should not be "easier for a man to get a licence to keep a wife than it was to get a licence to keep a dog." Using sentiments first expressed in *Social Welfare*, she condemned a society that made the unwed mother bear the stigma while the father was accepted in society, and she uncompromisingly defended the child of such unions.

At the conclusion of the speech, the Reverend Mr. Raney described her "peroration" as the "most eloquent" he had heard. After little Frances Grigg presented Miss Whitton with flowers the evening was completed by two solos, and the concluding remarks observed that "while a prophet may be without honour in his own country it did not seem true about a prophetess."

If Whitton had joined the Social Service Council at the beginning of its most vigorous period, she conveniently left it just prior to its decline. The most obvious causes of the Council's troubles were the continuing economic crisis of the 1920s and financial costs of the temperance campaigns that by 1923 had a forced national organization to act as a receiver for six provincial councils. An even more serious problem centred around the Council's links with the churches. Since there was little difference between the various social service departments of the churches and the SSCC and its provincial councils, the establishment of an Inter-Church Advisory Council in 1920 and the revival of the church union movement quickly raised the issue of overlap.[57]

By 1921, the Inter-Church Advisory Council's call for "a full-scale reorganiza-
tion of the national council" prompted the SSCC national executive to circulate
a proposal that called for centralized financing and budgeting and a unified
structure for national and provincial councils. Despite these efforts, the SSCC
was forced to cut its budget for 1923, and Shearer's death in March 1925
removed the driving force behind the council as the major voluntary social
service organization in Canada.[58]

Thus, Whitton's decision to leave the SSCC in 1922 for a position in Ottawa
was sensible on several grounds. First, the signs of financial difficulties ahead
were visible. Second, the creation of the Inter-Church Advisory Council suggested a desire on the part of the churches to bring social service more fully
under their supervision and to erode the line between non-denominational
social service and the work of the individual churches. Consequently, by 1922
the SSCC had little to commend itself to an ambitious man or woman who
hoped for a career in social service unencumbered by sectarian restrictions. On
1 July 1922, Shearer's "faithful and brilliant assistant secretary" was granted
leave, and the end of the year, Whitton's resignation was finally accepted. Her
place was taken by "another brilliant Queen's graduate," her friend, Elizabeth P.
MacCallum.[59]

3

AN OTTAWA MARRIAGE

*Marriage is not by any to be enterprised, nor
taken in hand unadvisedly, lightly or wantonly;
but reverently, discreetly, advisedly, soberly,
and in the fear of God.*

BOOK OF COMMON PRAYER.

When Whitton joined the SSCC in 1918, it had fourteen Dominion-wide affiliates and eleven provincial units (including Newfoundland and Bermuda), Shearer had become its full-time secretary, and its annual budget had been increased from $2,000 to $10,000, which allowed it to start publishing *Social Welfare* and to employ a paid staff at the national office.

Montreal and Toronto provided the Canadian forum for social welfare innovations during the first three decades of the twentieth century as well as a vibrant theoretical climate in which to test new ideas about the co-ordination of philanthropy and scientific charity organization. As environment superseded moral defect as the major explanation of dependency and delinquency, social workers were eager to discover the internal and external pressures which interfered with normal family life. If dependency and delinquency were the results of psychological and sociological disturbances, then intervention as a form of prevention was both possible and desirable.

Whitton's perceptions of the opportunities in social welfare were based on her awareness of the debates in the United States and Great Britain rather than the contemporary Canadian scene. American women were a particularly powerful example of female service in both national voluntary social service associations and a federal agency for child welfare. Canadian voluntary organizations, while neither as numerous nor as developed as their American counterparts, were not dissimilar in purposes, methods, and female participation. The most obvious distinction was the establishment of the United States Children's

Bureau (USCB) in 1912, which represented public recognition that trained professional women were the natural administrators and organizers of child welfare.

The SSCC's advocacy of a "children's bureau for Canada" allowed Whitton to become deeply involved in the debate over the nature of federal participation in child welfare. The founding of the Canadian Council on Child Welfare (CCCW) as well as the establishment of the medicalized child welfare division in the Department of Health in 1920 profoundly altered the course of Whitton's life in two ways. First, the final shape of the Federal child welfare division and the appointment of a medical chief, Dr. Helen MacMurchy, meant that there would be no such careers for social service activists such as Whitton.[1] In the United States, the Children's Bureau had offered leadership positions to female social service reformers. A medicalized Canadian agency destroyed a potential career path for a generation of Canadian women. Secondly, with the federal route blocked, Whitton was forced to turn to voluntary organization for a fulltime professional career. Her work with the Canadian Council on Child Welfare was the practical expression of ambition and intelligence driven into the private welfare sector and she proved herself more than equal to the challenge.

Although the Toronto years had been ones of initiation into social service, Toronto was not the city that would best facilitate Whitton's ambitions. Just as the United States Children's Bureau was situated in the American capital, Washington, D.C., so too the CCCW, if it were to become a voluntary equivalent of the Children's Bureau, must be housed in Canada's capital, close to patronage and to the major source of funding. Whitton's move to Ottawa, therefore, was the decisive act of her life. During the next three years she made personal and professional decisions that permanently shaped her future.

For many, Ottawa would be dull in comparison to Toronto. In 1921 its population was only 107,843 in comparison to Toronto's 521,893, and it had no burgeoning suburbs or easy connections with the major American cities. But Whitton was a political animal.

Whitton's ostensible job when she left the SSCC was as private secretary to liberal M.P. Thomas A. Low. First elected in 1908 and re-elected in 1911, Low had stepped aside to allow the Honorable George P. Graham to win a seat. By the time he was again elected in 1921, he was well-known as a Liberal Party organizer in Ontario. Tom Low, a lumber merchant and manufacturer from Renfrew, "needed a capable assistant, one who he knew and could trust implicitly." A daughter of a fellow townsman, Whitton had the ability, training, and experience. Moreover, Low remembered her as the bright graduate of the Renfrew Collegiate Institute who had won the Low medal in 1914. Ottawa and Low's offer represented a change in her fortunes and a return to the "Valley." When Low was appointed minister of Trade and Commerce on 17 August 1923,

Whitton went on the civil service payroll as a temporary appointment at $3,360 per annum.[2]

The fledgling CCCW, which had grown out of the attempt to organize child welfare nationally, had been located in Ottawa since its founding in 1920. Whitton, its honorary secretary, would now be in an ideal situation to convert her position into a full-time administrative role and transform the CCCW into the major Canadian child welfare agency. However, to play it safe, given that Low's appointment was only as secure as the Liberal government, Whitton requested leave of absence from the SSCC until she was more confident of a life in Ottawa. Her friend Emily Murphy wrote to her when she heard of Low's offer. After saying that Whitton's departure would be "a very vital loss" to the SSCC, she continued:

> We had come to look upon you as an indispensable part of the machinery and I know that Dr. Shearer was planning to lay even more responsibility on you. . . . I cannot well imagine your hiding your light under the proverbial bushel and I shall await the result with great interest. At any rate I am always happy to hear of your success and well being, for you may take it from me that no young girl in Canada is so well known and as widely beloved as you.[3]

The July 1922 issue of *Social Welfare* predicted that Whitton was destined to be a member of Parliament, perhaps even a cabinet minister, in the not too distant future.[4] Such predictions were not uncommon in the immediate years that followed, and without a doubt Whitton firmly believed them too.

Grier, now secretary to the Canadian Tuberculosis Association, moved with her. With their joint salaries, the women were able to maintain an apartment on James Street. Since salaries for women were always lower than those of their male counterparts, single women who chose to live alone either "boarded" or rented a mean little "bed-sitter." They could only maintain a comfortable standard of living as a "dual household." The economic imperatives behind such arrangements meant that not all women in such households were "women identified women" like Whitton and Grier. Such female households could include a widowed mother and daughter (as with Whitton's friend Hilda Laird), cousins or siblings, or companionate friends.

As Low's private secretary, Whitton accompanied him when he sailed for England on 10 June 1924. Although Low had originally intended to visit the Department of Trade and Commerce's commercial intelligence offices in Great Britain and Europe, negotiations in London for a government contract for a North Atlantic fleet caused Low to cancel his planned visits to Copenhagen and Hamburg. When the Government undertook to improve trade with the British West Indies, Low was appointed to head a trade delegation to the islands.

Whitton planned to accompany Low as part of the delegation in January 1925; however, Low decided to stay behind because of the opening of Parliament, and Whitton lost her Caribbean trip.[5]

At the same time as she was working for Low, Whitton spent all her spare time in the cluttered CCCW Plaza Building office with the secretary, Miss Kate Dixon, and Margaret Grier. With an annual federal grant of $1,000 for the first two years, raised in 1922 to $5,000, the Council would not be able to maintain an executive secretary until it increased its affiliates and subscriptions or generated monies by offering consulting services. Therefore, in a major effort to publicize the Council, Whitton devoted many evenings and weekends to mailing pre- and post-natal letters, brochures, and diet folders. Whitton solicited articles for and edited *Child Welfare News*, the Council's publication. For her efforts she received a $500 honorarium each year. Even before January 1926 when the Council was able to sustain a permanent office staff and an executive administrative officer, she wrote reports on child labour, published a summary of child and family welfare laws in an effort to standardize it, and analyzed juvenile delinquency under the counsel of W.L. Scott, the framer of the Juvenile Delinquents Act of 1908. In addition, the Council called annual conferences and published their proceedings, conducted studies of mother's allowances, published a national directory of child welfare agencies and a census of handicapped children's services, and planned social welfare surveys. A special contribution by the Montreal Woman's Canadian Club financed the Council's first survey into juvenile immigration.

During her first years in Ottawa however, she could not be sure that the CCCW would become a significant national agency, nor could she relinquish all thoughts of marriage. Whitton may have been tempted by the comforts of sexual intimacy, children, family relationships and domesticity; however, her experiences of marriage in the case of her parents must have influenced her overall perceptions, not of marriage as a viable institution, which she never doubted in the theoretical or the ideal sense, but as a personal state which did not necessarily guarantee conviviality. In an age without sophisticated birth control methods and, even more critical, without the moral and social justifications that allowed a combination of career with motherhood, there were few alternatives. Women either married or pursued full-time careers. Only in exceptional cases were they able to combine both. And Whitton, convinced that she could make something of her world, could not accept the anonymity of marriage.

If Whitton was temperamentally a woman whose primary relationships had been and would remain with other women, this orientation was reinforced by the objective conditions of her career, and if her professional interests contributed to her identifications with her own sex, Whitton's single status ensured that she would remain a woman-identified-woman. Judging by the evidence Whitton left in her personal papers, she intended the future to know that she made the choice of career over marriage with full consciousness of the consequences. Mo had predicted no less in their Queen's days when she noted Whitton's all consuming passion for service: "You must give all or not at all," she wrote, "yet that decision will involve sacrifice which will perhaps leave a place in your woman's heart forever unfulfilled."[6]

The decision to remain unmarried was not easy. Indeed from Queen's on Whitton developed a psychological safety device, a rationalization for her lack of interest in men as suitors. She called this safety device, her "program" and shared it with her closest friends and Professor Gordon. Apparently unable or unwilling to relinquish Bill King's affections altogether, she used it to stave off his attentions. By sharing her "program" with him, since Queen's she had been able to effectively postpone any emotional commitment. The "program" itself was clearcut. She would work for several years in order to put aside savings; first, to enable her two brothers and young sister to have a university education, and second, so that she might then pursue graduate studies. In a time when family duty was emphasized over personal needs, her program was not seen as excessive. She did not propose to pay for her siblings' education entirely from her own funds. Instead, J.B. was to go through university and in turn continue the process with Stephen. Stephen's responsibility was for Kathleen. However, Charlotte was prepared to advance loans if necessary.

After his return from France, J.B. did not go immediately to university, which was fortunate for Whitton could not have managed to support him on $100 a month. Between 1920 and 1924 his sister lent him $1,267.25, a considerable sum for those days. However, the autocratic manner in which she dispensed her loans caused resentment. Often berating her brother, whom she saw as feckless and selfish, she exacted a gratitude which chaffed him. Her father too was irritated at what he thought to be an overdose of moral rectitude towards the young man, and he chastised his "dear daughter" for cutting J.B. off ten weeks before his course at Queen's had ended. As a result Stephen refused to be indebted to his sister and balked at going to Queen's.[7]

The estrangement between brother and sister had been provoked by J.B. buying, instead of renting, a dress suit for a Science dance. On one occasion his sister fumed, "I asked you to be a little unselfish and do what others were doing for you, go without something." After peppering her reprimand with requests that he be more manly, decent, and honourable and stop leading their mother "a dog's life" she continued:

> You arrange to pay for your suit in the summer as soon as you get to work, where any man, who appreciated what his sister had done for him, and was trying to do, would be thinking of paying her back first thing. . . . I have done my best and gone without a new dress and am staying at home from

the Governor-General's drawing room. . . . Stephen goes down in the fall
and I am relying on your repayments to help me with his course.[8]

Responding to J.B.'s accusation that her tantrums would "shorten" their mother's
life, she complained that the family "used" her. With a bachelor of civil
engineering degree, J.B. became a town engineer for Renfrew, and later he
constructed and opened the Smelting Works in Kitimat, British Columbia.

Despite his sister's complaints, Stephen was able to go down to Queen's in the
Fall after all. Later, in 1928, he dropped out of his B.Comm. programme
disaffected with "being short of funds and relying on someone else." He
explained to his sister that he had "qualms of repugnance at continuing to
accept [your] aid."[9] It was not until 1936 that he finally received his degree.
Kathleen had entered Queen's in 1923 and received her B.A. with honours in
1926. Until then Stephen was a disappointment to Whitton and the only
impediment to the full realization of her "program." The following comment,
although made in 1936, is *apropos* because it describes the family feelings about
a sister who was such a success. When Whitton intervened in Stephen's life
during the Great Depression to obtain employment for him, the director of an
employment bureau wrote:

> My own unchecked impression is that deep in his subconscious is the
> feeling that he has got to find a job on his own without the help of his
> overwhelming sister. His sense of loyalty to you, however, represses this
> natural feeling. As Bernard Shaw's character replied when asked if it was
> not embarrassing for a doctor to have a waiter for a father, "Possibly, but it is
> more embarrassing for a waiter to have a doctor for a son."[10]

Charlotte was always "overwhelming," and family responses were mixed: admiration,
envy, resentment, and pride. If Whitton had any major besetting sin, it was her
unquestioning faith not only in her abilities but also in her *right* to make major
decisions for other people.

Bill King also chaffed at Whitton's autocratic tendencies. If J.B. called her "the
little Czar," King called her "Miss Judge" and also found it difficult to come up to
her standards. If he and J.B. both found settling down after the war difficult,
Whitton found it just as difficult to understand why. As a returned serviceman,
Bill King moved from being an engineer in Hamilton in a firm that went
bankrupt to Oakville, Ontario, where he established "The King Engineering
and Contracting Company," which did very well by the thirties.

While toying with Bill's affections, Whitton received another proposal from a
young doctor from Medicine Hat. In December 1923, Max B. wrote:

> Lottie I've wanted you since College days. I cannot say I was fully intensely

in love—more a great admiration and a wonderful sense of good comradeship, an understanding beyond all common ken, and don't you think that leads where we would go? Geo. Kelly and I were speaking on the subject in England and he said when your name was mentioned, he'd be afraid . . . to marry someone that was cleverer and knew more than he did. I thought that it was more a case of one's manhood matched with womanhood so to speak—yet it has caused me much thought.[11]

For a woman like Whitton, such a timid approach was bound to remain unconvincing, and she does not seem to have been even remotely tempted. Max urgently telegraphed "Please relieve the tension. Send a favourable reply if possible." In January 1924, she sent a terse and business-like response— "Received letter and wire, and appreciate both."[12]

The relationship with Bill King groaned finally to a painful halt. The long separations and the geographical and psychological distances between them inevitably led to "possibilities for doubt and uncertainty," just as the few social occasions that Whitton's frenzied schedule allowed them to be together led to an eventual disaffection. In 1924, seven years after having agreed to abide by Whitton's program, King reminded her that he had "never bothered her" but that his patience was running out. It was during that year that Whitton fully grasped the possibilities of her professional life when she launched the juvenile immigration survey with the Council.

In 1924, just before leaving for England as part of Low's delegation, Whitton determined that the CCCW would be the leading social agency in the crusade opposing juvenile immigration. G. Bogue Smart, Director of Juvenile Immigration, had aroused Whitton's attention by his report before the CCCW conference in Winnipeg. She told the executive in April that "the step now contemplated is a serious one and will undoubtedly involve the Council and its officers in an important public controversy." She did not doubt the political importance of the debate.[13]

Formerly, critics had stressed tightening up of supervision and placement regulations to ensure the protection of the children, their attendance at school and the enforcement of indenture agreements. The CCCW, however, came to believe that nothing less than a total cessation of the movement would do. Clearly Whitton and her associates were right. Many of the provincial child welfare departments, child caring agencies, and particularly children's aid societies insisted that they should have supervisory and placement rights instead of the British societies who acted for their youthful clients *in loco parentis*. In April, Whitton wrote to W.F. Nickle, Ontario's attorney-general, that

Our protest is motivated by two convictions. First, the conviction that all dependent children within the Canadian provinces should be equally protected and safeguarded and that therefore any agency bringing children for settlement in this province should submit to the same regulations and standards of placement as we exact under the various Children's Protection Acts for our own children. . . . Secondly . . . that all dependent children fall under the jurisdiction of the provinces and therefore the provinces have the right to enforce the same inspection of application of prospective homes.[14]

On the same day, she forwarded a lengthy memorandum to all the provincial attorney-generals seeking support and information. Once more she cited Dr. Erik K. Clarke's statistics and the survey of the Toronto General Hospital. In October, pursuing the subject again with Nickle, she insisted that, "Canada as a new country with a small population can afford even less than the Old Land, the creation of a weak and derelict section of the race."[15]

Over the next four years Whitton pursued an all-out offensive against the movement in the press, at welfare conferences, and through correspondence with the Immigration officials, harassing the British immigration societies and investigating the backgrounds of the children. It was a well orchestrated crusade which included child welfare workers from every province. No other survey conducted by the CCCW reflected Whitton's genius for political sensitivity or organizational skills.

There is no doubt that Whitton saw the juvenile immigration question as the most important issue of 1924. The headline, "Juvenile Immigrants Forced on Dominion," in the *Ottawa Citizen* on 4 June 1924, reflected her confidence. Speaking before the Toronto IODE King's Birthday dinner, she said:

> Most of the juvenile immigrants from the British Isles who are children of unmarried parents are sent out by a certain prominent institution. That institution is continuing to force these children on this Dominion. The women of Canada should not tolerate the gross imposition of this well-known home [Barnardo's].

Although Whitton suspected all the British emigration societies, she despised the Barnardo Homes, probably because they were the most aggressive and the most successful. While the IODE members may have responded to such misrepresentation, "D.P.T." wrote a letter to the editor of the *Montreal Gazette* on 7 June objecting to the speech.

> It does seem a trifle absurd to think that because a child happens to be born out of wedlock in Great Britain that his (or her) immigration into this country is to have a tainting influence.

With the CCCW inquiries into juvenile immigration underway, Whitton left for England. She intended to consult with the Overseas Settlement Board about the issue as well as convey Canada's point of view in her address to the British Empire Exhibition at Wembley on 23 July and through private contacts. However, over those next colourful weeks, her interest in juvenile immigration was diverted by her first introduction to the variety and the culture of Europe. Her journal for this period is full of touching naivete and excitement. She described the sights, colours, and atmosphere of New York as she left it on 12 July 1924 with the pier "jammed and the colours of the dresses [making] one think of an old fashioned nosegay cast down carelessly in the squalor and dirt" on the harbour. Remembering that night—the Statue of Liberty disappearing as the ship left the harbour—Whitton wrote:

> She is a busty lady from all but one angle. She could have been thrown in the face of coming people only by the inspiration of the United States, and only the U.S. with its force of Democratic Convention still warm in the pot, would fail to see the humour of their bold bronze assertion. Perhaps they satisfy themselves with knowledge of the great reconciliation that their bronze symbol of liberty is a perfect symbol of that it typifies, for it too is hollow.[16]

Within a few days of leaving New York, Charlotte missed "Margie's" company and vowed she will never go on a long trip without her again; she longed to talk to a fascinating woman on board just because she looked like Margaret; she wistfully found herself "thinking such a long letter to Margaret" and then absently added that she must also "drop a line to Max, poor lad." She was also thrilled that William G. MacAdoo and his wife, Woodrow Wilson's daughter, were aboard, and she sat with them at the captain's table. He had just lost the Democratic presidential nomination.[17]

On seeing the coast of England for the first time she recorded a sense of returning "home"—a common but profound sentiment among colonials with British forebears and education revolving around British institutions and values. During this, the first of her visits to Britain she enjoyed her second experience with Royalty, a more gratifying one than in 1901 when she had cried in disappointment. On the afternoon after her Wembley address, she was a guest at a Buckingham Palace garden party, and before that she and Low's son Bill went to the review of the fleet at Portsmouth where they saw King George V and Queen Mary at close range. Canadian politicians, N.W. Rowell and R.B. Bennett were at the palace also as guests of the British Bar Association. Such events and the auspicious company helped refocus her emotional and professional horizons.

The trip to England coincided with a psychologically critical period in Whitton's life for her journal suggests a heightened emotionalism which might be seen as a vital part of resolving her struggles about marriage. Two days after arriving in London, she experienced a metaphysical translation, represented by three events whose intensity could not be merely coincidental: a profound religious experience which sacramentalized her dedication to public work; the identification with a contemporary achievement-oriented role model who fuelled her own ambitions in the public sphere; and the projected assimilation of a romanticized historical figure who inspired her own vision. Nor is it coincidental that these three events occurred at Westminster Abbey, Whitehall, and the House of Commons, all symbolic citadels of political power. The three events are conjoined in what might be described as a transcendental experience which reinforced her determination to retain her independence.

On the morning of the 22 July Whitton attended religious services at St. Faith's Chapel, Westminster Abbey, where on receiving the Eucharist she was overwhelmed by feeling "one with all the mighty past" and "the communion of Saints." Anyone, she said

> Who touches the Sacrament in the Abbey drinks of no sacred but a sacrosanct vessel—holy all the cups that hold His blood but holiest the Chalice of the Empire, for in that consecration is the greatest concourse of the Church Triumphant there.[18]

The afternoon's social events extended the metaphor of the past—her communion of saints—into the present and joined the mystical with the practical. At Whitehall with the trade delegation, Tom Moore, president of the Canadian Labor Congress, arranged a meeting with Margaret Bondfield, the first woman cabinet minister in the British government, and Whitton spoke with her about the juvenile immigration movement. Bondfield represented the possibilities Whitton envisioned for herself in Canada. Measuring herself against a contemporary whose strong personality and energetic demeanour captured her imagination, Whitton provides in her description as much a self-projection as a perceptive pen sketch.[19] Whitton wanted to be like Bondfield; indeed, she felt that she already was. Overcome with admiration, she wrote:

> There are only two men in the Canadian Cabinet whom I think could "stand up to her." Amiable, pleasant, loveable woman, is the first woman member of a British Cabinet. She could handle men and circumstance with sense, judgement, tact, and no injury.

The following comments could be a description of Whitton herself.

> Miss Bondfield, a little thing, shorter than I, like a bird, but a strong, energetic, capable bird, with still body and bright, bright eyes. She comes in hurriedly and takes off her hat and coat. She has the brightest, darkest,

quickest eyes and carried her head forward, eager, quick, piercing, searching. Her hands are strong, and capable. When she sits down you forget she is short. She does not sit back in her chair, but upright, always. She has kindness, tolerance, and humour hid in her eyes, and the soft lines about them. And she knows, and you know that she knows what she is talking about and what is more, what you are talking about.

The difference between Bondfield and women such as Emily Murphy, Helen Reid, or Julia Lathrop was the difference between their social backgrounds and economic circumstances. Like Whitton's, Bondfield's background was modest; her career was made possible by sheer determination and not by family or spousal financial connections. Coming from a poor family, she had struggled from age thirteen when she left school to work in a haberdashery to become the sole woman delegate to the Trades Union Congress, delegate to the International Labour Conference in Washington, and the Socialist International Conference at Berne. After capturing a Labour seat in 1923, she became parliamentary secretary to the Minister of Labour in 1924 under Ramsay MacDonald and was Great Britain's delegate to the International Labour Conference at Geneva. Significantly Bondfield too was unmarried.[20]

At the time of their meeting at Whitehall, the two women's views on the juvenile immigration question seemed similar although they were to shift subtly once Bondfield, having investigated the situation in Canada, wrote a major report on it in the fall of 1924. What Bondfield, also an electrifying speaker, thought of Whitton's resounding address on child welfare and immigration at the Exhibition the next day is not known. As a Labour politician, she could not have failed to understand the drift of Whitton's views about restricting immigration to the right classes because the lower classes contributed to the enfeeblement of a young nation. Whitton proclaimed:

> Canada is making a determined effort to rid her youthful blood of this poison of mental deficiency with its attendant social evils, and to this end is taking every precaution against its national reproduction. Consequently, she is enforcing a stringent immigration regulation to guard as far as possible against the influx from other shores of the poison that she is combatting at home.[21]

Whitton returned to Canada on the same ship as Bondfield, who was to study the plight of British juvenile immigrants. During their trans-Atlantic crossing, they walked a mile on deck each evening. Later, their mutual interest was to cause some conflict, for despite her adulation of Bondfield, Whitton did not entirely approve of her juvenile immigration report. Bondfield did not advocate total cessation of the movement and placed blame on the Canadian reception of the children as well as on the British philanthropic societies' inadequate supervision of the young apprentices. Bondfield visited Winnipeg, Regina, Edmonton, Vancouver and Montreal in late September and October, but her investigations were cut short with the government's defeat in Parliament.

Whitton observed other women too. Mrs. Harrison Bell, who worked with the Overseas Settlement Board, was one Whitton thought could be duplicated ten thousand times in Canada—"a woman of ability, a woman who has known work and struggle, a woman in whom attainment has somewhat affected in a positiveness and pride of appointment."[22] But it was Bondfield Whitton wanted to emulate.

Another of Britain's postwar women, however, also at Whitehall that afternoon, decidedly disconcerted Whitton. Her own provincialism made her uneasy in the presence of Commandant Mary S. Allen "in her mannish attire determined to deny her womanhood, smoking like a furnace and causing . . . much perturbed amusement." Allen, a suffragette who had gone to prison for her beliefs, had earned a formidable national reputation as one of the founders of the Policewoman Movement in England alongside her co-reformer and intimate, Margaret Damer Dawson. During the First World War, Allen became "Commandant of the Women's Auxiliary Service" and worked with the WAACS as Her Majesty's Munition Factory Police[woman]. Portraits of her show a striking and handsome profile severely set off by her uniform and military cap. Florence Fisher of the Women's City Club of New York, anxious that Whitton should meet Allen, had written Charlotte only three months before. Enclosing a portrait which showed Allen's "remarkable personality and power," she added, "She is, besides, a cultured gentlewoman." Whitton always rejected pseudo-masculinity throughout her own public life, trying not to dress or behave in what she perceived as "masculine" ways.[23]

If Bondfield, a contemporary, fired her imagination, a mythologized version of the Virgin Queen did no less. When Whitton encountered the portrait of Elizabeth I in the House of Commons, she responded to her as "the first modern woman." Between Bondfield and Elizabeth I, Whitton saw a continuity of past and present and recognized that chastity and power were inexorably linked. Of the Queen she purred into her journal:

> She is beautiful, as I believe she was, her gold red hair crisping about her crown, her beautifully shaped hands showing clearly, as she holds out her coronation ring to the petitioning parliament . . . "With this ring was I wedded to the realm."[24]

Her sense of "service" to the nation was strengthened as was her resolve to remain unmarried. In resisting marriage she saw the path to autonomy, independence, and meaningful work.

She was not idiosyncratic in her views that singlehood gave greater scope to women with career aspirations; generations of women before her had sought a similar path, distinguished only by the *vocational* nature of their careers. One historian has observed that "Although never institutionalized, the Cult of Single Blessedness, with its affirmation of the vocational life of the unmarried woman and its celebration of celibacy, provided an ideological framework that upheld spinsterhood as a worthy state of being." Twentieth-century women demanded careers which, while salaried, retained aspects of this vocational meaning. Rhoda, the fictionalized heroine of George Gissing's *The Odd Women* (1893), described such a sensibility as the embodiment of ideas about "female chastity and womanly service" which, in turn, were strengthened by "the *choice* of a celibate life" and channelled into meaningful work.[25]

The summer in England and Europe was crucial at another level. As Whitton experienced a profound religious culmination, as her political imagination was stirred by the example of a contemporary role model, and as the link between the celibate life and service was reinforced by historical precept, a deprivation occurred in her emotional life. For five years Margaret Grier had increasingly satisfied the emotional side of Whitton's nature. Her commitment to this friendship is evident in her 1924 journal. Her longing to share every precious moment of excitement abroad with Grier pervades the journal entries. The places she saw, the people she met, the speech she gave, and the Buckingham Palace garden party were all marred by Grier's absence.

On the European portion of her tour, in early August, Whitton was overcome with loneliness. Her journal records her longing. While her trip to Paris filled her with astonishment about the simple everyday pleasures on the continent and she excitedly wrote about sharing her train compartment with "the frankest English-woman of the demi-monde I ever met. She does enjoy life—drank a bottle of Graves as though she were eating a blueberry." In Florence, her longing was so great that she wept on the Ponte Vecchio. Immediately she hastened to Genuzzi's to buy a "lapus Laxuli chain for my dearest Margie" for which she paid far too much, but could not resist buying a matching ring for herself. At the Uffizi, she remembered learning about art during the happiest days of her life at Renfrew Collegiate but then confessed that they were imperfect because they were "without Margaret." Lapsing into a romantic reverie about Mariotto's "Virgin and St. Elizabeth" who looked "so human, so fond of one another, so intimate and neighbourly confiding their secrets to the other," she thought of her friend in Canada waiting for her return.[26]

And as if there had not been a surfeit of excitement in London, there was more to follow during her holiday trip to the continent. She was in Milan "that day in August when Matteotti's body had been found." (Matteotti was the leader of the Italian socialists and an obstacle to il Duce's rise to power.)

Suddenly, everywhere, armed men were patrolling; and the picturesque

carabinieri quickly took their posts at each exit to the arcade where we were
having tea. I can still remember the strange sense of chill coursing through
me on that sunny Italian afternoon. It was my first experience of the revival
of the rule of the dagger and the sword to make clear the way of those who
sought control over men and nations.

In Genoa the political tensions compelled British tourists, Whitton among
them, to be escorted to the Hotel Bristol for protection.[27]

By December, three months after settling down again in Ottawa, Whitton had
resolved her emotional crisis. Bill King ruefully observed, "Frankly Lottie I
hardly know how to answer your more or less distant note written in everlasting
haste." He noted that he received only one letter from her while in England
which "was not in haste and I answered it; you never got the answer and you do
not seem to care what I said." He was probably right.

Returning to Canada and to Margaret Grier, Whitton was driven by new
inspirations which had reinforced her former dreams so that there was less
conflict about Bill King and marriage after the summer of 1924. Margaret
Bondfield's example was significant in shaping the decision that she would not
circumscribe her life by marriage, Elizabeth I symbolized the power over one's
personal life conferred by celibacy and service, and Margaret Grier was accepted
as the primary relationship in her life. And by 1925 the possibilities for her own
career were made clear by her inclusion in the first volume of the pioneering
Biographical Cyclopaedia of American Women.

From the outset, marriage between Whitton and the more relaxed and less
ambitious young man seemed unlikely. The letters showed that Bill recognized
in Whitton an energy that could not be diminished, a vision that would not be
diverted, an independence not easily relinquished, and, finally, a heart that was
not to be won. Rather than contemplating either romance or marriage, she was
proving to be "a glutton for work." Threatened by her success and by press
reports that she had "electrified her audience" or that "she ought to be in
parliament" or "even a Cabinet Minister," he was unhappy that she would
neither accept nor refuse his suit and hurt by the manner in which she fought
against their romantic attachment and her occasional coldness and indifference.
Taken up by her own needs and busy establishing contacts, she could, at times,
be thoughtless as when she invited him to a social evening at her Ottawa
residence but had omitted telling him that it was a formal occasion. She made
him so fully aware of her embarrassment at his inappropriate dress that he was
obliged to leave early.

Although it is plausible that Whitton's decision not to marry was based
partially on a feeling that Bill King was not "good enough" for her, that does not
fully explain her long temporizing. She often quoted the Book of Common
Prayer's exhortation that "marriage is not by anyone to be enterprized lightly,"

and her procrastination demonstrated her belief in the words. Whitton was, however, sorely tempted to marry, and she was strongly attracted to King. The decision represented a real crisis in her life. She also could not cavalierly turn her back on the social advantages of having a male escort. Although Bill King was not her intellectual equal and had less ambition or energy, few men could compete with Whitton on these grounds, and successful women frequently marry men who are less able or who have less social status. The term "spinster," even when applied to economically independent and successful professional women, had the power to ostracize. Whitton faced a formidable future, without the comforts of family life, where the path ahead was socially and economically disadvantaged and the prospects for old age were tenuous and lonely. A resolution not to marry, if consciously made, was not for the fainthearted or the compromising. Whitton was neither. Further evidence that Whitton *consciously* decided not to marry comes from her response to Max B.'s proposal. Although his location was even less attractive than Oakville, his *social status* was not in question.

Whether Grier's decision not to marry was of the same nature and at what point she realized that their lives would be united remain mysteries, but the repressed anxiety in her letter to Whitton in Toronto suggests that she was not certain that her younger friend would remain unmarried. Within eighteen months of Whitton's return to Ottawa, however, their compact was firm enough for Margaret Grier to bequeath everything to Whitton in her will, and she never saw any reason to alter its conditions.[28]

The relationship between the two women can be described as a "Boston Marriage." In *Surpassing the Love of Men* (1981), Lillian Faderman observes of this arrangement:

> The term "Boston Marriage" was used in late nineteenth century New England to describe a long-term monogamous relationship between two otherwise unmarried women. The women were generally financially independent of men, either through inheritance or because of a career. They were usually feminists, New Women, often pioneers in a profession. They were also very involved in culture and in social betterment, and those female values, which they shared with each other, formed a strong basis for their life together.[29]

The term itself comes from Henry James' *The Bostonians* (1886), a novel of friendship between two women that fictionalized the arrangement between his sister Alice and Katharine Peabody Loring. Other Boston Marriages existed between such notables as Mary Wooley and Jeanette Marks and Jane Addams and Ellen Starr. Because the sexual impulse and romantic love were not seen as necessarily related, these arrangements were not seen as suspect or disruptive of the social structure. Whitton's "Ottawa Marriage" bore the same characteristics of a marriage with its mutual interests, economic partnership, and social usefulness. Indeed, it contained graciousness, trust, and intimacy that would be envied by most.

There is no evidence that their life together included homosexual relations; in fact, there are strong grounds to believe that it did not. Whitton's public comments and personal views were consistently judgmental regarding the purpose of marriage and sexual activity, and she was intolerant of various forms of female delinquency and sexual non-conformity. Her commitment to celibacy was as passionate as her commitment to Margaret. A "poor little High Church hybrid," Whitton was further constrained by the sincerity of her religious convictions.[30] Radcliffe Hall may have found it perfectly comfortable to be a practising Roman Catholic lesbian, but Whitton and Grier, both devout Anglicans attending St. Alban the Martyr Church in Ottawa every Sunday, a parish influenced by British Tractarianism, could not have easily reconciled such sexual behaviour with their religious beliefs. As in so many other areas —social, political, and moral—Whitton was in this instance also a creature of her time. She was no iconoclast like Mary Wolstonecraft or George Sand, who were even exceptional among the *bas bleu* of the nineteenth century. It was imperative to Whitton that there be not the least breath of scandal that could "ruin" her for as a woman without independent means, she could not afford such a catastrophe.

Nevertheless, it is not the particulars but the *form* of the Whitton-Grier relationship that is significant. She and many of her unmarried associates, would have been less fulfilled and more lonely except for the strong affectional bonds among them.

Sometimes the exchanges between the partners in Boston marriages were as ardent as those between heterosexual couples, and while there is little correspondence between the two women, Whitton's feelings were expressed in poetry written in the early twenties.[31] One poem to "Dear Loveliness" laments that "each deep night is but the same/as yesternight for loneliness" and describes the "night's suffering spirit, sick with eagerness/for dawn's brief rapture with the day." However, this turbulence is juxtaposed with the words of another lyrical four-versed poem that plays with the fire on Margaret's hair, the radiance in her eyes, and the sweetness of her voice, concluding:

> Then from the pictures of that glowing screen
> Turning my thoughts enwrapt and eagerly
> I lose myself—fade all my gilded towers
> When sweet and aurealed in the light I see,
> The lovely face of Margaret.

In another poem she records gentle thoughts.

> I'd like to carry you to sleep
> With hands all full of touching yet most light
> And bear with me down the slope
> Of a smooth endless wave into the night.
>
> So softly your tired head would lie
> With gentle heaviness upon my breast
> And knowing but each others' arms
> Desiring nothing more we two would rest.

Whether or not these are to be interpreted literally, the depth of passion and sincerity of sentiment are unmistakable.

Apart from her puckish humour and a certain winsomeness, Margaret's personality is difficult to analyze. But her role in the relationship is less opaque. Her salary was important in maintaining the household, though she clearly saw Whitton's work as more valuable. Grier quietly maintained the domestic arrangements during Whitton's frequent trips abroad, across the country on her social surveys, or while on lecture tours in Canada and the States.

Although Margaret was less obtrusive, there is no evidence that Whitton acted the "masculine role." A capable housekeeper and an excellent cook, she was a gracious co-hostess for a coterie of friends and eminent Ottawans.[32] Margaret gave an abundance of loyalty and support, and Whitton returned it. She was psychologically dependent on Grier, and when Margaret went through emotional breakdowns and physical illnesses in 1933, 1939, and 1943, Whitton's personal anxiety affected her professional life.

Many of Whitton's friends and colleagues shared similar domestic arrangements. They wrote unselfconsciously to each other about their companions' illnesses and shared their companions' joys and pains with each other. Such couples assumed that they would be treated as a pair on social occasions, holidays, or visits. And when they were bereaved, they received consolatory letters as florid as any widow. Whitton and Grier were understood by their colleagues and friends alike to be a "couple." For example, when Wilhelmina Gordon visited them, her thank you note observed that "to be with your 'better half' was a pleasure in itself," and Emily Murphy, remembering a drive the three had enjoyed in Victoria, observed:

> It was St. Augustine who said 'Alpheus accompanied me for his presence did not disturb my privacy. . . .' At any rate that is how I felt with you and your fine pal. Remember me to her.[33]

On the other hand, the companionship and fidelity they shared imposed some limits. Commitment demands compromise. Married women sometimes use marriage, motherhood, and the male partner as excuses for their decision to leave the public arena for private life, but people are interdependent whatever the "household" is based on. Those who seek love, companionship, and permanence must sometimes sacrifice mobility and free choice. Whitton's relationship with Grier illustrates this dilemma.

Whitton's failure to pursue postgraduate education is telling given her adulation of degrees and unwavering respect for prestigious institutions. She saw such qualifications as a means of exerting influence, as was apparent in her emphasis on her "M.A." and her later insistence on being addressed as "Dr." after she received her first honorary degree. She had, moreover, received an offer of a four-month scholarship to study social and community work in the Graduate Department of Social Economy and Social Research at Bryn Mawr.[34]

But Tom Low's offer and the location of the embryonic CCCW in Ottawa were not her only reasons for abandoning further education. Her position as private secretary for the Minister of Trade and Commerce depended on the mood of the electorate, and there was no guarantee in 1922 that the Council would ever become influential. If CCCW was the reason for staying in Ottawa, Whitton was gambling on its future.

Some might argue that Whitton's sense of duty to her family, as seen in the emphasis she placed on her "program," was the reason she turned away from higher education. But the "program" may also have been her "fail safe" device to justify whatever choices she made. Her friends knew that she had good reasons for not achieving some of her high hopes, and her final decision certainly appeared altruistic.

But Whitton's decision not to leave Canada is best explained by the extreme importance she placed on her personal life. Despite her family loyalty, her commitment to Grier took precedence. Only a passionate sense of fidelity and a strong need for emotional sustenance could have tempered her ambitions. Whitton was unwilling to live apart from Grier. Perhaps she was uncertain that they would be able to take up their lives together with the same intimacy after a long separation; perhaps she foresaw the possibility of opportunities that she could not pass up which would delay her return either temporarily or permanently; or perhaps she felt that such a move would be a betrayal of their "arrangement." In this sense Grier's position was like that of a wife who gives up a career and personal income to accompany her husband when a job or the pursuit of higher education calls for it. If Grier followed Whitton, she might have truly become a "dependent." But whatever the reasons, this "Ottawa Marriage" circumscribed Whitton's ambitions.

At the same time as Whitton was resolving her personal conflicts and coming to a stage of emotional equilibrium, she was pouring her energies in the offices of the Council, and it gradually began to reflect her image. From 1920 to 1925 it expanded its horizon even as its honorary secretary expanded hers so that at the September 1925 CCCW conference, the council President, Ella Thorburn, observed that the history of the five years of the CCCW might be called the "Autobiography of an Infant Prodigy."[35] During this time a paper organization with a scattered, though enthusiastic, membership, had managed to affiliate nineteen national, fourteen provincial, and sixteen municipal organizations, as well as 191 individuals. Its budget had grown to include a reserve of almost $9,000, and it had pledges covering three years to assure an economic viability. Whitton had insisted when she became honorary secretary that she was not prepared to take a full-time position without such a reserve fund to conduct surveys and to provide her with some economic security. By the fall of 1925 Reid had enlisted fifty-two subscribers, mostly from Montreal, who alone contributed $2,935 each year. As Helen Reid worked to give the Council economic stability, Whitton tried to create an aura of national leadership. Thus, when Tom Low was defeated in the federal election in October 1925 and resigned as Minister of Trade and Commerce, Whitton was ready by December to move to the CCCW office. Within a month of her arrival on 2 December, the Council was well underway as the leading Canadian child welfare agency.

In the fall of 1925 Whitton also first heard that the League of Nations was opening up a position for a Canadian assessor on its newly established Child Welfare Committee, which was part of the reconstituted Advisory Committee for the Protection of Women and Young People. The committee studied questions and prepared international conventions relating to morality, education, law, and economic and political intervention as they affected child life. These conventions included principles regarding the return of young people whose lives had been disrupted by war to their homes and affording indigent foreign minors equal treatment with minors of the country in which they were residing. The committee's chief task was a comparison of different child caring methods and institutions for dependent children through a series of investigations and questionnaires about administrative and legislative practices.[36]

Just as Whitton's tenacity and energy generated her career with the Council, these same traits gained her the Canadian assessorship in 1925. No one could have worked harder or more efficiently than Whitton at exploiting the mechanisms of the CCCW as she manoeuvered to gain the nomination. Whitton had learned that Canada could have League representation on the child welfare committee circuitously. Edith Abbott, chief of the United States Children's Bureau, urgently informed her in September 1925 that Dr. W.A. Riddell, the Canadian Advisory Officer to the League, had recommended that the SSCC make nominations for the position. The newly appointed Under-Secretary of State O.D. ("Sandy") Skelton, former political science professor and Dean of Arts at Queen's, also alerted her of the opening. Whitton acted at once. Alarmed that the SSCC had been chosen to make nominations, she convinced Skelton and Abbott to write to Riddell and delay matters until the question of who would make nominations was settled.[37]

Whitton also persuaded Ella Thorburn, whose family had been involved with child welfare in Ottawa for over half a century and who was a Canadian delegate to the International Labour Organization, to write to Dame Rachel Crowdy, the British convenor of the child welfare committee, requesting a postponement. In addition, she solicited the president of the Trades and Labour Congress, Tom Moore, who had co-operated with Whitton on a variety of social issues and on the juvenile immigration question, to use his contacts at the League of Nations. Whitton asked those she approached to make it clear to the League that the CCCW represented such diverse interests as the National Council of Women, the Victorian Order of Nurses, the Girl Guides, the IODE, the Red Cross, the Federation of French Canadian Women, the Catholic Woman's League, the TB Association, the Trades and Labour Congress, and the Saskatchewan Co-operative Creamery. She insisted that a grave "error of judgment" had been made in choosing the SSCC for such an important task and that this error would eventually embarrass the Canadian government. Marjorie Bradford, the secretary of the SSCC, did not know about Whitton's moves, and copies of the exchange of correspondence between Riddell, Skelton, and the proposals to the SSCC itself were also held up at Whitton's end. The delay in reaching Toronto was just long enough for some solution to be reached regarding the "error."[38]

Writing to Mrs. Thorburn, Riddell explained his part in naming the SSCC as the Canadian organization responsible for nominating the Canadian candidate for assessorship. The original suggestion had been that one of the American National Conference on Social Work's nominees be a Canadian. Riddell had rejected this "very humiliating" plan, arguing that the SSCC was the only plausible Canadian organization equivalent to the NCSW. Finally, Riddell agreed that a compromise was essential since any delay would be "fatal to Canadian interests." The compromise would be in the form of co-operation between the SSCC and the CCCW.[39]

Not wanting to discredit an organization she had served for four years and of which she was a corresponding member, Whitton too argued for "joint representation." The calorific descriptions Whitton gave of the CCCW and her position in it in the fall of 1925 were not entirely accurate; for example, she was not yet its full-time executive secretary. In a letter to the under-secretary of state, Whitton requested that Skelton not send her comments on to Miss Bradford. She remarked on the apparent chaos at the SSCC offices, which confirmed that since Dr. Shearer's death in March, no one knew "with whom to deal with the SSCC." She also noted that, unlike the CCCW, "by far the greater part of [the SSCC's] finances and propaganda had been devoted to the more repressive aspect of social reform" and that its interests were more in the traffic of women than in child protection. Whitton made a point of attending the executive meeting of the SSCC in Toronto to discuss co-operation. Since the nominating agency was required to pay the assessor's expenses to attend League sessions, she recommended that it would be preferable to nominate persons who had joint membership with the SSCC and the CCCW so that the two agencies could each contribute half. This shrewd compromise also had pragmatic importance because neither the SSCC nor the CCCW could have funded the enterprise separately. And so Whitton had little difficulty in convincing the executive of the prudence of her recommendation.[40]

In one way Whitton's argument was true. The SSCC certainly had more limited representation than her council, and it was through the latter that she orchestrated so many nominations in her favour. In October 1925 she claimed that the CCCW "were certainly *the* child welfare people . . . and more similar to the National Conference on Social Work of the United States than the SSCC," which had no provisions for individual membership, represented only the major Protestant churches, had no Jewish representation and excluded Roman Catholic and organized labour groups.[41] Although these claims were not entirely accurate, they all contained germs of truth.

Whitton moved quickly as soon as joint representation was agreed upon. Together the SSCC and the CCCW solicited names from child welfare groups and individuals across the nation. She circulated the requests for names among her affiliates, emphasizing requirements of the position which pointed to herself. First, the financial aspect: were the organizations willing to pay the expenses should a member of their group win the nomination? Second, maintaining that government officials were excluded, she effectively disposed of Dr. Helen MacMurchy. Predictably, the Child Welfare Division resented Whitton's strategies. Whenever MacMurchy was requested to submit official Dominion reports about child welfare work to the League in the following years, Whitton attempted to undermine their credibility by implying that the data were wrong. Consequently, supporters of the Child Welfare Division and some medical officers began to regard Whitton as an "upstart" without official health or medical qualifications.

The League assessorship was coveted by many Canadian child welfare workers, and resentments and rivalries between individuals and interest groups inevitably surfaced when the final list of Whitton, Helen Reid, and David B. Harkness, Secretary of the Manitoba Social Service Council appeared. Reid generously withdrew her name in favour of her young friend, but Harkness did not. He never forgot the fact that he lost this appointment to Whitton, and his antipathy surfaced three years later when they met again in Manitoba.

Others such as Maude Riley of the Calgary Council of Child Welfare and Judge Ethel MacLachlan of Alberta were also hostile to Whitton's nomination.

Whitton never forgot Mrs. Riley's opposition, and Mrs. Riley clearly suspected that things went a little *too* smoothly in Whitton's favour.[42] By stressing, with deliberate obtuseness, that government officials were excluded from nomination, Whitton promoted confusion among several people, including MacLachlan, who remarked in exasperation, "Having the facts so clearly in your own mind may possibly have led you to think they were clear in mine." Mrs. Riley pointedly wrote, "I take it that you are not eligible for the nomination still being a government employee." However, by December Whitton was able to report to Grace Abbott, "I am glad to tell you that on December 1st I took over the executive secretaryship of the Council."[43]

In addition to campaigning for the nomination, Whitton also altered by hand votes given to people who were not on the final list so that they became votes for her. How the final decision was reached cannot be satisfactorily determined. However, in December, Whitton had been informed that she was to be Canada's assessor.[44] Between 1926 and the collapse of the League, she served Canada on the child welfare committee and several sub-committees dealing with traffic in women, illegitimacy, and nutrition.

The path of Whitton's professional ambitions was not smooth. With the failure of a major federal initiative in child welfare to create a Canadian Children's Bureau, prominent advocates of child welfare seeking significant professional careers were compelled to create the means in the private sector by which this was to be accomplished. Of all the new generation of professional social welfare women, Whitton demonstrated the greatest energy and determination in turning apparent defeats into advantages. Her move to Ottawa had allowed her to assume control of the fledgling Council and transform it gradually. If Canada was not to have a Children's Bureau, then Whitton was determined to make the CCCW into its voluntary equivalent. The next years were to see this happen.

4

THE EMPIRE BUILDER

*We have three imported experts saddled upon us
by Miss Charlotte Whitton et al., and whose wages
are paid with public funds . . . I would very
respectfully suggest to our City Council that they
pack off all our expensive imported experts to
Ontario . . . and operate home produced
welfare machinery.*

SAINT JOHN TIMES-GLOBE, 1930.

During her five years as honorary secretary, Whitton had made herself indispensible
to the CCCW by strengthening its organization and expanding its interests
nationally. Consequently, when funds were finally available for a full time
executive officer, she was the logical choice. While the council had proven
viable under her part-time leadership, with her appointment as permanent
executive secretary in 1926 it had a new authority. Under Whitton and her
associates, the council became the acknowledged leader in social welfare across
the nation between 1926 and the Second World War.

Coincidental with this realization of professional ambition was the move of
Whitton and Grier from their modest apartment on James Street into 326C
Rideau Terrace, a charming lead-windowed house in an elegant and quiet
neighbourhood near Government House. The home that the two women
created was largely a reflection of Margaret's tastes. While the study was Whitton's
domain, "elsewhere Margaret ruled." The furniture consisted of pieces of old
French of exquisite design, a petit-point stool, Irish candles in old brass,
numerous china figurines from a variety of countries, and splashes of green
potted ivy and indoor flowers, "and over it all a sense of muted color, a delicacy
and daintiness, for Margaret's favorite colour was pastel green, and in her
bedroom . . . and in the living room the same softness." In contrast, Whitton's
study was cluttered with parliamentary papers, statutes, pamphlets, scrapbooks,
numerous sharpened pencils for writing her drafts, and a library of 1,000

volumes, one-tenth of them about Elizabeth Tudor. Portraits of Elizabeth decorated the walls, and the queen's death mask was kept on a shelf.[1]

While choosing to lease rather than purchase a city house, they did buy a cottage on McGregor Lake where Whitton could escape from the oppressive summer humidity of the capital—to canoe, swim, walk, and write and to plan strategies for future assaults on anachronistic child welfare conditions across the country—but still be close enough to Ottawa to keep an eye on council affairs. Named "Wensleylea," after Wensleydale in Yorkshire from which the Whittons had come, the cabin was set in white pines and birch with the only access by boat across the lake. It was, as Whitton said, "the very nearest thing you can get to crawling into your own 'hole' and pulling it in after you." There was a simple joy in taking the "rowboat on a sunny morning, when the lilies [were] afloat and the turtles sunning on the banks and mudflats." She believed that McGregor Lake would be where her soul would rest after death.[2]

In 1926, she was receiving $3,500 per annum, raised to $4,000 by 1928. That it was generous can be seen in comparison to contemporary academic and clerical salaries. At McGill University, a lecturer received approximately $1,200, an assistant professor, $2,500 to $3,000, and an associate professor between $3,500 and $4,000. In 1922-23, McGill's director of nursing earned $2,500, which was raised to $3,000 in 1933. A stenographer on the CCCW staff was earning $960 by 1928, the assistant secretary $1,700, and the office secretary $1,500. Dr. Harry M. Cassidy, who Whitton viewed as a rival, was offered $3,000 at a starting salary in the School of Social Work at the University of Toronto in 1929. In 1928 Elsie Lawson was appointed supervisor of Child Welfare in Manitoba for a salary of $2,200, and Gwen Lantz, the executive secretary of the Halifax Children's Aid Society, earned only $1,800 in the same year.[3]

The CCCW divided its work into sections to deal with such critical aspects of child welfare as the protection of children in need of special care and defective, neglected, and delinquent children. One section, consisting mainly of religiously oriented members and clerics, issued reports on the "ethical development of children," while others studied the problems of children in industry, child hygiene, and matters pertaining to education and recreation. The council sponsored annual child welfare conferences, and Whitton, by now a respected leader in the North American child welfare community, participated in similar conferences held in the United States.

The council co-ordinated child welfare programs among its affiliate members and distributed brochures, pamphlets, instructional materials, and copies of social surveys as part of its educational program. Its contributions to child welfare legislation and juvenile justice stand out as its most effective work. W.L. Scott, drafter of the federal Juvenile Delinquents Act of 1908, was retained as legal adviser in these matters.[4] Between 1928 and 1934, there were three major investigations of the juvenile court system and inquiries into family allowance systems, the rights of illegitimate children, guardianship of dependent children and state wards, and the protection and education of the handicapped child. The child welfare committee also maintained close liaison with the International Labour Organization with regard to child labour and related questions.

From 1927 to 1929 Whitton was personally engaged in the conduct of three surveys. The juvenile immigration survey whose groundwork had been started in 1924 was financed by the Montreal Women's Canadian Club and completed in 1928. In June to November that same year Whitton travelled between Ottawa and Winnipeg as the investigator for the child welfare section of a Manitoba royal commission into social services, and at the same time she supervised a survey of the Ottawa Children's Agencies and directed a New Brunswick survey.[5]

The juvenile immigration survey was a political *coup* for Whitton and her council although her part in stopping this form of immigration reveals her prejudices as well as her sincere opposition to child labour. Her larger immigration philosophy meant that her concerns for child welfare were not free of class and racial biases. In her early writings for the SSCC, Whitton had identified those unfit for Canadian life: those who would not stay on the land unless they were people of capital; those who required assisted immigration; those who were not of Anglo-Celtic origin; and those who were not of the right "stock" or "class" even though they were of the right nationality. Despite their nationality and age, the immigrant children from Great Britain were among the "undesirables" who would pollute the "blood stream" of Canada. She re-iterated these views when she wrote to Bertha F. Nicholson, the national secretary of the IODE, requesting that her words be kept "confidential to the national executive," although as national immigration convener she presumed it would agree with her sentiments:

> I am not a person who does not believe that people of other races cannot contribute something to our national life, but I do think that we should decide whether the characteristics of that national life are to remain as they are or whether we are gradually to allow ourselves to be welded into a race that will not be predominantly British, or at least Anglo-Saxon in character.[6]

These very views apparently caused some unpleasantness on her first visit to Geneva when she aired them before League of Nations delegates. Writing to Frederick C. Blair, the assistant deputy minister of Immigration from Basle, Switzerland, Whitton fumed that:

> There is a dead set of misrepresentation, etc., of our immigration law, regulations, etc., in some of the European countries, and in the United Kingdom, I imagine, though I have not been there yet. I have had great pleasure in explaining that we have the best system of family and unaccom-

panied women immigration in the world. Italy is certainly "annoyed" with us—that much to our credit anyway.[7]

At the IODE national meeting in June 1928, she insisted that since Canada needed landworkers and Britain did too, immigration should be restricted "unless we are to have foreigners galore," and the following year her report declared making "public the pride of our prejudices."[8] She wrote to F.C. Blair again that it was a "singularly unhappy thing to have brought [into the country] hundreds of thousands of persons, two or three centuries behind the civilization and social development" of Canada.

> Constantly one encounters the most disturbing evidence not only of a standard of living but of standards of public and private morality far below those of our own community. This disparity is not a question of the poverty of a European peasantry, and its depressing environment. It is something deeper, the inevitable chasm between advanced and backward peoples.[9]

Among the most disturbing of Whitton's views about Central Europeans are those found in this confidential memorandum written during her child welfare investigations in Manitoba. Asserting that she was only recording her "impressions," she continued that she could not "conscientiously ignore the immigration significance of the nasty soil atop some of the furrows" while she was "ploughing a field for other grain." The memorandum discussed immigration and demographic trends that were beginning to make Central Europeans overrepresented in western Canada. The data had been part of the Royal Commission and was not public, so, not unnaturally, she was anxious that Blair not reveal his sources.

> I would ask you, especially, not to allow this material to go on the Department files but to retain it for the information of the Minister, Mr. Egan, yourself, and Miss Burnham. I am giving it to you, on this understanding, and also that the source of the information will not be revealed.

Such immigrants were the prime recipients of mothers' allowances, public monies for dependency and unemployment, and benefits from state institutions. She warned Blair that Central Europeans were contributing to all manner of immorality. Also, being highly politicized, they subsequently influenced government officials.

> Some of the most ghastly cases of immorality and incest, with very young girls involved were encountered among these groups. The frankness with which the most disgusting relations were discussed by the people concerned, and by others of the same race in the district was appalling. Things known

to exist were allowed to go on, taken for granted as they would be in the open sex life of a Russian village.

No doubt Whitton's opinions were commonplace. Still, the fact that she urged *confidentiality* suggests that she realized there was something unusually prejudicial about them. Two of Whitton's close associates, Julia Lathrop and Grace Abbott, did not share her negative views of immigrants. Consequently, her correspondence with them and others associated with either the League of Nations or American organizations were remarkably free of such observations.

Therefore, while understanding that Whitton did not stand alone in her views, what is significant about them is the extent to which they represented conservative class interests. On child and social welfare issues Whitton was a progressive, but on broader political issues she was not. The dissonance is perhaps not unusual since social work by its nature is more concerned with social adjustments than with radical change.

Whitton's views on immigration were stable and consistent. In general, they represented a Canadian version of scientific racism, that is, a belief in the existence of racial stereotypes, acceptance of the myth that certain races possess a monopoly of desirable characteristics, and a belief that racial differences being caused by heredity are resistant to any modification. In her public and private statements on immigration, Whitton betrayed emotional intensity. For Whitton, undesirable immigrants provided an explanation for Canada's social and economic problems. Faults inherent in Canadian society could be safely ignored; there would be no troubling guilt and self-doubt.[10]

Although Whitton's views on immigration reflect her times, there is more to the tale than that. The ideas she derived from school, family, friends, and the media need not have been translated into these stereotypes. Whitton herself believed in free will and individual merit, not in a blind evolutionary process. In addition, during her life the interpretation of human nature moved from inflexible deterministic hereditarian explanations to environmental explanations of man's social behaviour. Finally, Whitton's ideas of the 1920s continued to shape her attitude towards immigration into the 1940s as is demonstrated by Irving Abella and Harold Troper in *None Is Too Many*.[11] Whitton played a significant role in preventing refugee Armenian and Jewish children coming to Canada.

Nevertheless, the juvenile immigration campaign was a *tour de force*. At no other time in her career, except in Alberta, did Whitton so reveal her strategic and political skills, and never again, except in Alberta, did she use such a politically volatile topic so well to advance her own career. Whitton demonstrated her ability to exploit popular prejudices and the sentiment of the child welfare profession as well as the council's ability to conduct a successful investigation of a social problem. The image of competence was important in promoting the council's fee-based survey services.

After it was agreed that the movement should cease at the October 1928 conference, Whitton was able to concentrate her efforts on the home front and proceeded to expose inadequate placement standards in 1928 to 1930 surveys in New Brunswick, British Columbia, and Manitoba. These surveys were powerful indictments of institutional child care and led to a more rapid adoption of foster care practices. All of the surveys emphasized the usefulness of the Children's Aid Society model of child care. CASs were in place in many provinces, although the suggestion to utilize volunteers and community input on a similar model did not sit well in Alberta, which favoured a more "centralized" control over child dependency. By the 1930s, the CAS model was defunct in Alberta, and placements, supervision, and financial support were under the auspices of the provincial government and a superintendent of child welfare. Children's aid departments replaced the former CASs. Whitton was not happy with this trend in Alberta.

The surveys were important because they pointed to the discrepancies that emerged between legislation and practice as well as in the different provincial legislations. The surveys recommended standardization of child care practice and child welfare legislation, increases in professional staff, more generous public funding, and examples of how to implement scientific attitudes in welfare, community work, and family life.

Throughout the hectic and exciting period that Whitton was supervising provincial surveys, attending League sessions in Europe, travelling to Winnipeg to conduct her Manitoba study and planning the last stages of the juvenile immigration survey, she was also organizing national CCCW conferences, working on immigration committees of the NCW and the IODE, attending meetings of the Queen's Trustees at Kingston, performing her duties as historian for the Canadian Women's Press Club, giving numerous public addresses, and producing a voluminous correspondence on child welfare problems. It was no wonder that on 3 November 1928, ill with an abscessed tooth and nearing a collapse through exhaustion, she wrote Elizabeth King, "I am nearer being submerged than ever in my life and faced with the utter necessity of going West with my [royal commission] report finally drafted, on the 13th."[12]

She must also have known she was making enemies. Unavoidably, Whitton's handling of the council surveys sometimes alienated the sympathies of social workers. Her efforts in Manitoba, in particular, first as a consultant with the Royal Commission on Social Welfare in 1928 and then between 1929 and 1930 when she prepared reports on female juvenile delinquency and on child caring agencies, earned her a reputation for autocracy.[13] Her clumsy criticisms of the competence and qualifications of the public welfare staff caused considerable resentment among Winnipeg workers, and she was identified as an "Easterner," seeking to create jobs for Ontarians in hard economic times. While these were grossly oversimplified reactions, they were not uncommon. Social workers in Alberta and New Brunswick shared Manitobans' suspicions. Whitton was not unaware of the growing rift between East and West, but she remained unsympathetic to it. Emily Murphy, on the other hand, writing from Edmonton, knew the issue was a delicate one.

> Maybe someday, I'll get up a kind of symposium on the relations of East and West. The subject is highly diverting to say nothing of being loaded.[14]

In fact, rather than making Ontarian appointments, Whitton searched for trained and experienced *Canadians,* including those who were working in the United States, to fill the posts her surveys created. Her major concern was the "Canadianization" of social welfare for she was committed to the view that social products and institutional forms should reflect the organic community and the political reality of Canadian society. For instance, in 1930 she brought Lillian Thompson back from settlement and charity work in New York to become the director of the Social Service Exchange in Saskatoon after her first two choices, Gwen Lantz, a Dalhousie graduate whose experience had been in Montreal and Halifax, and Marjorie Moore of the Toronto Neighborhood Workers Association had both declined the offer. She brought Elizabeth King back to Canada from the Brooklyn Charities to assist the council in its survey work in Manitoba, Montreal, and New Brunswick. King, an Acadia graduate, had furthered her education at Simmons College, Massachusetts, and had worked with the Ottawa Welfare Bureau in 1917 and then on the Ontario Mothers' Allowance Board before returning to the States. There was no deliberate policy on Whitton's part to place Easterners, but most of the welfare models had been established in Toronto and Montreal, and it was the Toronto School of Social Service that graduated the majority of social workers in the 1920s. Likewise, many Easterners had gone to the United States for training and experience and returned to agencies and organizations in Canada.

In Winnipeg, Whitton further estranged D.B. Harkness, who had wanted the League of Nations assessorship. Harkness, who had helped in the passage of the Manitoba Child Welfare Act that served as a model for other western provinces, was a formidable enemy. As judge of the Manitoba juvenile court and later as representative of the Social Service Council of Ontario, he had first become involved with Whitton on SSCC and CCCW committees in the twenties. Reverend James Mutchmor, secretary of the Welfare Supervision Board in Winnipeg, also saw her tactics as highhanded. He believed that Whitton created positions which were in her friends' rather than in child welfare's interests, and he thought that her control over recruitment and training programs primarily represented the interests of Ontario.[15] He also considered Howard J.T. Falk of the Montreal Council of Social Agencies, who later became director of the

Vancouver Council of Social Agencies, to be in "cahoots" with Whitton. Falk's connection with social work dated back to the previous decade; he had been the first secretary of the Associated Charities in Winnipeg in 1908, and later the first secretary of the Manitoba Mothers' Allowance Commission and the Social Welfare Commission of Manitoba. Apart from his relationship with Whitton, Mutchmor probably disliked him because of his high-pitched outbursts and "outpourings of wrath." Impatient, Falk entirely lacked tact, and his rages could be unreasonable. Given the similarities of their personalities, it is surprising that he and Whitton developed such a close association. Perhaps the fact that he was a British born Oxonian, educated at Rugby and Balliol College, and could boast of relatives such as Arnold Toynbee and John Howard, may have neutralized the potential for clashes between them.[16]

A. Percy Paget, who had been the president of the CCCW in 1923, also objected to the heavy-handed tactics in Manitoba that stirred up such ill feeling and resulted in his demotion. When Mutchmor replaced Paget as temporary acting director of child welfare in the early part of 1929, he recorded Paget's disgrace in his memoirs. "The child welfare director, A. Percy Paget was a good man but his administrative efficiency according to Dr. Whitton was not up to par." He also included an anecdote about the chairman of the Winnipeg Welfare Supervision Board who was asked by a colleague, "Miss Whitton is she *some* person?" He had promptly replied, "I would say two or three persons."[17]

But though government personnel in Manitoba suspected Whitton's motives, the Good Shepherd sisters of West Kildonan were overwhelmed by her civility and understanding. Sister M. du Coeur de Jesus thanked her in May 1929. "You so kindly took us for what we want to be," she wrote, "and the friendly feeling was not only on our side."[18] This is just one of the many examples of Whitton's tact with regard to the work of the religious sisterhoods in Canada. Apparently, these women recognized in each other a sense of vocation that warranted deep mutual respect.

Her accomplishments in Winnipeg, despite the difficulties, gave her no little pride. When Whitton left in 1929, there was a move afoot to establish a case work agency, and a private central family exchange, and there was talk of a central council of social agencies in addition to the re-organization of the provincial child welfare division. Her reputation was such after this experience that she was called to Saskatchewan to consult with the Commissioner of Child Protection; she was asked to advise on New Brunswick's Children's Protection Act and the New Brunswick Boys' Industrial School; and she was asked to conduct a survey of the problems of youthful offenders in Canada.

Simultaneously, she was building her role at the League of Nations. Several historical actors played important parts on the stage of Whitton's international child welfare career until the League disintegrated with the hostilities that led to the Second World War. Sir Austen Chamberlain, the British rapporteur of the child welfare section, proved an obstruction to any effective transformation of child welfare policies, since he was committed to views that were antithetical to Whitton's or, indeed, to most North American experts. Dame Rachel Crowdy, chief of the Opium and Social Questions section of the child welfare committee, held essentially the same opinions. In addition, she was a strong-willed older woman with autocratic tendencies, and her antagonism towards the younger, equally strong-willed Whitton surfaced in the first session of 1926. Crowdy did not think Whitton, a Canadian, understood her "place" in the imperial scheme of things and Whitton, usually deferential to things British, refused to take a back seat. When it came to welfare work, she did not have a colonial mentality, seeing herself as part of a *vanguard* of experts, mostly North Americans, who were working to transform child welfare from the philanthropic mode to one of scientific organization and research. Dr. W.A. Riddell, the Canadian advisory officer to the League, played the part of conciliator in the drama that ensued between North American pragmatism and Old World certitude. Whitton, who was later advised "to rest" more by a Hungarian associate, was also described as "the personification of the New World."[19]

Among other players were Grace Abbott, Julia Lathrop, and Katharine Lenroot. Inspired as at previous stages of her life by other magnetic women, Whitton found in these three both mentors and peers she sought to emulate and impress. Indeed, from 1926 to 1939 at different times each of these three American child welfare reformers saw themselves in a vigorous alliance along with the Canadian representing New World social philosophy.

During the first years of the League, Julia Lathrop was the assessor for the United States, representing the American National Conference on Social Work. Her support, like Helen Reid's, substantiated Whitton's efforts on the Advisory Commission for the Protection of Children and Young People. She was sixty-eight years old when she and Whitton renewed in Geneva an acquaintanceship begun some years before in Toronto. Lathrop's interest in the younger woman was flattering because of her substantial reputation. Grace Abbott, twenty years Lathrop's junior and sixteen years older than Whitton, had been initiated into social service through the example of Lathrop and Jane Addams in much the same way as Whitton had been with Reid and Murphy. She and her sister, Edith Abbott, later Dean of Social Service at the University of Chicago, had stayed with Lathrop at Hull settlement house. One biographer discussed Grace Abbott's appointment to the League of Nations.

> [She] was the first American to serve on any committee of the League of Nations and as such her appointment was heartening not only to those who wanted to see women in important posts but also to persons who had been disappointed at America's decision not to join the League and who still hoped that American points of view would be heard through the League of Nations.

Grace Abbott emphasized the need for facts as the basis for the Committee's recommendations. The European men on the Committee in 1923 were hardly prepared for the American delegate, who, while courteous, was unimpressed by their aura of authority and negotiated herself ably through the formalities common to international governmental meetings. She was not a simple person to deal with. Furthermore she had always managed to interpret her own point of view informally and organize her own nucleus of support before the meeting.[20]

Whitton's close identification with Grace Abbott did not endear her to Rachel Crowdy, the British chief of the Social Questions Committee. Crowdy was hostile because Abbott was on the committee by invitation only owing to America's anomalous status with the League. When Abbott had persuaded the original committee on the traffic of women and children in 1923 to divide into two committees, one dealing specifically with children and the other with the traffic of women, another British delegate, S.W. Harris, "who had been influential in the committee from its inception," had been "firmly opposed." Abbott had also strongly advised the use of non-European and non-British assessors on the two committees. Because she was "able to garner financial support for part of the child welfare program from a grant by the American Social Hygiene Association,"[21] Abbott quickly earned a reputation for efficiency and a "scientific" approach to social questions.

Owing to her responsibilities with the Children's Bureau and because League meetings "were held in the spring at the same time as a new presidential administration was taking over or when congressional appropriations for the Children's Bureau were in a critical stage of debate," Abbott did not attend any of the sessions between 1925 and 1930. Consequently, the appointment of Julia Lathrop as assessor ensured a more adequate representation of North American interests at the League's child welfare activities.[22] In 1934, after Lathrop's death and Abbott's retirement, Katharine Lenroot became the delegate as the USCB's new chief. Lenroot was assistant chief and Acting Chief of the bureau in 1927 when Abbott came down with tuberculosis. She was of Whitton's generation and a great affection developed between them that transcended the limits of collegiality and which continued into old age. Lenroot was born in 1891 in Wisconsin and received a B.A. in 1912 from the University of Wisconsin. The political acumen she learned from her father, Senator Irvin Lenroot, provided an effective role model, and she had worked for the bureau since 1915 as a special investigator.

Whitton's optimism about the League of Nations reflected Lathrop's. In 1926 Lathrop wrote to her enthusiastically, "the League is so indispensible; its social science functions promise so much for an indefinite period ahead and I must feel sure of the future."[23] Years later Whitton, reminiscing about their optimism, sadly observed that as much as we had hoped and longed and dreamed that we might recapture something of what seemed at this distance, the comparative security of the pre-war world, that chimera was vain and idle longing. We, who are of the war's generation, cannot still in our lifetime the furies that it loosed. . . . We must face and deal with a social organism, permanently weakened by these holocausts that we have known—war and economic collapse.[24]

It was, therefore, with considerable enthusiasm that Whitton left to attend her first League sessions in Spring 1926 with Margaret Grier accompanying her in order to conduct research on heliotherapy at Leyson for the Canadian Anti-Tuberculosis Association. Whitton remained in Europe for two months, and following her stay in Geneva, she drove from Nice to Genoa at the same time as the attempt on Mussolini's life took place. As they drove into Genoa she was overwhelmed by a surging multitude of singing fascists in the streets—25,000 Italian men at arms—joining in marching songs and concluding a rally in a powerful rendition of the "Magnificat."[25] To add to the excitement she found herself caught up in the confusion of the General Strike on her stopover in England.

Whitton's third visit to Italy during the 1928 session of the League proved as colourful as the previous two. On this occasion she visited the Doge's place at Venice as an observer of the Fascist Labour Day celebrations in April where, mesmerized, she saw thousands of black shirted children parading in San Marco Square.[26]

During her first years in Geneva, although subjected to greater bouts of frustration and depression than the more optimistic Lathrop, Whitton had not yet succumbed to the moroseness that was to increase during the 1930s; however, that a serious *impasse* had been reached between the North American "offensive" and the Europeans can be seen in a memorandum she wrote to Sir Eric Drummond, secretary-general of the League of Nations, around 1928. Observing that the "New World" might appear to League members as "too impatient and anxious to make progress too hastily" and that she herself might seem to reflect "the impatience of young and too energetic countries with the necessarily more considered and deliberate pace of old nations, or the caution which must characterize a general international experiment like the League," Whitton wrote that she must continue to object to certain attitudes displayed by the Europeans. She felt that the child welfare committee consistently turned away from "the scientific attitude to what might be described as the incidental aspects of moral and social reform problems which can only divide, not unite us." Neither was she alone in her frustration about the work of the committee.[27]

Consequently, the estrangement between the North Americans and the Europeans in Geneva can be seen as a reflection of opposing views of social service and not merely the clash of strong personalities. The Europeans clung to modes of philanthropic service which had been rejected by North Americans in favour of social science research; however, Whitton's impatience did little to pacify certain members of the Child Welfare Committee. She did not find compromise easy, and her impetuousness was often tempered by the more tactful Lathrop and, later, Lenroot. Nevertheless, on the issue of a scientific approach Whitton's impatience with the European attitudes was justified.

If the European delegates found it difficult to appreciate the differences that existed between unitary states and North American federalist systems of political organization, they were particularly insensitive to the historical and geographical differences, and they found it incomprehensible that different provinces or states would have different standards and approaches. More importantly, since the most inferior provincial standards or methods of care were always taken as the basic norm in describing Canadian child welfare, Whitton was humiliated. Returning to Canada, she worked even harder to implement child welfare reforms that would clear up provincial discrepancies.

As early as the first session she attended in 1926, Whitton and the three Americans had formed a united front at Geneva identifying themselves as *North American progressives* whose world-view and style was antithetical to European views of child care. As Lathrop wrote in 1926

> Perhaps we do not realize how different the European views are from ours and it may be a longer struggle before us than we anticipate. I confess I wonder if anyone in Geneva has an adequate conception of the business of a child welfare committee. In my mind it is a committee for scientific social research and for publication.

Lathrop, who occasionally signed herself "always your admiring friend," wrote that the United States and Canada should "form a little offensive, a defensive alliance on the basis of a mutual admiration society with two members. Here is my membership."[28]

Although the status of assessor was not as significant as that of a delegate, Whitton still had considerable input into discussion as well as representation on sub-committees such as the legal sub-committee established to examine matters pertaining to family allowances, child labour, infant life, repatriation of foreign minors, and the age of marriage and consent. Whitton so immediately impressed others with her acuity that soon after her arrival she was appointed to this sub-committee. An assessor's function was to contribute expertise to discussions and to evaluate various reports. Over the twelve years that Whitton worked with the League, first on the child welfare committee and then on a re-organized social questions committee as well as on various sub-committees, she contributed to discussions and reports on legislation, cinematographic performances, illegitimacy, guardianship, juvenile justice, institutional care for delinquents, children in "moral and social danger," bi-lateral agreements regarding indigent minors, assistance to foreign minors, and the development of a library on child welfare in the Secretariat.[29] Despite all the discussions and reports, little international reform emerged. Finding the generalities and the inability to achieve concrete results frustrating, the North Americans blamed European conservatism for much of the committee's inertia.

The North Americans felt estranged on several accounts. The Americans were at a disadvantage because the United States was not an official member of the League and because it had no policy in relation to the League although national representatives of government agencies such as the Children's Bureau were given delegate status on certain committees. The Canadians were at a disadvantage on different grounds. Before the Treaty of Westminster in 1930, it was not uncommon for the British to wonder why Canadians should have national representation on any international organization where the Mother Country was a member. This partially explains Crowdy's attitudes. The geographical and cultural separation between trans-Atlantic countries exacerbated the estrangement. Abbott, Lathrop, and Whitton uniformly felt that the confusion of such categories as child welfare, the traffic in women and children, and a sub-committee on the opium traffic tended to diffuse discussion. "White slavery," prostitution, drug abuse, venereal disease, and child welfare seemed oddly incompatible.

A decade was closing and with it some of Charlotte Whitton's more intense experiences and gratifying achievements. Yet as the decade closed, it contained the seeds of a controversy which would not culminate until the 1940s and which would wreak havoc in her public life. Out of these years of frenetic travel, innumerable professional exchanges, and memorable accomplishments, her views on the social contract were being formulated. They were to constitute the foundations of a coherent world-view which eventually might become unfashionable but which could boast of a long, respectable intellectual tradition.

Whitton's reports, including those of the New Brunswick Survey and the Manitoba commission of inquiry, generally supported mothers' allowances; however, in 1929 less tolerant views on the system of family allowances began to emerge publicly and they would culminate finally in a determined crusade in the 1940s. She sharply distinguished between a system of mothers' allowances based on need and the extension of a universal principle of family allowances.[30]

Purporting to be "representative" of Canadian social workers, Whitton, Robert E. Mills, director of the Toronto CAS, and Mrs. M. Kensit, Secretary of the Children's Bureau of Montreal, appeared before the Parliamentary Committee on Industrial and International Relations to oppose the principle and the establishment of family allowances for Canada. A 1929 resolution endorsing the system had been introduced into the House of Commons by J. Letellier and seconded by J.S. Woodsworth. Although the brief was presented by the three on behalf of the Social Service Council of Canada, it was undoubtedly composed by Whitton for she re-iterated much of its sentiment when the matter was debated and became law in 1944. The opinions expressed in the brief deserve extensive quotation for they are the precursor of later articles on the baby bonus. They reflect an incisive grasp of the tensions between individual freedoms and social responsibility.

> Such a measure [family allowances] would impugn upon the sanctity of the institution of marriage and the home by reducing them to the level of economic relations and rendering them capable of economic exploitation.
>
> The principle of the measure is subversive to the position and privileges which woman enjoys in most of the provinces of Canada, in that it reduces her from the position of an individual citizen, with personal rights, to one whose interests are to be regarded and preserved because she is the potential mother of future producers and consumers.[31]

Attending the hearings of the Quebec Commission on Social Insurance in 1930, Whitton was asked to present a council brief on guardianship, mothers' allowances, and child welfare organization.[32] The embryonic statements on family allowances of the previous year were developed further. While her views on the family allowance as a citizen right—that is, to be given to all families without means tests—were forthright and appear reactionary, in context they were not entirely so. Whitton did not readily accept popular assumptions. In the case of the family allowance, arguments were bandied about that the allowance would improve standards of living of working families, lighten child-rearing costs, and increase the birth rate without further immigration. She saw no concrete evidence to support such claims, protesting instead that if the State was really interested in problems of women and motherhood it should prohibit the employment of women in low paid and arduous industrial and agricultural work and at the same time increase their health insurance throughout pregnancy and after the birth of a child. Moreover, she found it distasteful to think that "a bad worker [is] compensated for extra children in a raised income which would not dignify marriage or motherhood or family life." The woman's "present status of an individual personality, with citizenship rights" would be reduced to that of a "person who would be cared for and maintained as the slave woman in Rome."

> Not for herself and because she had a human body and a divine soul, but because she mattered greatly to industry and the State, as a potential mother of future slaves and employees.[33]

Despite the work of social reformers to separate childhood from economic considerations, she believed that the family allowance reduced children to an economic asset for a parent's benefit. As in the resolution before the 1929 parliamentary committee, the CWC memo presented to the Quebec commission re-iterated Whitton's views on the function of the State.

> It is not the function of the State to assume itself the maintenance obligations which its laws impose upon parents; it is rather the duty of the State to see the distribution of wealth and the conditions of labour, housing, etc., within the State are such that it is possible for parents to discharge their legal obligations to their children. . . . Family Allowances are an admission by the State that the wages within its areas are not and cannot be made sufficient to support the average family according to minimum standards of health and decency, and therefore the State must, by subsidy, redistribute resources, the equitable development and distribution of which it cannot control.[34]

There was a certain moral fastidiousness in Whitton's genuine revulsion to the idea that the protection of women was being advanced on the basis of "reproduction" instead of "production." She insisted that Canadians were "a young, strong virile people . . . provident, thrifty, wholesome and ambitious. They are not the weary and sophisticated population of old and jaded nations," and she called upon the Quebec government as she would the Dominion government in the 1940s to believe that energy, independence, discipline of mind and body "will be born of her people and not [to] seek in our youth reliance on the social palliatives of older, less energetic lands."[35] She was concerned lest the working man be overburdened in his support of less productive citizens. Mothers' allowances were already eating up public funds.

> Every dollar expended by the State in this service, can come from one source and one source only, the pockets of the taxpayers upon whom also rests the responsibility of maintaining a decent standard of life and citizenship. The most intricate social philosophy cannot befog the hard facts of the situation that every dollar provided for public funds, for the payment of allowance to a mother in need, or any form of public aid, comes directly, but not unquestionably from those of the community who are not in receipt of any form of social assistance. The balance of social justice must be held even.[36]

It is only in the light of present-day political and social thought that Whitton's suspicion of state intervention appears unusual for someone in a social welfare position. In the late 1920s, before the massive dislocation of the Depression compelled many involved in social welfare policy to develop new models to deal with the enormity of economic problems, her views were not startling. Indeed, her political thought was beginning to emerge more clearly in the broader social context, framed by an intellectual conservativism which argued that the state should interfere minimally in the lives of its people while maintaining satisfactory living standards for its citizens. Moreover, Whitton was sincere in her concerns that women would compromise their legal identity by claiming subsidies for "the breeding of baby crops," just as she was committed to preventing "the Russian Soviet doctrine of *State ownership* of children, except for those for whom you cannot get guardianship through the duly incorporated societies." She saw incursions of state control as "a vicious principal that means ultimately the death of the private agency." Just as she consistently defended women as "persons," she maintained a similar position on children. She objected to the view of children as a national resource.[37]

In the submissions to the parliamentary committee and to the Quebec commission on social insurance, her socio-political views were refined and clarified. The similarity of these views and those of Edmund Burke, whom she had studied at Queen's, becomes apparent. With Burke she believed in the seamless fabric of organic society, a partnership between generations of the living, the dead, and those to be born (her "communion of saints"). She was beginning to frame political beliefs in a metaphysical system that united the social contract

> of each particular state [which is] but a clause in the Great Primaeval, connecting the visible and the invisible world, according to a fixed compact sanctioned by the inviolable oath which holds all physical and moral natures, each in their appointed place.[38]

Like Burke, Whitton was a conservator of the species who believed in an unusual constitution of civilized peoples. She had a reverence for the divine origin of social disposition which relied on tradition as well as a commitment to social equality and personal liberty. In fact, her ideas thrived in the auspicious company of some of the great conservative minds of eighteenth- and nineteenth-century political and social thought.

5

A LARGER STAGE

I pledge myself to the service of those whose respon-
sibility is entrusted to me. I promise always to place
their needs before my own desires. I vow my loyalty
to the service in which I am retained and should
my honour conflict with this duty, I promise to
withdraw therefrom, and as far as in me lies, to
bear myself without malice toward it. And I ask
my God to give me knowledge of truth, faith in
goodness, and the power to do good in His service.

SOCIAL WORKER PLEDGE, 1936.

That Whitton's ambitions usually coincided with her perception of the common good can be seen in the meteoric rise of her child welfare career and the expanded role of the CCCW. Committed to promoting social reform on a larger stage, this complementary and socially productive relationship between self-interest and society's interest carried into the 1930s. In contrast with the youthful, vibrant, and productive 1920s, however, the next decade was a time of social ferment, economic stagnation, and intellectual re-evaluation as Whitton came into her maturity.

Since 1928 the council had been interested in adding family and community welfare services to meet the criticisms of those rival organizations and welfare workers who had claimed that its child welfare work was too limited.[1] In 1929 the council changed its name to the Canadian Council on Child and Family Welfare (CCCFW) to describe its new functions. In April 1931 Whitton and the council's president, Ella Thorburn, were able to initiate efforts to establish this section. As some indication of the strength of the council in the ten years since Whitton had led it, its income had increased from $4,822.64 to $29,930.68 per annum, and its membership income from $173 to $1,204. In the three years from the time she took up her full time position, that is from 1925 to 1928, the affiliated membership had grown from 19 national organizations, 14 provincial organizations, 16 municipal agencies, and 191 individuals to 25 national, 35 provincial, 108 municipal, and 661 individuals. One historian has described the council as "the beloved octopus." Its many tentacles may have made the octopus an apt comparison, but "beloved" is hardly appropriate.[2] Curiously like its prime mover, the council itself evoked extreme reactions, divided into those who admired its work unequivocally and those who were suspicious of its motivations. The CCCFW had taken on a persona that was the lengthened shadow of Charlotte Whitton.

Belief that she was an empire-builder was harboured by some council affiliates. In June 1931, Maude Riley of the Calgary Council on Child Welfare, whose antagonism towards Whitton dated from the League nomination procedures, complained there was insufficient input from affiliate members. Her feelings were shared by others in the West who thought that provincial branches should operate on a model like that of the National Council of Women. They felt isolated and cut off from the decision-making processes, and Riley pointed out that financial support was not enough, that "enthusiasm comes from participation."[3]

With religion and morality so intertwined in her life, it was with considerable enthusiasm that Whitton accepted an invitation to conduct a survey for the Ontario Synod of the Anglican Church on the pastoral needs of women between the ages of twelve and twenty-five and particularly those between twenty-one and twenty-five. Assisted by Kathleen Snowden, who had worked in B.C. for the council during its mothers' allowances investigation in 1931, and Vera Moberly of the Toronto Infants' Home, Whitton had her report ready by September 1932. Using data from her immigration surveys and from the Mercer Reformatory and Alexandra Industrial School in "The Better Provision for the Protection of Girl Life," Whitton attempted to link incorrigibility, immorality, illegitimacy, and the dangers surrounding girls such as British household helpers, who were living away from home.[4]

In the midst of this confusion of morality, sexuality, and social matters, Whitton nevertheless championed the concerns of single, working girls which were ignored by the Church. Her advocacy of their interests thus at first appeared somewhat incongruous. She emphasized the minimal social lives and housing standards of poorly paid factory, shop, and office workers whether they lived at home or in boarding houses and hostels. She championed the cause of the immigrant household help, whose sense of cultural isolation made them particularly vulnerable to exploitation and unmarried parenthood. For such women she urged that her church "have the courage and foresight to pioneer in this field by an experiment in the provision of personal services for the unmarried mother and her child" rather than resort to institutionalization.[5] There is no evidence that the church attended to Whitton's concerns.

It has been noted that Whitton's initial experience with the League of Nations had been chequered and that she and her American colleagues felt geographically and philosophically isolated from the European perspective on child welfare. Nevertheless, by 1931 Whitton was campaigning for full membership and encouraging Skelton, undersecretary of state for External Affairs, to press for it also. She felt that the executive officer of the council at any given time could fulfil the new mandate. "This would be myself at the present time, but I feel that any membership which I hold should not be personal, but exercised by the executive director of this Council, since that was the understanding on which my nomination went forward for assessor."[6]

Her feelings of isolation increased in 1932 when Lathrop resigned from the advisory commission of the League shortly before her death, and Abbott threatened to resign unless a more scientific approach was taken. Whitton informed Skelton that she felt her own work had been rendered "futile." In this year Whitton was invited by the International Labour Office to join a committee of experts on women's work to advise on matters pertaining to female employment, and while she did accept and occasionally advised, there is no evidence that she attended any meetings.[7] Probably she saw that her authority would be increased on the ILO committee if she had membership and not just assessorship status with the League so she continued to press the case. It is likely too that the demands in relation to her relief survey for the Bennett government took up so much of her time that Whitton was compelled to limit her European efforts.

Whitton never tired of arguing that social work as a profession rested on objective and scientific principles in the same manner as engineering and public health. Such skills and knowledge were the product of university professional training and field experience under competent supervision. The Depression demanded a massive extension of professional social workers to all the new or greatly increased bureaus of relief and employment established by the provinces and municipalities. Even if the required army of social workers could not be recruited, Whitton was confident that a cadre of highly able and experienced women was available to provide the leadership desperately needed if the relief services was to achieve the desired results. Whitton obviously saw herself as the most prominent candidate for a leadership position in the professionalization of relief services within the dominion and provincial governments.

The search for nationally significant service led Whitton to accept appointments with both R.B. Bennett's Conservative government in the summer of 1932 and, later, W.L. Mackenzie King's Liberal government in 1936. Her relief work for Bennett, however, is particularly interesting in light of the special relationship based on mutual interests and a real affection between Whitton and Bennett. Bennett saw her as capable, energetic, and committed to those conservative principles that were his own. Since 1926 he had been a patron of the council and an admirer of its leader. Therefore Whitton's service with his government was an exercise in mutual self-interest.

Offering Bennett the council's consulting services in April of 1932, Whitton suggested that a conference be organized under the council's auspices to discuss relief problems and to collect accumulated data. Ten days later, Bennett made the arrangements for a western tour which took place from 3 June to 17 August 1932. While Whitton toured Winnipeg, Weyburn, Brandon, Calgary, Swift Current, Medicine Hat, and various remote B.C. locales and prepared her report, Ethel Dodds Parker and Elizabeth King ran council affairs.[8]

In the spring of 1932, at the very time when more and more skilled workers and middle-class members of society, having used all their resources, were forced to seek relief, the Bennett government abandoned funding direct relief. Although Bennett acknowledged the effects of the Depression on unemployment, he maintained that the "ease" with which people accepted assistance demonstrated that "the fibre of some of our people has grown softer and they are not willing to turn in and save themselves."[9] Such views were strikingly like Whitton's. She called this loss of morale "pauperization" and "devitalization." These opinions were shared by many conservative Canadians in the Depression. In a report to the League in 1933 discussing family life and unemployment, she noted:

> One of the subtle but quite definite cost of such conditions [economic depression], especially to a democracy [is] the rebuff to courage and initiative and the stunning of independence and resourcefulness involved in a long period of complete reliance on social aid, and a complete submission to administrative control over the minutest details of life.[10]

She also criticized government programmes that merely provided large-scale mass treatment of economic problems "with provision only for the mere material elements of life," decrying the "blind crucifixion of human values and of individual character." Only one who had these "mere" material elements of life —food, shelter, clothing, and work—could utter such facile nonsense.

Moreover, during her relief studies, Whitton surveyed child welfare problems in Victoria. Reprimanding F.E. Winslow of the Royal Trust, who was helping to organize a soup kitchen, she commented:

> I think that you will find that your soup kitchen without any investigation of beneficiaries and without any other service related to it, will prove a very demoralizing and expensive venture . . . In a community as generously supplied with provision for relief in the child's own home as in Victoria, you will find that women who are taking their children there are generally the women who are too lazy or too slipshod to prepare meals at home or are simply using the rooms as a convenient place for a lunch when they are out shopping or at the movies.[11]

Of course, there were much more than nineteenth-century attitudes about dependency and sapping the nation's moral fibre behind Bennett's anxiety. Like Mackenzie King after him, Bennett feared the financial collapse of the nation if the federal government committed itself to indiscriminate relief. Similarly, Whitton's reports were more than attempts to ingratiate herself with the two prime ministers by providing a rationale for limiting federal responsibility for relief. The Bennett-Whitton relationship was based on an affinity of social and political views, which was in sharp contrast to the basically impersonal one she had with the Liberal leader. That Whitton would proffer the same advice to both men suggests that her reports represented deep-seated views and not mere political expediency.

Since it was the "only detailed unemployment relief study" ever commissioned by Bennett, James Struthers has claimed that Whitton's findings "had enormous influence in conditioning his subsequent response to the depression."[12] At the same time, it is obvious that Bennett's perceptions and actions were set well before Whitton offered her services and that the outcome was not particularly different from what it would have been without her. Indeed, Whitton's failure to persuade Bennett and, to a lesser degree, King to act on her professional advice was the first in a series of political disappointments for her. Just as her efforts in writing on social security for Canada would be dismissed in the 1940s as representing a social worker's perspective, so Whitton found the federal leaders in the 1930s indifferent to what she judged to be the soundest and most logical conclusions drawn from social work.

Always concerned with classification of clients and their problems, adequate diagnosis, and proper casework, Whitton sought to apply these principles to the destitute of the great depression. As a first step, the traditional recipients of relief were to be distinguished from the victims of "the present emergency." Whitton maintained that since the former class had relied formerly on voluntary, municipal, and provincial agencies, support for them should properly come from these traditional sources of relief. Only the true victims of the Depression, that is, those who were normally neither underemployed nor dependent, represented a proper call on federal funds.

Whitton's views on relief for even the true victims of the Depression were astonishingly similar to the views of the nineteenth-century advocates of scientific charity organization, who also had denounced "indiscriminate" almsgiving. Suspicious of cash relief and convinced that over 50 per cent of people receiving relief were "in receipt of earnings," she insisted on thorough investigation of clients (which virtually amounted to detecting). She also charged that many men lodging in camps were sending money out of the country to families and that while cash relief was appropriate for many, nevertheless for 30 to 40 per cent, "the best interests of the whole family are safeguarded by relief *in kind*." In a council pamphlet published in 1934, she re-iterated her belief that "cash relief wipes out the last distinction between the family on relief and the struggling low paid wage earner's family."[13]

Such a position was consistent with those she had held in the previous decade against the extension of mothers' allowances to women other than the unwed, deserted, or widowed. Instead, she insisted that labour must fight for decent wages, and legislation must ensure better work benefits, compensation, salaries, and insurances so that working men did not have to resort to allowances or government "hand-outs." It was a position she would apply in the following decade to family allowances, one that was inspired by her organic view of a society consisting of smaller units which maintained themselves without resorting to massive state intervention into family life and which took upon themselves tasks better performed by individuals and communities. Whitton's views in many ways were singular, not easily placed into opposing ideological camps of left and right. A complex woman, not surprisingly she had complex social views, and unlike many of her fellow conservatives, these reflected a view of human nature itself rather than of crass economic self-interest. Yet too frequently—if taken out of the context of a total social philosophy—they came down on the side of the right, especially in the case of the casually employed. To convince others, she often resorted to arguments that reflect economic expediency.

Like her nineteenth-century predecessors, she systematically divided the recipients of relief into the categories of the worthy and unworthy poor—or the "genuinely unemployed" and the "casually unemployed," and like her predecessors, the data and information she received was gleaned from relief officers whose sympathies were closer to hers than their clients. The "casually" unemployed were those able-bodied young men (the "potent poor" of the past) who either stayed at home idling their youth away in dissipation or apathy or became homeless men whose plight had been caused by their misguided "spirit of adventure." The "glamour of tramp life" was "leading thousands of young chaps into the eddy, and thousands of them will be lost to lives of usefulness and self-respect."[14] Convinced that the separation of relief and unemployment was imperative since dependency was a permanent social problem merely exacerbated by the Depression, she agreed with Tom Moore, the vice-chairman of the National Employment Commission, when he observed in 1937 that relief must be separated from unemployment to distinguish between these out of work owing to the economic crisis and "the hard core of social dependency." He added that "the fact is that it required a depression to bring this dependency to the surface." In November 1937, he was quoted as saying that employment figures were "conflated" and not as bleak as they appeared because "there had always been unemployment but today we [are] more conscious of it than before."[15]

During the 1920s unemployment varied from a high of 8.9 in 1921 to a low of 2.6 per cent in 1928. The overall average for the decade was 5.4 per cent in contrast to the 18.1 per cent for the thirties. After rising to 25 per cent rates in 1932 and 1933, unemployment dropped steadily before hitting a decade low of 12.5 per cent in 1937 and rising again in 1938. Only in contrast to conditions of 1931-36 could the 1937 figures be described as "conflated." Moreover, since the participation of Canadian women in economic activity remained low before the Second World War, the impact of unemployment would be greater on families. Finally, by contrast unemployment rates in the period 1953-72 averaged 5.2 per cent.[16]

Insisting on registration, Whitton objected to supporting men who left their towns of residence to find work, even if those towns were economically stagnant. The duty of citizens was clear; they were to report "panhandlers" to registration centres, and any man "riding the rails" was to be handed over to the authorities. Banks were to be warned against authorizing monies to be sent out of the country, and permanent work colonies were the cheapest way to contain the unemployed, that is, "by their gradual segregation into semi-penal work colonies or camps, subject to rigid discipline, where they will be retained on a self supporting work basis." With a utilitarianism that competed with the meticulous nineteenth-century Jeremy Bentham, she expanded this idea in her observations that the able-bodied younger men could construct the work colonies to earn their keep while the older derelicts would occupy them.[17]

It did not escape Whitton's notice that many of the homeless men whose discontent had to be contained in work colonies were foreigners, and the anti-immigrant prejudices endemic in Whitton's social thought figured prominently in her relief reports. She was obsessed with large congregations of single foreign males and believed that "the sturdy foreigner" crowded the cities when life on the land became too strenuous for him "and relief was better than that which characterize[d] his natural diet and mode of life."[18] Arguing that foreigners had a tendency to segregate themselves, that their corporate loyalties were not in the best interests of Canada, that they were susceptible to seditious propaganda, and that they had a "known proclivity" to hoard money, she asserted that it was difficult to ascertain their actual need for relief. Subsequently, they were "among [the] troublesome clients," and the "foreign peasant" drove his young daughters out to work rather than supporting them at home, with the result that single transient foreign women constituted another relief problem.[19]

Several consistent concerns make Whitton's general analysis understandable. First, Whitton accepted a version of "less eligibility" that had framed the English Poor Law of the nineteenth century. In brief, she was determined that the underemployed and seasonal workers, that is, the marginal labour force, should not improve their status vis-à-vis the skilled and middle classes. If they had any call on relief during slack seasons, it was from traditional sources of relief not beyond their usual standard of living during difficult times. She was convinced that there was a "slackness" in investigations and was dismayed that many families received assistance after a month's unemployment. For someone involved in social work, this seems extraordinarily callous; of all people, she must have realized that, even in normal times, the absence of one week's wages could be disastrous to a working class family who were not able to accumulate savings or invest in insurance premiums. Whitton's determination to prevent marginal workers from abusing the dole led her to exaggerate both the extent of abuse and the levels of subsistence provided by relief. She claimed that while indiscriminate relief demoralized "the sturdier workman," it encouraged "the loafer."

Second, she was concerned that the most basic principles of social service were being undermined by political interests. Whitton had no real interest in economic issues or in radically changing the existing order in order to prevent similar catastrophes in the future. The dislocation caused by the Depression called for the professional application of scientific principles of social work, not for a basic restructuring of the economic and social systems. It was, partially, this perspective that marked the difference between Whitton and the social critics of the political left. Whitton's opposition to political opportunism and radical change was predicated on a view of social problems and individual distress in which social ills, being transitory and individual, were best met by personal and community adaptation.[20]

The suffocating and unbending conservatism that seemed to atrophy Whitton's sensibilities during the Great Depression is the hardest part of her personality with which to sympathize, the most difficult to understand, and the easiest to "judge." During this worst of times, Whitton clung to views about dependency that thoroughly undervalued the enormity of the situation. For the first time, a whole section of the middle class (including her own brother Stephen and her father, John Whitton) either experienced or came perilously close to penury and identified with the plight of the unemployed and the dependent. While her views on the residual aspects of social programmes were common among the business community, as a recognized leader in social welfare Whitton's pronouncements were increasingly at odds with the growing sensitivity and positions expressed by other prominent Canadians.

Regarding the provision and administration of relief in Western Canada, Whitton charged that lax administration had allowed "thousands of casual workers who were normally unemployed six to eight months of the year to swarm . . . into relief . . . on a 'year round basis' and thus raise their standard of living 'beyond anything they have ever known.'" The laxity she perceived to exist was derived in part from the desperate financial situation of most municipalities, the fear of social unrest, the existence of large scale federal relief aid, and the inexperience of politically appointed relief officers. Whitton's answer to administrative and financial irresponsibility was "to place trained professionals [that is, social workers] in charge of relief administration throughout the entire country."[21] If the dole were professionalized, greater efficiency would result as well as reduced costs.

Bennett's response to Whitton's lengthy report was disappointing. Fearing that the rising cost of federal relief, which had reached $42,341,690 in 1931, would bankrupt the nation, Bennett seized on her exaggerated charges of abuse to initiate reductions in federal relief. In 1932, federal relief disbursements were cut to $25,927,573. Indeed, only one of Whitton's recommendations, the establishment of relief camps for unemployed single men, was implemented.[22]

As Bennett's administration drifted aimlessly from the spring of 1932, responding only to crises, pressure for action gradually mounted. By November 1933, Bennett was proposing that Ottawa embark on a "reasonable policy of public works" in the spring. Others, however, were more concerned with relief reform. Sir Charles Gordon, president of the Bank of Montreal, fearing the undermining of municipal, provincial, and even national credit, called for the consideration of " 'some system of unemployment insurance, 'if only' for our general self-preservation [and] . . . if it can be done soon, so much the better.' "[23]

Whitton argued that municipalities, the major instruments of unemployment relief, were "the units of governments most susceptible to direct political control and manoeuvre." The solution was simple: the federal government should require professional standards of administration in return for future relief grants. Such conditions would force the provinces to establish independent provincial commissions or provincial departments under the control of social workers. To support her view, Whitton argued that an unemployment insurance system would not solve the problems associated with the casually employed. Moreover, the uninsured would come to demand equivalent benefits and bankrupt the scheme.[24]

More important, Whitton claimed that the federal government could reform the system of relief without assuming any permanent responsibility by establishing a normal unemployment rate and restricting federal contributions to those times when that level was surpassed. Such federal grants would, of course, be carefully proscribed by strict administrative requirements. Despite her hopes for an active federal role, Whitton's recommendations only confirmed Bennett's belief that federal aid encouraged fiscal irresponsibility on the part of local governments.[25]

The opening that Whitton longed for out of all of this was to head a federal bureau or division which would administer and co-ordinate the investigation and supervision of provincial and dominion relief. Although she did not suppose that massive relief programmes would be a permanent fixture on the economic landscape, such an opening might have been a stepping stone for other dominion appointments. Any such opening, however, was to be with the future Liberal government and not the troubled Conservative one.

Despite disappointment about Bennett's attitudes towards her relief recommendations, when he was soundly defeated in the fall of 1935 Whitton's overall admiration for him had not wavered, nor had he for her. Whitton's admiration is seen in a 1933 note to his secretary, Alice Miller, asking that a message be conveyed to the prime minister. The message from a prominent relief worker in Saskatoon said:

> But what could any one do without our great leader Mr. Bennett? Even when I was very ill and weak they brought the radio to my room so that I did not miss any of his great speeches. If Canada rejects him at the next election she will deserve the fate that will surely befall her.[26]

And in turn, a year later, he was still able to tease her affectionately by saying in a memo, "Just why you, of all people, should sign yourself 'your obedient servant,' I do not know."[27]

In later correspondence, after Bennett had retired to England and accepted a title, she addressed him as "milord" and criticized Prime Minister King because he had substituted "chicanery, shrewdness and smart practice" for honour, courage, and responsibility.

> Not the true and the right as you saw them and their exposition and your destruction, . . . as you witnessed steadfastly for them but, what you can get away with and "win" as the rule of conduct. The appalling lack of any sense of honour to a pledge, the utter disregard of the interests of Canada and humanity, the backing and edging, the indecision and review of our own party—or what was that great Party.

Assuring Bennett that she would expose any attempts to "traduce" his reputation, Whitton continued that she was determined to write a pamphlet, "Our Greatest Canadians: Macdonald and Bennett."[28]

Those social workers moving left of centre during the depression or who had Liberal sympathies viewed Whitton's work for Bennett with jaundiced eyes. In the summer of 1933, finding herself at odds with the CASW executive on the issue of professional over academic training, Whitton complained to Helen Reid that she was "nearly killing herself for the CASW" at the expense of the council and that the CASW executive showed "little loyalty" even though she had "sacrificed" so much for the profession. She wrote similar grievances to C. Jean Walker, the executive secretary of the CASW, but the executive continued to be suspicious of Whitton because of her insistence on the council's autonomy at social work conferences as well as her political involvement with the Bennett government.[29] J. Howard Falk had warned her of this state of affairs years back when he expressed concern about the *expansion* of the council. She should, he insisted, "convey the impression" that she depended on council affiliates "as a national group." Because she was busy cultivating prominent people and governments she had come to be seen as "a professional social worker."[30]

Her ability to fend off the adverse consequences of criticism had diminished by this time, and her letters in the summer of 1933 reflect the uncertainty of Whitton's life as the comparative domestic tranquillity she had shared with Grier for the past thirteen years threatened to disintegrate. As secretary of the Canadian Tuberculosis Association, Grier had studied sanatoria management in the West, taking a trip which coincided with Whitton's western relief tour. Apparently healthy then, within twelve months she suffered the first of a succession of physical ailments which were to culminate in the cancer that would take her life fourteen years later.

Surgery to remove an obstruction to the bowel proved so radical that Grier was on the brink of "a bad emotional crack up" for some time after. For her convalescence the two went to McGregor Lake in early summer, and Whitton drove twenty-four miles each way daily trying to keep council affairs running smoothly during this trying time. "She has to get back her confidence and get away from the psychology of inferiority . . . about her own powers and responsibilities," Whitton wrote in June to Edna Moore, the chief public nurse for the city of Toronto, asking Moore to keep an eye on Grier if she decided to attend a public health conference. In November, with Grier far from recovered, a concerned Whitton wrote fretful letters to Kennetha Haig in Winnipeg and Nell in Edmonton (now Mrs. S. Gandier) in an attempt to alleviate her anxieties.[31]

At the same time as her personal life seemed threatened by Margaret's ill health Whitton's professional life seemed robust. The council continued to grow, this time in an unexpected burst and in an unlikely direction. In September, Dr. Murray MacLaren, minister of pensions and national health, met with Whitton to discuss a replacement for Dr. MacMurchy, chief of the Child Welfare Division (CWD), who would soon be forcibly retired. It seems probable that Whitton's conservative party connections influenced his offer and Bennett's positive recommendations as well as her relief study probably opened up the first tentative negotiations for the council to take over the work of the federal division. The merger was startling because it is rare that a governmental service allows itself to revert to the private sector. Responding to MacLaren's suggestion that she take the post, Whitton wrote a letter that set the stage for the elimination of the division. After thanking the minister for "the opportunity which you have opened for me," Whitton pointed out that while the council's work had broadened with pressure and changing social conditions, the CWD had continued to work almost exclusively within a narrow definition of child welfare, that is, maternal and child hygiene. Moreover, she pointed out that even this work— except for a study of maternal mortality in 1927-29—was limited to publications of a kind that were being "extensively developed by most of the provinces, and larger municipalities, and by this Council." Having deprecated the division's work, Whitton logically questioned its existence. Dismissing the possibility of reorganizing the CWD she asserted that the government should recognize that the council would "be more effective in rendering the service . . . [which] rest[s] within the sphere of federal action in general social welfare problems." Indeed, the council could provide the present services of the CWD at 50 per cent of the present budget of $12,000.[32] During its final years, the CWD operated on a budget of $12,000 to $13,000 of which $10,000 to $11,000 went for salary. In comparison, the council's budget was $35,000 with only $8,100 supplied by the federal government. With continuing budgetary restraints likely, Whitton saw little reason for preferring the CWD to the council; however, she saw every reason for absorbing the CWD as part of the council.

The issue of the Child Welfare Division took up only part of Whitton's letter. Since the Pensions Division was concerned with the provision of pensioners' and veterans' services, Whitton asserted that although her interest in relief qualified her for service there, she doubted that a permanent appointment was needed. She then combined her views on the Child Welfare Division and on social welfare with the Pensions Division to recommend that she be appointed, temporarily, acting chief of the CWD, that her duties would not be the circumscribed ones of the present division, and that if possible the Division's name be shortened to Welfare Division. Although this amazing bit of self-aggrandisement failed, the Conservative government did eliminate the division and concluded an agreement with the council to transfer its functions to the private organization.

Unfortunately for Whitton and the council, the reaction by medical and public health organizations and professionals was uniformly negative. The transfer was attacked in professional and popular journals and in Parliament. In particular, public health advocates saw the move as a retreat from federal responsibility for child and maternal hygiene, and medical practitioners decried any scheme that placed a layperson in charge of any medical or public health agency. Consequently, Whitton, finding herself defending the agreement and her motives, was never able to enjoy the fruits of her success in the matter.

Nineteen thirty-four began far more happily. Charlotte Whitton was included in the New Year's honours list as a recipient of the Commander of the British Empire. Bennett's recommendation to King George V, who issued the annual Commonwealth honours, merely affirmed the opinion he never ceased to hold that Whitton was "probably the most capable woman engaged in social welfare in the Dominion."[33] Bennett had thus demonstrated his confidence in her three times: in appointing her to his relief survey; in supporting the transfer of the child welfare division to the council; and in recommending her for a CBE. He would intervene once more in her life before he left politics by exerting pressure for League membership.

Letters and telegrams of congratulation from individuals, admirers, prominent citizens, political leaders, social agencies, and women's groups poured into her office from across the nation. Hundreds of women identified Whitton as most deserving among the women singled out by the Bennett government. Although

Agnes Macphail cynically remarked that women needed these honours "as much as pigs need skates," Whitton wrote to Bennett that "every pig is better for a nice curly tail."[34] And for every Agnes MacPhail, there were dozens of women such as Elizabeth Barley Price of the Federated Women's Institutes of Canada, who wrote to Bennett applauding the good sense of his recommendation and saying that "we women of the press consider Miss Whitton one of the most brilliant young women in Canada today." The institutes represented "thousands of women," and one individual voice, that of Ella Percival McLeod, represented many more when she wrote to Whitton that she had predicted many years back that one day she would be "Prime Minister of Canada."[35]

Whitton was to display her CBE and later service medals and ribbons on her breast at public occasions and state affairs with obvious pride over the next decades. The most disappointing incident of 1934 was that she was unable to attend the investure ceremony at the governor general's residence because it coincided with a League conference in Geneva. The elation she felt after being awarded the CBE had barely worn off by early spring of 1934. In a letter to Bennett she said: "It is amazing the difference that decoration has made to the Europeans especially. So many would come up and say 'Vous êtes été decorée n'est-ce pas?' It certainly gives your work standing in their eyes."[36]

With the defeat of the Conservative government in October 1935, the fate of the transfer of the child welfare division was sealed. The widespread condemnation that had seriously damaged the reputation of Whitton and her council was soon to be a thing of the past. Aware that the transfer had been a pyrrhic victory, Whitton was also aware that the federal attitudes towards relief had not appreciably changed with the new Liberal government. The centrepiece of King's policy on unemployment relief was a National Employment Commission supervising relief expenditures and ultimately reducing federal funding "by ensuring its administration would become more 'efficient and economical.' " Given royal assent on 8 April 1936, the National Employment Commission Act gave the commissioner three basic duties: "to register and classify those on relief; to allocate stricter conditions to grants-in-aid to the provinces; and to supervise and audit provincial and municipal relief expenditures in order to 'avoid overlapping and abuses.' "[37]

Rather than conduct a complete registration of all unemployed, the NEC opted for a partial survey and hired Whitton to report on reforming the relief system at $500 a month plus expenses. Since the council had recommended a study under the aegis of an independent advisory national commission as early as 1931, Whitton eagerly accepted the offer.[38] As she was paid by the commission, the council was run during her absence by the director of Toronto's Public Welfare Department, Ethel Dodds Parker, with the assistance of Bessie Touzel and Marjorie Bradford.

Given the predominantly male appointments to the NEC, Whitton must have realized quickly that if the commission did succeed, she would have little chance of playing an important part in its hierarchy. Influential men such as O.D. Skelton were patrons of other Queen's men such as W.A. Macintosh, whom he nominated as an NEC member. Although the federal government in the 1930s was greatly influenced by this network, it did not necessarily extend to promising young women.[39]

In less than a year Whitton submitted an eight-chapter report consisting of 194 pages with 21 pages of Introduction, 27 tabulations, and 12 charts. It was a mammoth effort, but it contained few surprises.[40]

Given her commitment to reforming relief administration and practice by social work professionalism and stricter conditions attached to federal aid, Whitton proceeded to propose a scheme that would meet those requirements.[41] As in her first report to Bennett, she argued the need to divide those on the dole into those who could work and those who could not. Ottawa's responsibility would be limited to assisting in the relief of the former and to concentrating on getting them back to work. The actual administration of unemployment relief would remain with the provinces and municipalities because a national admin-istered system could not keep payments below regional and local wage rates. In this she disagreed with the growing interest on the part of Canadian social planners for increased federal control.

In order to encourage the movement from relief to employment, Whitton recommended that practice of unconditional grants for relief—introduced by Bennett in 1934—be replaced by new agreements with strict and comprehen-sive conditions for all federal aid. Federal supervision would ensure that work was more attractive than relief by careful monitoring of local units and by setting standards based on local or provincial standards of living.[42] Earlier in the year she had reiterated her views about relief monies. "We must realize," she stated in an address before the Empire Club, "that a State cannot treat its dependents better than its earning contributory tax payers of low income."[43]

Determined to advertise her position with the NEC, in September and October 1936 Whitton attempted to gauge public support for her views. Antici-pating much of her report, Whitton prepared a series of eight articles for the *Financial Post*. Examining issues such as national health schemes, the challenge of land settlement for unemployed youth, the plight of homeless men, and the eradication of graft in relief programmes, the *Financial Post* articles were moder-ate expositions when compared to the confidential views presented to the prime minister or the chairman of the NEC. With catchy titles such as "Human Relief Vultures," "Two Meals and a Bed," "Canada's Health Maze," "The Plight of Youth," and "Whither Canada?" the articles were excellent summaries of a good observer who recorded those social problems that took up most of her time and energies in the 1930s.[44] What they failed to do was explicate her views on just how to deal with such real problems. Their intention was to convince her audiences that she could contribute in some way to solving the country's malaise.

The *Financial Post* articles are also interesting illustrations of the fears of riot and instability, of disorder and class conflict that had come to haunt Whitton during the Depression. In 1934 she had optimistically written that economic recovery must be close but that "essential to the coming of that time is the maintenance of stability and order in the life of today." Continuing this theme in "Two Meals and a Bed" two years later, she was less optimistic as she warned her readers that "Canada's floating population must be collected, sorted, and salvaged," as if people had become refuse. She felt that the relief camps were overcrowded with an "inchoate aimless movement of transient men"—a "churning mass that threatened stability."[45] Such views and fears were shared by those who saw the security and privilege that they had hitherto enjoyed threatened by the continuing depression. In some ways these fears were understandable. In this decade the Canadian Communist Party had attracted many of the alienated and disaffected into its membership and sympathizers and the Social Credit and CCF parties had emerged on the prairies and the Union Nationale party in Quebec. Such populist movements were challenging the mainline party system just as the "On to Ottawa Trek" of hundreds of protesters had forced many to reassess Canadian working class attitudes. At no time was there any real threat of revolution, but the circumstances were extraordinary enough to exaggerate conservative perceptions. The 1935 On-to-Ottawa Trek, which culminated in the Regina Riot was still fresh in the paying public's mind although with investigation, interpretation, and hindsight the immediate threat has been shown to be exaggerated. When respectable intellectuals could approve the Regina Manifesto of 1933, which founded the CCF and spoke of a new social order replacing the profit motive and restructuring the capitalist system, Whitton and others like her magnified its revolutionary potential.

The NEC report, "Organization of Aid to Persons in Distress" (1937), evoked hostile responses. Informed that the *Final Report* advocated that Ottawa take over unemployment relief, Mackenzie King worked vigorously either to have the recommendations changed or at least to undermine agreement within the NEC. His reason was simple enough. They would prove to be too expensive. Moreover, he saw the recommendations as part of a conspiracy within the federal civil service in which Norman Rogers, minister of labour, O.D. Skelton, undersecretary of state for external affairs, W.A. Macintosh, Queen's University economist, and W.C. Clark, deputy minister of finance, "all of whom are Queen's University, Department of Economics, have come together, and have been working jointly to seek to bring about change in constitutional relations which will lead to a centralization of power and away from the present order of things."[46]

Membership on the League of Nations' newly formed Social Questions

Committee which Bennett had secured for her prior to his defeat in 1935, gave Whitton an opportunity to influence the direction of the child welfare committee.[47] She could not know that within three years the League would fall apart under the threat of war; however, as a rapporteur on the advisory committee on social questions, she made the following observation on the BBC in May, 1936.

> There are those who say that the League is a failure, but though it has failed, and will fail again, that does not write it down a failure of it- self . . . Is the League a more extravagant toy then, than the armaments with which mankind may ultimately destroy mankind? Is the League's slow and patient progress along humanitarian lines to be decried at a time when man's ingenuity is being increasingly devoted to the study of more and more methods of mutual extermination?[48]

Her enthusiasms for the League were also expressed in a series of twelve articles, "Social Work at the League of Nations," for the Toronto *Star*. Although Whitton's optimism could not change the course of history, in two short years, from 1936 to the end of 1938, her contribution was significant.

In Paris, in April 1936, at her urging, the advisory committee reorganized itself to become the committee on social questions, and it was agreed that Whitton would be the chairman of the committee on placing in families as well as the rapporteur of a significant study coming out of this committee, "The Placing of Children in Families." In 1937 she joined the League's mixed committee on the problem of nutrition. This appointment added to the dismay of deputy minister of health, Dr. R.E. Wodehouse, for he believed that only agriculture, economic, or health experts should sit on this particular committee. Nor was he happy in 1937 when she became Canada's delegate on the social questions section. Yet on this committee Whitton asked that the definition of "child welfare" be expanded to include far more than the mere "protection of the health of infant children." She argued instead for

> the desirability of emphasizing the importance of a positive approach through preventive and constructive measures to the whole problem of child welfare and general social betterment, visualizing the appeal of normal family life and child welfare effort rather than remedial action along what, in contrast, might be described as negative lines of treatment and control.[49]

Her contribution to such redefinition of the future work of the social questions committee was praised by Katharine Lenroot who wrote:

> The report of the work of the First Session [of the newly organized section]

is . . . the most adequate and comprehensive report the Committee has ever had. I think very good progress has been made in getting the scope and work of the Committee on a dignified and more adequate basis, and I know that it is due to you.[50]

By 1938 a two-volume, scientifically researched, seven-chapter report culminated from a survey of child placement methods in several countries. It was accompanied by a film on child-placing methods used by the Toronto Infants' Home, which was supplied by the home's director, Vera Moberley. Robert E. Mills of the Toronto CAS was used as a technical consultant along with Elsie Castendyck of the U.S. Children's Bureau. Acclaimed as "the most important inquiry completed this year in regard to child welfare," this judgment was not shared by one member of the British Foreign Office.[51]

Mr. W. Garnett had been a member of the Overseas Settlement Board when he accompanied Margaret Bondfield during her Canadian juvenile immigration investigation in 1924. He had been unimpressed with Whitton's campaign then, a view that had apparently not changed. He claimed that some of the material in the report "was extremely prejudiced and biased," not specifying on what grounds except that it had been supplied by a "voluntary" organization, the council (renamed the Canadian Welfare Council [CWC]), and therefore did not represent official information supplied by the Canadian government. He suggested that the report "was compiled with great haste, and, in fact, the main committee agreed to its publication without having had an opportunity of considering it."[52] However, nothing came of his protest, and while Garnett was perceptive about Whitton's role a decade earlier, he had allowed personal antipathy to colour his assessment in this particular case.

The last important contributions Charlotte Whitton made to the social questions section of the League were a resolution on the reaffirmation of the Declaration of the Rights of the Child and the provision of legal data supplied by a Montreal legal adviser, Elizabeth C. Monk for the Equal Rights International Committee.

Just as the League of Nations faltered in the late 1930s, so did the council. Despite Bennett's spirited defence of the transfer of the child welfare division, the council's maternal and child welfare division never really got off the ground, and with the defeat of the Conservatives, the special arrangement between prime minister and the council was broken. Although Mackenzie King appointed Whitton to the National Employment Commission, his sympathies stopped there, and in 1937 the Liberal government moved to reassert federal interest in child welfare with the appointment of Dr. Ernest Couture as chief of a new division of maternal and child hygiene. With this reassertion of dominion authority, any lingering hopes for a Canadian Children's Bureau ended, and with it Whitton's social service career lost much of its impetus.

Two significant statements a few years earlier, "Notes on Social Work" (1934) and "The Social Worker Pleads for Faith" (1935), had exhibited a pervasive melancholy. In "Notes" Whitton referred to a sense of a "great weariness" and the "deeply seared scars" she now bore after bitter disagreements with some of her associates despite sixteen years of "fine friendships." She reflected that "a man's enemies most generally are to be found in his own household."[53] Had she heeded the warnings of Falk about being a "professional social worker" and of Wodehouse about the "jealousy" of other national groups, as well as Emily Murphy's words about relations between East and West, the impasse might have been averted. Had she listened to Helen Reid's gentle chastisement about being a politician or Maude Riley's caustic one about overlooking council affiliates she might not have felt so embattled by the late thirties. But it was not Whitton's nature to listen to advice. Ironically, had it been, she would not have done so much in so short a time for social and child welfare.

By the mid 1930s Whitton was seen as an anachronism by some of the very professionals she had helped to create. The new social philosophies shaped by the Depression demanded state intervention, particularly at the federal level, more expertise, more government controls, and more public funding. Increasing numbers of ambitious technocratic men with advanced university qualifications in such areas as labour and economic planning entered the profession, undermining the power of the established nucleus of female social workers who remained in family and child welfare areas. Whitton had been particularly bold in asserting herself in social planning, an area presumed to be the domain of males. As these new policy areas expanded, the "feminized" occupations and those avenues deemed as "women's sphere" were devalued by comparison.

There is a certain pathos in this situation when Whitton's dedication to social welfare is contrasted with the fading ethos of social stewardship. A world separates the bureaucratic mentality from that best summarized by a "pledge" that Whitton, Ethel Dodds Parker, and Dorothy King agreed was appropriate for one embarking on a social work career:

> I pledge myself to the service of those whose responsibility is entrusted to me. I promise to place their needs before my own desires. I vow my loyalty to the service in which I am retained and should my honour conflict with this duty, I promise to withdraw from, and as far as in me lies, to bear myself without malice toward it. And I ask my God to give me knowledge of truth, faith in goodness, and the power to do good in His service.[54]

Moreover, even before the council's submission to the Rowell-Sirois Commission, the CASW executive had begun to separate itself from Whitton. Consequently, in 1937 she declined to renew her membership.[55] The CASW executive was suspicious of her political involvement in relief questions, her consultant status with the NEC, and her role in the child welfare division transfer. Their repudiation of her work was painful and humiliating. Inferences that she was not a trained social worker had compelled her to ask in "The Social Worker Pleads for Faith":

> Is a man or woman of good intellect, sound character, proven capacity and experience who has spent the better part of his or her life in doing social work, recognized as such in the community, to be denied as a social worker and decried as an amateur or volunteer because he or she lacks training, a formal certificate, from some approved school, when at the time of his or her entry to social work there were no such schools, because he or she may even have helped to make the very school itself and evaluate its very training?[56]

Elsewhere she decried the social workers' "extra-territoriality," which excluded both professionals and volunteers unless they had "taken a course" or done casework. She saw this as untenable because it ignored "many persons of brilliant capacities, and thorough education of the mind, as if it were argued that the head of a railway could be recruited only from locomotive engineers." Fearing the implications of such attitudes with regard to those volunteer services that were organized by the religious social services of the Anglican and Roman Catholic Churches, she despaired for a society that discouraged lay participation by overemphasizing expertise, technical intervention, or professional monopoly.

> The most deadly, the most undermining, the most fatal tendency in certain communities today is the extent to which the professional workers get together, consult, discuss, confer, decide, with very, very little fresh air from the lay point of view infiltrated into the atmosphere, and then agree that because they have so concurred, the problem is settled . . . the volunteer group would save us from our own 'inbreeding.'[57]

She had felt intimations of the consequences of professionalism as early as 1932 when she had written to Ernest Blois, superintendent of dependent children in Nova Scotia:

> I believe that for our own generation at least there will have to be a special recognition for the great group of us who have our own type of education and equipment and long experience, but not professional training in social work. In this group there would be yourself, Mills, myself, and many others.[58]

The apparent contradiction between Whitton's insistence on professional staff for social work positions and her own lack of specialized social work training can be understood as a separation of those who were responsible for carrying out the operation of welfare agencies from those who were responsible for educating and executing the acceptance of scientific standards of child and social welfare by public and private agencies. This latter elite group, of which Whitton clearly saw herself as a leading spokesman, needed not a narrow training in social work but rather a university education in subjects relevant to social service.

Also, while insisting on professional standards, Whitton had always been careful to separate effective volunteers from those who were "casual or careless" or those who were led by "religious or emotional importunity" in a "sort of vicarious vice of the pure in heart." Although suspicious of volunteers who were "just thrilled by social work" or who were members of "the same bridge club," she equally deplored the replacement of the volunteer spirit with the "expert complex" that made knowledge claims based on technical skills and an esoteric language which was becoming increasingly sociological and mystifying.[59]

Whitton's commitment to the Children's Aid Society model was based on her belief in the volunteer as the "leaven" that humanized public welfare agencies. Her espousal of professional social workers also included the view that professional, not lay, leadership was essential if social services were to be provided effectively and efficiently. Like the earlier "deans" of Canadian social work, J.G. Shearer and J.S. Woodsworth, Whitton found herself overtaken by events she had helped set in motion. Unlike Woodsworth, who moved into a new arena, or Shearer, who died before professionalization had taken hold, Whitton was at the height of her powers when social work training became essential for leadership.

As the thirties neared their conclusion, Whitton's opposition to state intervention increased. While attending League sessions she observed the resort to fascism, and after a brief flirtation with Mussolini's syndicalism, she ultimately refused to be seduced by any populist fervour that subordinated individual impulse to the state. She believed absolutely that handing over this impulse would result in a bureaucratic outlook that was both impersonal and manipulative. Inordinate state assumption of the parental role was a retreat into collective subservience and public dependency. In short, the acceptance of state socialism was a sure sign of the bankruptcy of the human spirit and intellect.

Believing that citizen input and community effort put the human face on an otherwise impartial collectivity and that they were necessary to a society alienated by urbanization and industrialization, she asked whether voluntary effort was to become

something so outworn, of so little value in the whole structure of the national life, as to be blithely left to one side, as of such small size and significance as to enter nowhere in the picture of adjustment? I, for one, am not prepared to accept any such premise, particularly after close contact with States where this development has come.

Canada was a nation turning its back on the possibilities of rejuvenation except through massive state-aided programmes; a nation that wallowed in spiritual inertia; a nation that lacked faith and imagination; and finally, a nation that trivialized the significance of God. As her need to escape this wasteland of political panaceas increased, her need for religious support gained strength. Social reconstruction was destined to ultimate failure unless equal weight were given to moral reconstruction.

> Individual relationships to one's God and to the source of strength outside oneself may vary, but surely it can only be the result of very superficial thinking for humanity to imagine that mankind has so far come upon this road without some predestined purpose in an ever enduring plan and that the sum total of all humanity's ingenuity from the dawn of time until today is patently ineffectual in these times and that there must be some setting of the life of the individual and the raising into accord with some underlying divine harmony? . . . that social work particularly deals more than anything else except the church itself, with the spiritual adjustments of individual souls.[60]

For Whitton, her work was more than a career. It was a vocation best regarded as a *stewardship*, begun at Queen's and nurtured by the Queen's ethos of service. This inspiration sustained her during what she saw as betrayals by social workers enthusiastically agreeing to more state intervention and during the painful period of her growing estrangement from members of the council who eagerly embraced state welfarism. Without her belief that human history followed a divine plan and that individuals played an important part in it—both as witnesses to its truth and as a means to their ultimate self-expression—life would have been intolerable for Whitton. She could not have endured existential absurdity.

The 1930s had been frustrating for Whitton in many ways. With the onslaughts of the Depression, not even the transfer of the child welfare division was enough to ensure the hoped for expansion of council. Her dreams of a children's bureau for Canada vanished as she realized that the council had reached its peak and that she could expand it no further. Alienated from the new professionalism and from many of her colleagues, she found social welfare work confining and the advance of the welfare state threatening. At the very time that Whitton gained full membership at the League of Nations, it was already in the process of disintegration. The Italian invasion of Ethiopia and the Spanish Civil War sounded the death knell for the League as well as for Whitton's hopes on the world stage. Her international ambitions were dashed by historical circumstance; her dreams for the council obliterated by the Great Depression; and her hopes for a ministerial or government post vanquished by Bennett's defeat. Even her domestic tranquillity had been threatened by Grier's ill-health. Neither the CBE in 1934 nor the honorary doctorate from King's College Halifax in 1939, which allowed her to be addressed as "Dr. Whitton," rejuvenated her.

Although in December 1939, she submitted comments to the Montreal Council of Social Agencies to be used in proposals for Child Protection Legislation in Quebec, her suggestions lacked the bite of her previous work.[61] Charlotte Whitton was tired. She was also deeply unhappy. A decade that had begun with depression was to end in war, and Whitton's years from maturity to early mid-life seemed to reflect the uncertainties of the times.

Yet, despite the thwarted dreams, these had been useful years. As she struggled with her disappointments, frustrations, and perceived betrayals, Whitton was compelled, for the first time since Queen's, to articulate her social views, to debate them publicly, and to organize them into a coherent social philosophy. This philosophy, with its amalgam of ethics, religion, politics, and economics, was balanced by a wealth of practical experience. The next decade was to see it fully developed.

6

CAREER IN CRISIS

*You had a dream in your more youthful days, a
large part of which has been realized—more than
is given to most of the dreamers of this world—and
you have furnished the foundation; one which will
endure for others to build on. The children of the
future will benefit by your work, even as they do
today, and live to bless and we hope to continue,
the structure that you started.*

LAURA HOLLAND, 1941

If the first twenty years of Charlotte Whitton's adult public and private lives were
the best of times, then the years immediately following were the worst. In 1939,
the very year that she was presented to the King, the CWC board rejected her
budget. She did not see the action as a result of war time economizing and a cut
in the government grant but as a criticism of her leadership. Whitton's difficulties with the CWC governors were partially of her own making. The move to
recruit more businessmen had substantially shifted power from the old coali-
tion of social workers and public spirited women such as Ella Thorburn to men
such as Philip Fisher and C.S. MacDonald who were less sympathetic to
Whitton's style of leadership. Moreover, her professional problems were compounded by a deterioration of Grier's health.

Despondent and needing reassurance, Charlotte wrote to Viscount Bennett
complaining about the council and asking him to return to Canada. He replied,

> I like you Charlotte, as you know; you amuse me at times but God has given
> you a fine brain which you use as the spirit moves you! You have done
> much valuable work and can do much more and even better. You are
> envied; but that is a tribute to your capacity. . . . As for wanting me back
> that is sheer nonsense Charlotte, and you must know it. They gave me a

great 'send off' for many reasons. Some for conscience sake; some for real regard, some glad to be rid of me. But it just became a bit of *mob manifestation*: 'Hosanna in the highest' and 'Crucify Him, Crucify Him,' a week later.[1]

She saw the rejection of Bennett as a rejection of herself. She wanted his return to give her life meaning, perhaps to give her work of national importance once again. Meanwhile, she marked time, delaying her inevitable resignation.

However, her words to George Davidson in the spring of 1939 were resolute: "I have no other plans . . . I must enter gainful occupation as soon as possible, but I am quite definite in this; *if I break service with the Council, I break all connection with Canadian social work* and, like Joan of Arc, am determined to find my way in other paths." Despite these brave words, Elsie Lawson wrote from the Manitoba Department of Health and Welfare that Whitton seemed to be very "run down."[2] The CWC board of governors strongly recommended she resign or take a leave of absence, but Whitton convinced them to give her an unpaid temporary leave. The board felt that she was out of touch with new ideas and that the council needed re-organization under new leadership. Whitton was right in seeing her leave as a vote of non-confidence.

Believing that she was indispensable to the council and that it would founder without her, Whitton wrote to Frank Stapleford of the Toronto Neighborhood Workers' Association that should she be absent for even forty-eight hours all interviews, correspondence on social work, and administrative processes would *cease* until she returned.[3] She correctly observed that as far as the affiliated agencies and the board were concerned, "a certain element of support turns about the Council because it turns about me."[4] Elsie Lawson merely affirmed this when she wrote, "You have lived so strenuously . . . I cannot think of you and the Council ever being separated and of course it will never be so, because the structure is of your building."[5]

By November 1939, Nora Lea of the Toronto CAS was also concerned about Whitton's health, gently chiding her that she was "driving" herself, that it was "a waste of human energy and ability for you to go at things so terrifically hard and spoil your own effectiveness. Do, for goodness sake, slow up a bit." She continued:

> So forget this bogey of rejection or discrimination or whatever psychological term you wish to describe it, and recognize the fact that the Council has to have limitations and that particularly at the present time [the war effort] localities must be left to work out their own development with their own local group.[6]

By 1940 Whitton also found herself quarrelling with her good friend Frank Stapleford, who was president of the council that year. She and Stapleford had first become colleagues and friends in Toronto twenty years before. In March

1940, obviously preparing herself for the worst, Whitton wrote that her previous angry letter was not the result of "nerves or annoyance" but of the realization that she had "come to the end of the road and it had to be faced."[7] Histrionically she asserted that her doctor had warned her of a possible "crack up" and that she had not slept for ten nights before bracing herself to write. Clinging to the last vestiges of hope, she threatened resignation and demanded that if the council was not re-organized to meet her demands it would go into "liquidation without her."

Claiming the CWC was faced with "continuous drift and gradual inevitable collapse," Whitton accused the governing board of inertia, the president of capitulation, and the staff of incompetence. Annoyed, Stapleford impatiently responded to the charges:

> I do not know exactly what you are expecting me to do under the circumstances. Your letter pretty clearly infers that neither officers or members of the Board are taking any interest in the work, and are leaving you to sink or swim the best you can. That is hardly a true picture of the situation.[8]

He pointed out that because of the war funds were short and that she was allowing a multitude of imagined problems to work on her mind to the extent that she visualized "a complete collapse" of the council's work. She was getting "keyed up higher and higher," and in the end she must "break from overstrain." If the council was disintegrating, he went on grimly, this would be taken by the board as a reflection on her and, as far as he could tell, there were "more rocks ahead." He clearly did not think that she could navigate them.

The passionate, even abrasive, tone of her exchange with Stapleford was not out of keeping with her character even during better times. Whitton was consistently confrontational, a trait which normally got things done: indeed, without which very little might have happened. During her work with the CWC she had similar misunderstandings with subordinates such as Marjorie Bradford, her assistant, and with Eunice Dyke, secretary of the maternal and child hygiene division. She also had sharp exchanges with associates outside the council such as Rachel Crowdy at the League and Dr. E.W. Montgomery, minister of health and public welfare in Manitoba. She quarreled with George Davidson before he took over her position with the council and with Harry Cassidy who was seen as a rival in social welfare. Whitton's impatient nature had antagonized many throughout her social welfare career and would again in the future.[9]

Within the month a further blow weakened Whitton's psychological resilience; she lost the re-election as a Queen's trustee, a position she had held for over a decade. Queen's historian, Frederick Gibson, noted her service as a Trustee from 1928 to 1940. In this capacity she contributed to "the continuing inheri-

tance of the Queen's community . . . an important governor of its destiny."
This contribution was recognized in 1941 when she was awarded an honorary
degree at the University's centennial. Nevertheless, neither her participation in
1940 as the Canadian delegate to the White House Conference on Child Life in
Washington nor on the board of the Family Welfare Association of America
could lift her out of despondency.

On 31 December 1941, Charlotte Whitton and the council officially separated after twenty-one years. Her notice of resignation contained a report of the
council's affairs in which she observed that the council's retiring director could
only feel a deep sense of failure in her inability to have developed within the
board that sense of corporate responsibility necessary to assure financial support and working conditions that would permit adequate discharge of the
council's obligations under its letters patent.[10] It was a restrained and reasonable
letter.

The lavish praise she received after her resignation provided cold comfort.
On 1 January 1942, Dr. Charlotte Whitton, now in her forty-sixth year, found
herself a single woman without a salary, without prospects, without definite
plans, and without a pension. A daunting enough situation for the young and
courageous, Whitton was now exhausted and humiliated, with all her dreams
and ambitions turned to ashes. Although like the phoenix she was to rise, it
would be almost nine years later before she would again enjoy financial
security. This was her most desolate period. Whereas in the preceding decades
she had been productive, confident, and visionary, the keywords between late
1941 and late 1948 were distress, fear, and, above all, panic, which was manifested in the unremitting demands she placed on herself as if sheer activity was a
defence mechanism.

For a brief period in January 1942, Whitton worked as a liaison between the
War Time Prices and Trade Board and the women's groups in the area of
consumer education. Her brother-in-law, Frank Ryan, who was a member of the
board, influenced the appointment. Finding neither the dealings within the
board itself nor the obscure and mundane nature of the work to her taste, she
was no longer in its employ by the middle of the same month. That this
interlude was so brief was not surprising for Whitton's milieu was hardly
preserving vegetables, keeping lard, or rationing domestic supplies to fit the
wartime economy! However, one of her objections to the board was over
another issue. She protested that the "honorary chairmen" appointed to preside
over the mass meetings she was to speak to in the West were to be men and that
they condescendingly "advised" women. Indignantly writing to Donald Gordon,
chairman of the board, she said,

> In my judgement this will destroy the characteristic feature of the
> plans . . . and the force of your own vital challenge to the women of

Canada. The project ceases to be a women's undertaking entirely, and each centre loses the fine idea of a rallying force . . . taking on rather the aspect of a city meeting, under the local mayor.[11]

She asked to be relieved of the responsibility of the meetings in the West and withdrew her services. She was, however, quite nonplussed to hear that her sister, Kathleen, Mrs. Frank Ryan, would be taking her place. In a letter to Byrne Hope Sanders, editor of *Chatelaine*, she noted that she was "no party to, but was shocked to find that my sister had gone to the West to these other preliminary meetings. Nepotism is rampant at Ottawa these days, and I greatly regret that Kay should have let herself into this, and when her husband is on the Board, and I was there too."[12]

Not one to be inactive, Whitton began the first of the many lecture tours she would make during the 1940s for income and for publicity. First she lectured in Burlington and Cleveland, and by April, 1942, the executive director of the Welfare Council of New York City had organized enthusiastic audiences as she embarked on a tour which included Omaha, Kansas City, New Orleans, Dallas, Houston and Des Moines. She also spoke before the Iowa State Conference, the Oklahoma College of Women, the Ohio Probation Association, Catholic charities, family welfare bureaus, councils of church women, branches of the YWCA, and the English Speaking Union of Chicago. She met the challenge of being publicized as "Canada's Welfare Ambassador Extraordinary" with style and vigour. In the summer she lectured in Vermont, and within two months she was in Los Angeles where she broadcast an address and discussion on children and youth, having captured an audience at the Conference on Children and Youth in Wartime. The American press poured adulation on her, with the *Los Angeles Times* describing her as a "noted authoress, educator and social worker" who had been "decorated by two kings." No one in her audiences could have dreamed that this short, stocky, dark haired, and large eyed woman with her "commanding brilliance" harboured deep resentment and a feeling of rejection as she spoke so energetically and humorously.[13]

Of all her lectures in the fall of 1941 and 1942, the most important was a series given at the McGill School of Social Work. These lectures are a superb summary of the historical development and state of social work across the country and succinctly elaborate Whitton's own social philosophy. They also list the outstanding personal and collective achievements for which she could take credit. But more importantly, the lectures celebrated the work of a whole generation of social workers who had been predominantly female. It is surprising that these lectures were never turned into a text book for social work students unaware even in the 1940s of pioneering work of Whitton and her generation.[14]

After Cleveland, California, and the Western States between October and December of 1942, her relentless pursuit of fame and income continued in a lecture tour under the auspices of the University of British Columbia extension department. Vancouver, Victoria, Saskatoon, Chilliwack, Prince Rupert, Nelson, Trail, Calgary, Regina, and Winnipeg . . . exhaustive and exhausting . . . and so her train rattled on to Fort William, Parry Sound, and south again to Milwaukee. Her itinerary was frantic. She lived constantly out of a suitcase and spent long evenings in hotel rooms or making small talk wherever she happened to be billeted. She sipped tea and nibbled *petit-fours* with clubwomen, and she entertained comfortable dowagers in their service clubs. Her lectures ranged from the facile and mundane to the provocative and thoughtful. The calibre depended, not on the fee, but on the audience. She took the professional clubs more seriously than the Soroptomists, and the IODE (of which she was a favoured daughter) more seriously than the Rotarians. Given Whitton's religious convictions, the highlight of these presentations must have been her address, "Canterbury and Social Armament," delivered from the pulpit of Christ Church Cathedral in Victoria on 18 October and broadcast a week later from the Anglican Cathedral in Vancouver in which she rejected the "authoritarian concept of man as a mere material resource of the state." In contrast, Whitton saw democracy as evolving out of a "respect for the personality and the expressed will of free men" and, therefore, "able to draw upon energy available from the concept of the human soul."[15]

Besides lecturing, Whitton turned her hand to contract writing during these years. She produced a study of the lumber industry in Ontario that chronicled the Gillies family operations. Despite its rather inauspicious beginning, *A Hundred Years A-Felling* (1942) proved to be a competent piece of historical writing.[16]

In the following year she continued her frantic activity. In March 1943, the *Chicago Sun* referred to her commanding persona which enthralled audiences and to her gesticulating hand movements that were constantly "weaving a pattern for women of nations to follow." She was said to be on a "good will tour" bringing American and Canadian women closer.[17] In an emotional and dynamic tempo, she spoke with a confidence that must have, at times, verged on bravado given her precarious future. Neither was she silent on the homefront in 1943. When the Justice Department passed a ruling that a child born out of wedlock had no legal status and that tax exemptions could not be claimed for it, she cried out against the injustice of children "crucified on the cross of some strict legalistic ruling." "Why," the Ottawa *Evening Citizen* quoted, "did children have to bear the brand and pay the penalty of adults?" Her eloquence moved the Ottawa Women's Club on this occasion.[18] The end of 1943 saw Grier unwell again and Whitton's anxiety increasing.

It might be expected that this deliberately cultivated celebrity status and the excitement of touring would have elated her. She was, after all, appreciated and recognized, which was necessary balm to her "wounded pride." But she found superficial socializing unsatisfying and tiresome; her satisfactions were in the goading persistence of a hornet rather than in the ceaseless activity of a gadfly. None of this life amounted to the "service" she believed she was still capable of giving to her country. The many friends she made on her tours and the understanding she gained of the lives of ordinary women living without professional support systems could not replace the inspiration service provided. Neither could it ease her frustration; accustomed to significance and power, she now felt invisible except to the particular audiences she addressed. Alienated, no longer playing a significant social role, she ached from the lack of professional recognition. Nor did all of this burst of compulsive activity provide her with permanent income. When it ceased, as surely it must—what then?

Just as during the Great War Whitton was preoccupied with her immediate world and creating a niche for herself, during the Second World War she sought to re-establish herself. Her uncertainties consumed her, and there is again little evidence that she had a profound awareness of the larger world being torn apart by war although there is a sense of growing cynicism about human organization, a tiredness that verges close to despair.

If habits and work patterns were difficult to alter, temperament was impossible to change. While working on a never to be completed biography of a Manitoba aviation pioneer, Whitton mused about her approach to tackling problems. Her remarks show that for her, mediocrity was confining, conservative attitudes as "woolly headed" as liberal ones, and life too brief to settle for "prepared pablum."[19]

> Margaret always laughs at the way I work at a jigsaw puzzle. She picks out her straight edges and fills out the frame. Then she starts filling in. I get all sorts of little piles, each horded up, of similar colours, etc.,—she says looking like an idiot's flowerbed— and then I start and lift them all in great pieces into the pattern which I have in my mind's eye.[20]

While lecturing in 1943 "to put money in her purse," she was bringing together all her intellectual resources and gradually formulating a cohesive social philosophy which was shaped by her accumulated experiences with relief, the NEC, the CWC, the League, and the Rowell-Sirois Commission.[21] But more than these, her personal moral and religious commitments were to be the mortar that would bind them.

In 1943, John Bracken, Progressive Conservative leader, commissioned Whitton to produce a comprehensive statement on social security. By that time, the two leading Canadian scholars on social welfare, Leonard Marsh and Harry Cassidy were working their own analyses of the inadequate response to contemporary social requirements and recommendations for the establishment of a comprehensive social security system. Marsh, working with the Advisory Committee on

Reconstruction, submitted his *Report on Social Security for Canada: The Requirements for Post-War Planning* to Dr. F. Cyril James, committee chairman, in April 1943. Cassidy's *Social Security and Reconstruction in Canada* and Whitton's *The Dawn of Ampler Life* were published shortly afterwards.

In *The Dawn of Ampler Life: Some Aids to Social Security*, she examined existing welfare schemes and the bolder plans for state welfare of Great Britain's Sir William Beveridge and Canada's Leonard A. Marsh, and proposed an alternative for social security—the "Whitton Plan."[22] Although the plan was dismissed by some because of its sponsorship as Tory propaganda and by others on grounds that it reflected a "social worker's" mentality, such critics were not altogether fair to the deeper philosophical framework in which Whitton operated.

Many readers of Whitton's book would be genuinely perplexed by the odd mixture of conservatism and social re-organization. Whitton's sources were very conservative indeed. It was from men such as W.R. Williamson of the Social Security Board in Washington and V.R. Smith of Confederation Life Insurance that she gleaned her ideas about fiscal matters. She confessed to Bracken in April 1943 that Williamson, Smith, and H.H. Wolfenden, who had been on retainer to the Canadian Medical Association, had supplied her with data for the manifesto. Moreover, knowing that such advisers would be suspect with the critics, Whitton decided not to mention them in the final draft because she would be "unfairly attacked by some of the extremists on the contention that advice had been obtained from those with the greatest stake in the country." She admitted to Bracken that Smith was associated with the "extreme right" and that Wolfenden was "fundamentally opposed to social insurance." As the report was essentially "non-political," she thought this was irrelevant![23]

Unfortunately, if social reformers were suspicious of Whitton's political connections, few conservatives thought in terms of the social organization she envisaged as part of a total ethical system and worldview. Yet to grasp this worldview is to catch a glimpse of her complexity. A devout Anglican, Whitton was immersed in the apostolic and catholic tradition of Christianity, a tradition which embraced in its systematic theology a rational view of the world, individual volition, and human society. Adherents of such a tradition, which boasts more of its catholicity than its protestantism, were bound to translate knowledge into action through "intelligent and informed citizenship." In short, Whitton's personal views cannot be isolated from her religious views on society and citizenship.

Two statements demonstrate the cohesive frame of reference—the moral universe—in which Whitton operated. They explain her feminism and constant admonitions to her own sex to exercise and claim full citizenship; they explain her preference for small units such as children's aid societies, for voluntary participation in community services, and for the active involvement of ordinary citizens in governance; they explain her wrath with increased federal power and centralized provincial systems such as in Alberta; and they explain too her opposition to cash benefits in the form of family allowances. The first statement was written in 1926:

> And two attributes must distinguish good citizenship. It must be an intelligent, informed citizenship, and it must be an active citizenship. The educated, informed member of a State, who withholds himself from an active citizenship within the community, is equally culpable with the person who more flagrantly abuses his privileges as a member of a civilized, organized state . . . This then is the theme of my statement on citizenship—that it is a high and well-nigh sacred thing, and that to be effective and safe it must be both informed and active.[24]

The second statement found in the rough draft of a manuscript written some years later was less general and to the point: "human beings are not the creatures of the state but the state is rather their creation, a scheme of life and a structure of government whereby their lives can be lived".[25]

Such remarks are found throughout her writings and speeches from her earliest in the *Queen's Journal* and *Social Welfare*, through her justification for reforms in the social services during her CWC surveys, to ideas explored in the last decades of her life. They are the kernel of her social thought, the pivotal point around which all else revolves, the high ground from which she surveyed the human dilemma and the lacunae in social policy. Terms such as "a high and nigh sacred thing" reflect the unity of the sacred and the secular just as reference to effective and safe citizenship was merely shorthand for the confessional churches' view of the duty of its members to argue on grounds of conscience only after a strenuous endeavour to develop a "well formed conscience." At the risk of oversimplifying a philosophy that has embraced the ideas of an impressive array of great social theorists and has many hundreds of volumes devoted to it, a brief explanation of where Whitton fitted into political theory is necessary.[26]

An explication of the political and moral principles of *subsidiarity* (or solidarism) will make Whitton's view of society clearer. Based on a metaphysical view of the organic concept of State and society, subsidiarity stresses a relationship of mutual rights and duties whose integral observation serves to order the entire social system. The community is seen as a moral organism whose dynamic enhances the lives of its members without impairing their existence as individuals. That is, the solidarity of the individual with the social interest is supported by natural laws that unify family and individual interests with those of the state.

Subsidiarity, then, can be viewed as a political version of Christianity, not a party system but a law of reciprocity which can have a socialist orientation stressing the dignity of human labour, wage injustice, and trade unionism *or* a capitalist one, stressing individual rights and private property. Subsidiarity emphasizes the subordination of self-interest when it is not in the interest of the total welfare, but it does not seek to eliminate private enterprise or property so long as they meet the needs of the common good. If private enterprise is corrupt, inept, or socially harmful, it must be replaced.

This view, therefore, is not a reactionary political ideology since it holds that humanity has unrestricted practical freedom to realize these principles and a *moral duty* to exercise such freedom. Subsidiarists would deny that a particular economic system can be read into the Gospels just as they would reject ideas of a "True State" as neo-romantic and mythological fantasy. That is why Whitton, who was at first attracted to Mussolini's corporate vision of the state because it was supposedly based on solidarism, was quickly repelled by the perversion of its principles. Essentially, subsidiarity dignifies humanity and interprets work as a form of service or stewardship for which individuals are immediately and ultimately accountable on moral grounds.

The Dawn of Ampler Life is imbued with this metaphysical spirit. Whitton constantly claimed that wherever "the State steps in other support steps aside," that an overdependence on State subsidization diminishes individual effort to help one's neighbour, and that the vacuum would be filled by an impersonal bureaucratic machinery that dehumanized services and reduced the common person to a mere cipher. George Orwell's *1984* predicted no less.

The 1940s saw a rapid secularization of western society with a subsequent decline of interest in moral or metaphysical systems, and those who may have previously dabbled with subsidiarity were alarmed by the distortions and excesses of fascist states which sometimes apparently emerged from such views. *The Dawn* de-emphasizes the power of the state to enforce the social good. By locating and differentiating between community and individual needs (for example, the Maritimes from Southern Ontario, or the seasonal worker and self-employed from the salaried and professional) Whitton stressed subsidiarist principles. Different conditions require individual analysis and response rather than impersonal decisions made by an administrative expert. She believed that a productive nation ought to depend less on politically defined restraints and more on ethical principles, social justice, and co-operative and communal supports. Government intervention encouraged an unhealthy reliance on authorities and perverted the fundamental principle of the voluntary association of people to do what they *want* to do. And the tribulations of the modern welfare state have proved her caution to be well founded.

The debate over *The Dawn of Ampler Life* proved Whitton's singularity. In a decade where women were entering the work-force in great numbers and where many were involved in wartime emergency organizations, few were testing themselves in the political domain. Whitton entered what was perceived as the male world of economic planning, political restructuring, and important social comment. While men such as Drs. J.J. Heagerty (who proposed the re-organization of health administration), Marsh, and Cassidy could safely enter the social security debate, Whitton stepped in where few women had trod. One reviewer recognized this remarkable entry and was impressed enough to compare her with Beatrice Webb: "There are few precedents, but a great deal of logic in a woman writing such a plan, for women in welfare, in religious endeavour and in their social hobbies have always tended to make up to the unfortunate for the insecurity created by society."[27]

Both Marsh and Cassidy have been called Canadian Fabians who were committed to large scale state intervention in the field of social and economic planning, to careful research in order to establish a firm factual basis for progressive social reform, and the key role of "an efficient and well-organized bureaucracy of experts who would . . . direct and manage the . . . social engineering." Their commitment to centralization, state intervention, and state bureaucracy over community responsibility clearly separated them from Whitton.[28]

Since *The Dawn's* proposals were reasonably argued and thoughtfully conceived, the failure to invite Whitton to speak on Marsh's proposals before the Canadian Institute on Public Affairs during the summer conference at Lake Couchiching must be construed as both a sexist rejection and a Liberal suppression of alternative discussion.[29] Marsh's and Cassidy's plans were praised while Whitton's was consistently underestimated. On the other hand, conservatives such as Ernest Manning, Social Credit premier of Alberta, who praised Whitton's ideas, entirely misunderstood their drift. Manning agreed with her protestations about increasing *centralist* tendencies, but he merely identified these with increasing *federal* power. Rhetorically, he rose to the occasion and decried "leftism," the introduction of the socialist state, conspiracies against individual freedoms, and the "curse of State dictatorship."[30] Whitton, who viewed Alberta's centralized social welfare system as the most alarming in Canada, must have been very surprised to realize that she was identified as the political bedmate of such an unlikely partner. At this stage, however, she wrote nothing to disabuse Manning.

Given the public praise for such men as Marsh and Cassidy, whom she identified as "favourites" of the liberals and camp followers of the socialists, as well as the overall lack of serious discussion of her social security alternatives, Whitton's exasperation with these two men, and particularly Cassidy, is better understood. By February 1944, the recognition of Cassidy's work and his public criticisms of *The Dawn* put them in opposing camps. The hostility erupted the year following their publications. Whitton patronizingly advised Cassidy to read the American economist and politician Paul Douglas's views on family allowances, suggesting that he had probably been "in high school" when they were first discussed. This time, goaded to extremes, Cassidy responded:

I was in the trenches at the time you were thinking of, trying to make the world safe for sentimental girls at Queen's, and in the second place Paul Douglas did not write his book until 1923 or 1924! . . . Occasionally, As you will see from this letter, one of your shafts hits home, and I am driven to qualify my general affection and admiration for you with a sharp expression, 'Damn that woman!'[31]

Cassidy unwittingly expressed what many men had muttered to themselves and to other men throughout her social welfare career and what many men were to mutter again to each other throughout her second career, "Damn that woman!"

The Dawn of Ampler Life deserves to be thoroughly analyzed and honestly contrasted with the debates begun by Beveridge and assimilated by Marsh and Cassidy. But it also says as much about Whitton as it does about social security in Canada. Whitton's conclusions about the discussion in 1945 were to the point:

Ever since the Beveridge Report, immature social and political "experts" in this country have been outbidding in clamour every half developed emotional conception—I wish I could say immaculate—of this and that Tom, Dick, and Harriet who chooses to don the garment of welfare. . . . It's like Kipling's "Jungle Tales." You remember; every animal but the elephant starting rushing across the swamp. He was the only one with brains enough to be afraid.[32]

She too had "brains enough to be afraid." She was afraid for a society that accepted new truths about social re-organization without question, afraid of the bureaucrats who would order the lives of the common people, afraid of the ideologues who dreamed of transforming the world into their own images; and afraid of men "of honest and right inclinations" who, inexpert but open-minded, relied on "men like Cassidy." Whitton's fear was encapsulated in two letters, one to the Very Reverend Dean R.H. Waterman of the Anglican Church in 1945 and the second to Viscount Bennett in 1946. In the first she said, "I am convinced that nothing but a revitalizing of spiritual power will save our Christian civilization," and in the second, she wearily reported that "a great fatigue is on the land."[33] The moral inertia and spiritual poverty that she had struggled against in the 1930s became the spectre that haunted her personal wasteland of the 1940s.

The "Whitton Plan" revealed its author's sensitivity to the vexing question of dominion-provincial relations and her thorough knowledge of Canada's legal and constitutional arrangements, which she believed should not be tampered with at the whim of idealistic social planners. Although her past experience with social and child welfare legislation had taught her this, she was naturally sympathetic to the idea that the smaller the unit able to manage its own affairs, the better for the individual and the society. Recognizing both provincial and municipal needs, her plan endorsed the principle that the provinces and the municipalities should administer a "social utilities" system under the guidance of a Dominion Assistance Board. She argued for a flexible system of public assistance rather than a standardized system of cash allowances administered by a large-scale dominion bureaucracy. Although the argument between her opponents and supporters polarized into a "Beveridge or bootstraps" polemic, Whitton never subscribed to a belief in the untrammelled free play of economic forces. She consistently argued that employers must be made to pay their employees living wages that took into account the number of dependents so that profits might be more equitably distributed and dependence on the state minimized. In turn, the state must legislate a living wage and fix prices to prevent exploitation. While the Cassidy and Marsh supporters argued for a modified welfare state with universal cash benefits and allowances, Whitton adamantly disagreed. Instead, she advocated "utilities," that is, universal *services* available for anyone in need. Whitton never ceased to view cash benefits intended for children with the suspicion that had surfaced during her relief work. She could not uphold distribution of child allowances because there was no guarantee that children benefited directly.

Other aspects of the Whitton Plan included a modified version of medicare as a social utility (or "service in kind"), a concern that all income taxpayers (including the self-employed like herself) and not just wage earners be entitled to income assistance, and the belief that because of regional economic differentiations, utilities were more appropriate than uniform cash benefits. Throughout the Whitton Plan there is an emphasis on provincial disparities in contrast to a Canadian social security modelled on a highly urbanized and industrialized Old World country such as Great Britain. Thus, she rejected Beveridge.

Although the proposal was structurally undeveloped, she did suggest that two boards administer the plan: one, appointed by the Civil Service Commission and removable only by Parliament, to administer utilities and children's services, and a second to administer assistance with the director of the first board sitting on the second one. Had such a scheme eventuated, Whitton envisioned herself as the director of the first board.

Her insistence on "social utilities" rather than cash benefits was often interpreted as an extension of existing social welfare programmes and as a means of opening positions for social workers. But neither the CASW nor many of her former social welfare colleagues were happy with the idea.[34] It is nonsense to argue that *The Dawn* "reflected" a social worker's mentality, given that Whitton went into social work because she already had a mental set conducive to such interests. Her sense of service was born out of and grounded in this point of view, and it became more articulated and systematic as the years passed and gave her Plan its own inner logic. She was correct in being annoyed with Cassidy who described her plan as "dubious." Surely, she argued, it was "novel and untried"—but "dubious"? She further objected to his use of the term "questionable." Surely, it was "debatable or open to question" but "questionable"?[35]

Objections to the Whitton Plan from social welfare critics were swift and brutally frank. Esther Kingsley, in the University of Toronto's *Varsity Review*, for 27 January 1944, contemptuously noted that "Dr. Whitton reverses the ortho-dox procedure in security planning. In doing this she has grossly misjudged the psychology of the dependency situation." Whitton had called for a reorganiza-tion of the Canadian economy in which national standards for wages and primary products would be set, for improved collective services (social utilities), and for a system of social assistance that would provide cash grants on the basis of need for various kinds of distress. Her rejection of a system of social insurance meant to protect wage earners, and espousal of services and assis-tance were condemned as representing social policy "which implies investigation, proof of need, and carries with it the taint of charity." A snide review in the Toronto *Daily Star*, on 30 October 1943, ridiculed it: "Under Dr. Whitton's plan there will be a very long night before the Canadian masses will detect the dawn of ampler living." This commentator cavalierly dismissed positive aspects of the plan by saying that Whitton was against maternity benefits, against the federal takeover of social welfare, against family allowances, and against national health insurance. No matter *what* Whitton actually said, there were those who would reject her ideas out of hand. As Cassidy conceded, her suggestions on the national health question were the most embracing, so much so that on 26 October 1943 the *Montreal Gazette* had published a piece saying "Dr. Whitton Suggests Medicine is a State Paid Utility" and that Whitton was incensed at the "medical fascism" which led the medical profession in Montreal to call her views "socialized medicine under another name."[36] The comprehensiveness of Whitton's recommendations on health provisions is another example of her personaliza-tion of social issues. The costs of Grier's medical care had driven home the need for government support for health and medical services. It seems, then, that critics were not to be persuaded on any matter contained in the Whitton Plan.

Whitton received better treatment from general academic reviewers. Sociologist, S.D. Clark, reviewing Marsh's *Report* and Whitton's *Dawn*, observed that the two could be viewed as majority and minority reports on Canadian social welfare and that Whitton's minority report exhibited "a much more imaginative and critical type of thinking than that displayed by the majority report." Clark also recognized that Whitton's views had "the character of being proposals formu-lated in terms of a very definite social philosophy and a very clear understand-ing of Canadian problems" while Marsh's were "a very good example of the sort of thinking which grows out of a very adequate knowledge respecting English experience in the field of poor relief and social insurance and a very inadequate appreciation of the distinctive type of problems presented by the Canadian economy and Canadian society."[37]

J.A. Corry, professor of political science at Queen's, noted that Whitton's conclusion that the Canadian people would be unwilling "to pledge a large part of their resources to the maintaining of a minimum income by collective action" represented "a profound insight, hitherto missed in Canadian discussion of these matters." Corry also maintained that the discussion of social utilities and social assistance made "out a formidable case against much of the Marsh Report." Charging that Marsh had evaded the issue of dominion-provincial relations by plumping for social insurance, Corry concluded that Whitton had failed to discuss the dilemma fully because "the truth is that the economics and politics of social security implicate a wide range of considerations which have not yet been adequately explored, and Dr. Whitton is not so sure of foot in the territory as she is in the narrower field of social security measures and their administration."[38]

It was over questions relating to social security that her relationship with Harry Cassidy began to deteriorate. She did not trust Cassidy, whom she saw as part of the parade of younger males who passed her by in the 1940s, getting all "the plush executive jobs" and replacing women in a field that had been, if not a preserve of women, then certainly a profession that consisted mostly of them. She also saw George Davidson who had replaced her at the CWC as part of this parade. Although in his discussion of the *Dawn*, Harry Cassidy hesitated to describe the work and its author as categorically conservative, his *Social Security and Reconstruction in Canada* was seen as a refutation of Whitton's basic tenets for social security. In a review article which he forwarded to Prime Minister King, entitled "Three Plans for Social Security" before its submission to *Public Affairs*, he generously conceded that as for a scheme of medical care "on this point, Miss Whitton, in spite of her conservative sponsorship is the radical." She wanted a system of universal health care which most other social planners saw as too costly. Elsewhere, he cautioned critics:

> A Conservative document? Scarcely, in spite of its auspices. Rather a highly independent report by a brilliant woman with conservative leanings who knows a great deal about her subject and who has much to give to those of different political views if they will study her ideas carefully.[39]

To "study her ideas carefully," however, was precisely what her social welfare critics would not do.

The debate over the various plans on social security and especially family allowances continued in 1944. Whitton's speeches, lectures, and journalism kept her views alive if not exactly robust. When the Family Allowances Act was passed in the summer of 1944 (to be implemented on Dominion Day, 1945),

Whitton felt used and cynical. The Progressive Conservatives, including Bracken, ultimately supported it. That 40 per cent of the House was conspicuously absent when the vote was taken did not diminish the enthusiasm for the bill—it received unanimous approval.

Once the bill was passed, Whitton would have been prudent to accept it. Instead, a sense of betrayal on the social welfare front, described by Nora Lea as a "bogey of rejection," was now reinforced by thwarted political aspirations. On 7 February 1944, the *Ottawa Citizen* informed its readers that "Charlotte Whitton May Be Candidate in Next Election." It continued that she would be a "natural" as Progressive Conservative minister of social welfare since they had already retained her as a part-time consultant on welfare problems. The press could not know of that Whitton felt that Bracken had used her views on family allowances in *The Dawn* as a barometer to test public opinion. By late summer, 1944, she had declined an offer of a Conservative constituency because of her disagreements with the party. These included the family allowance "backdown" by the Tories, the matter of "British Relations," that is, the party's concessions to Quebec ridings on the conscription issue, and party structures which prevented the full participation of women, effectively reducing them to an auxiliary function. Whitton also refused to head Women's Organization and Activities within the Party's National Office because she viewed the offer as patronizing.[40] She and Winnipeg Alderman Hilda Hesson agreed that the party only supported women candidates if they stood "in slaughter house ridings" where they would not seriously compete. When Agnes Macphail, the first woman in the Parliament of Canada, urged her to enter federal politics in February 1945, Whitton replied that she would do so if "the party would stay put long enough to get aboard its boat." Though Macphail was a member of the CCF and their views on most issues were far apart, she wrote:

> I wish you were in the Federal House of Commons. You ought to be. I don't always agree with you but I always give you credit for great ability and sincerity. And I get pretty fed up with men in government. They are a selfish lot taking them by and large. I don't know whether women in large numbers would be any better but I'd like to try them and see.[41]

Nora Frances Henderson, a member of the Hamilton Board of Control, also urged her to reconsider.[42]

Whitton did contemplate running as an independent in South Renfrew, however, she knew she had damaged herself in the social welfare controversies. In 1943 Whitton had confided to the party's national organizer that she would always feel in the future "that I was not standing on a rock but a cliff of butter that would melt in the heat. I would not be able to convey confidence where I had none."[43] In the aftermath of the Tory defeat in June 1945, she wrote to Senator

A.C. Hardy of Brockville that Bracken was the man who "diddled the baby bonus on both knees" while losing the election:

> John Bracken takes as long as your letter to make up his [mind] and then keeps his 'make up box' handy in case he wants to put on a different face. So like your leader's tactics I think the country saw little use in shifting from an experienced to an inexperienced quick-change artist.[44]

Whitton believed herself to have been Bracken's sacrificial lamb because he had not appreciated that "through and on his instructions and request" she had made clear her own deep convictions on social security and family allowances although at the time she had not done so with "any projected ultimata."[45] To Hilda Hesson she wrote that, "after weeks and months in which I worked like a Trojan and was given not a sou, and actually lost hundreds of dollars in [earning] time," she had been left out on a limb.[46] She never fully understood the limitations of dispensing patronage or recognized that even if Bracken "owed" her, there were more urgent debts to be paid. This sense of betrayal was still strong in 1946 when she wrote to Bennett that Bracken had lost to King because "the Canadian people [would] not put out an experienced opportunist to elect an inexperienced and fumbling one."[47]

Forced to give up her political ambitions for the time being, Whitton redoubled her attacks on what she saw as "bonussed breeding" or, as she had said in 1942, the policy of people being remunerated on "their powers of reproduction instead of production." She continued to argue that family allowances attempted to "subsidize the moral condition of the community"— children and family life.[48]

The Ottawa *Evening Citizen* of 29 June 1944 pointed out an ironic twist to the debate, namely that it had been Whitton's fiery stand against the justice department on the rights of illegitimate children which had given *all* children, including the illegitimate, the right to access to the family allowance. Three weeks later, on 18 July 1944, it said she believed no citizen had the right to spend without restrictions *non-earned* monies such as government grants. The *Trail Times*, 13 July 1944, reported her statement that there was an illusion of "getting something for nothing" in the family allowances bill while, in fact, 20 per cent of the taxes would be spent on administrative costs and benefit a well-fattened bureaucracy. The path Whitton was travelling was professionally and politically suicidal, but her views were never to alter.

Indeed, in the 1929 brief on mothers' allowances, which she implied represented the views of "social workers," Whitton had rejected that the state should assume the obligations of the head of the family but that it was its responsibility "to see that the conditions of employment, the development of resources, and the distribution of wealth within its territories are such that it is possible for the wage earner to discharge these obligations, and then to enforce his discharge of them."[49]

She wrote to Bracken in the same vein describing Mackenzie King's liberalism as "dead at the heart" lacking "the energy to face [the] challenge" of reconstructing social services without resorting to the panacea of cash benefits. "Take more from the people so that we may control their very lives and have the baby under our bureaucracy from birth," she sarcastically wrote.[50] She saw an alternative in the expansion of social utilities such as medi-aid, dental clinics, educational facilities, land settlement schemes for Canadians, low cost housing, community nursing, universal food subsidies (for example, milk), and tax relief for low income earners which were "burdens to none but services to all."[51] This argument was consistent with the one she had presented in 1932 before the B.C. government on mothers' aid, which she also believed should go to the unwed, deserted, and widowed, but not be generalized as a citizen right. There was "no alchemy whereby generous impulses [become] financial resources" and "the balance of social justice must be held even . . . lest in relieving the obvious need of one group in the community, undue and oppressive burdens are imposed upon other groups, who may thereby be depressed beyond a modest standard of living, laboriously attained."[52]

The difference between the mothers' aid and the family allowance argument was that the allowance benefitted everyone; therefore, the appeal of discriminatory taxation was inappropriate. She insisted that family allowances were an admission by the state that wages and income were too low to support a decent living standard and that government was helpless to intervene in prices and wages. This could only operate to depress legitimate claims for a basic minimum wage while those already profiting from labour benefitted equally. Ironically, working people would be returning their taxes to support the children of the middle class. While not denying the necessity of benefits to the needy, she completely misunderstood the attitude of the middle classes on this matter. What she did not realize was that the extension of family allowances, and later medicare, as a citizen right to all would be as enthusiastically embraced by the well-off as by the needy. She was quite wrong when she noted to C.P. McTague, the national Progressive Conservative chairman, that "those who want their breeding bonussed are in sections of the population to whom we would not appeal and the great middle class just want a clean, practical statement of a few simple decent lines of social justice."[53]

The following year did little to restore Whitton's confidence and closed as dismally as the one before. In February 1945 George Drew, premier of Ontario, sent her a telegram asking for a breakdown of figures on provincial allocations of mothers' allowances. For a while, she clung to a false hope that the Progressive Conservatives would renew the fight again.[54]

The more she wrote and talked about the issue the further to the right she moved. In the end, she had placed herself in such an indefensible position that even Ernest Manning disassociated himself from her views. In March 1945 he replied to Whitton's description of the "sinister" situation the allowance would perpetuate by telling her that it was "bad strategy" to attack the allowance "due to the inequalities and undemocratic features of the wage system as the sole means of distributing incomes."[55] In the 24 March 1945 *Saturday Night*, she maintained that other measures were more urgently needed than the baby bonus—that the infirm, incurable, and failing aged were sorely neglected, yet unlike the child they would not move out of dependency into self-sufficiency. She pointed out that the measure ignored those 750,000 homes that had no children, consisted of "dual" households, were one member homes, or family-less homes (where children had left) but which were to be equally taxed to subsidize homes with children.

Whitton irrevocably alienated herself not only from Cassidy but also from many social workers in 1945 when she published a pamphlet in the Ryerson Press *The Canada Must Choose Series*. Whitton's *Baby Bonuses: Dollars or Sense?* was not only provocative and disturbing but also identified her with the Reverend C.E. Silcox of the SSCC, the author of the racist *The Revenge of the Cradles*. Together Silcox and Whitton pointed to the eugenic risk of the subsidized breeding of "morons and mental and moral defectives" and the advantages that would go to non-Anglo Saxon immigrant groups and racial stocks with large families. Whitton protested what she called "a subsidy to the birth of defectives" because the "prolific birth rate of the defective, especially of the sex moronic is common knowledge." Such subsidization, she claimed, went to the hinterlands where children were "bred and reared too often at the standard of brute creation." She advocated instead, the containment of defectives and resettlement policies for underprivileged families living in isolated and poor areas.[56] Religious groups with high birth rates and views against birth control were not overlooked either. Whitton was more cautious on this ground, being careful not to condemn one of the "basic stocks" of Canada—the French Canadians; but Silcox's very title was taken from the Quebecois purported strategem—the *revanche des berceaux*—to outbreed their conquerers. In his crude appeal to racial and religious bigotry, Silcox argued that the family allowance was a political ploy by which the Liberals were wooing the French vote. Quebec's leaders, he said, wanted nothing but "medieval fascism" to encourage large families which would be subsidized by the rest of the Dominion. He gave dire warnings about declining birth rates of the "right stock," asking whether "morons will inherit the earth" and "cuckoos lay their eggs in the nests of decent and self respecting birds"?

In her article Whitton subtly confounded conscription and the family allowance question. Arguing that the French Canadians enjoyed a demographic advantage because they opposed "equality of war service" and that English speaking provinces had suffered a grave reduction in basic birth rate because of their "spontaneous response" to the call for military service, she added that, "It is neither dishonourable nor mischievous frankly to face these facts." Whitton had strong feelings on the conscription issue (as befitted a member of the IODE) and such loyalties were admired as far away as in the *Boston Globe* which commented on her in the headline that a "Canadian 'Joan of Arc' Battles for Overall Draft."[57]

In March 1945 Whitton reiterated her immigration views, which, like those on mothers' allowances, had not perceptibly altered since the late 1920s. In a message to Premier Drew she cautioned that the content was "so confidential" that she said she was compelled to "inflict" her own typing on him. She deplored the alarming prospect of "the racial content of this country in the next generation unless there is substantial selected immigration."[58] Her concern this time was that the scheme assisted the worst classes and races to propogate themselves while the middle class of British stock had few children.

In *Baby Bonuses* she claimed that the family allowance was a fiscal and not a social service measure. Insisting that "We must have intelligent maternity and responsible paternity," she pointed out that Canada's generalized scheme could not be fairly compared with those of Australia or New Zealand, which were tied to a basic wage, required means tests, and in Australia were only given at the birth of the second child. Besides, she claimed, both countries had lower living standards than Canada or the United States.

The third Ryerson pamphlet, *Fact or Fiction*, by Cassidy's colleague, Margaret Gould, was a scathing attack on Silcox and Whitton. Whitton, who construed the attack as inspired by Cassidy, complained to Lorne Pierce at Ryerson who admitted that her accusations were not entirely unfounded.[59] In June, 1945, the month of the Ryerson affair, she resentfully wrote to Edith Abbott of the Chicago School of Social Service that many had "discovered the social services as the last preserve of patronage," and to Vic Smith:

> The trouble here is that the Canadian Conference on Social Work, the Canadian Association of Social Workers, and the Canadian Welfare Council are now in control, all of them, of a small clique, largely Harry Cassidy and a few of the very aggressive and superficially informed extreme "lefts," many of whom have very inadequate education—in Toronto, Montreal. Responsible mature thinkers like Stapleford, Mills, Laura Holland, etc., just "don't bother" because they are just shoved round if they open up and are such a minority. George Davidson for various reasons is using neither the intelligence nor integrity which he really possesses.[60]

The furore over the family allowance continued from summer to fall of 1945, and the 16 October *Ottawa Citizen* reported Whitton's indignation that a bank in

London, Ontario, was blatantly advertising that it would pay higher than ordinary interest rates and chequing privileges for family allowance deposits to encourage parents to put their benefits aside for the proverbial "rainy day." Could anything more "fantastic in the fiscal policy of a State be imagined" that gave monies to families who obviously were not in need of it and were not even required to spend it on the child? Such platitudes evoked a pithy response two days later from Mr. F.C. Wilson of Eastview, Ontario.

> Miss Whitton's articles are always a joy to read, not only because they are so delightfully one sided, but also because the other side sticks out so plainly that one is tempted to believe Miss Whitton is really only trying to be funny.

Could she be serious about "saving cheques" while "poor single persons and childless couples are taxed to provide the money for such saving"? He believed that Canadians were repelled by the alternative—"humiliating" means tests.[61] But Whitton was not trying to be funny; she was desperately trying to persuade the public of the correctness of a lost cause.

During 1944 and 1945 Whitton's career remained in crisis. Nothing promising had opened up which could be seen as an adequate substitute for her position with the CWC.

7

MID LIFE RESOLUTION

[Margaret] faced the final crossing over without me when we had never taken but one holiday apart in our thirty years of life together . . . it will have to be a great good for the children of Alberta that ultimately results to compensate for that.

WHITTON, 1948.

Throughout 1946 Whitton continued to write articles for *Chatelaine* and to give addresses to such groups as the Department of Welfare, Chicago, on "Public Welfare's Goal: The Preservation of the Dignity of Man," and she chaired a fund-raising committee for a new wing at Queen's.[1] The most pleasing event of 1946, however, was the celebration she and Grier hosted at Rideau Terrace on her fiftieth birthday on 8 March 1946. It was a gracious affair for which Whitton had silver coins minted as anniversary gifts for "the Silver Seven of the Round Table," who had shared her youth at Queen's. One guest wrote thanking her:

> especially the honour it was to be included in [a party] marking a high spot in your life. There was no flaw—flowers so gay and beautiful, and two hostesses blooming like the loveliest of them. I never saw either of you looking better. . . . So I say 'thank you' for having been born and long may you enjoy the good things of life.[2]

In November 1946, Whitton was the keynote speaker at the annual Queen's dinner, and her stirring address, "The University Graduate as a Responsible Citizen," was published by *The Queen's Review* in January, 1947. The sentiments she expressed echoed her own troubled existence:

> We are not so different from the inebriate, who was found searching, with that persistent singleness of purpose which inebriation often brings, for a

fifty-cent piece, four blocks from where he thought he had lost it. He explained to the policeman that the light 'was a lot better here' than where he had dropped the coin. There can be little hope of progress until we rediscover meaning and purpose in life and with them our sense of direction.[3]

Between late December 1941 and the close of 1946, Whitton had sought her own particular fifty-cent piece blocks from where she had lost it. After an unhappy detour, she rediscovered her purpose and her sense of direction. Given her bitter promise that she intended to "break all connection with Canadian social work" and her determined efforts to do so, Whitton's return to it was an indication of her desperation. In Alberta during the winter of 1947, she renewed her involvement with child welfare in an extraordinary scenario which restored her national reputation as child welfare leader. During a two-year period in which she almost collapsed, Whitton endured vilification at the hands of the Alberta government, enjoyed the vindication of a commission of inquiry into her work, and emerged from a series of crises applauded by an admiring public. The unexpected and extraordinary drama that was played out between January 1947 and December 1948 had antecedents that can be summarized briefly.

The Canadian Welfare Council had conducted social surveys in Calgary and Edmonton in 1929, 1931, and 1944. Each time the surveys recommended radical reorganization of municipal and government structures and a thorough restructuring of services, and each time the government ignored the recommendations. Well aware of Whitton's views on child welfare in Alberta, Premier Manning distrusted both her and the council. Her 1940 criticisms of the government's handling of the British Overseas children were not forgotten either. The CWC, Whitton, and the Calgary Council of Child Welfare under Maude Riley's leadership had made their criticisms well known. They opposed the enormous powers of the Department of Health and Welfare and the superintendent of the Child Welfare Division, and they believed the centralization of power was exacerbated by the anachronistic philosophy of child care held by Charles Hill, the superintendent of the division. In 1944 and again in 1945, the *Toronto Daily Star* reported his views in articles such as "Let Love Not Science Rule in Adoption." Lack of qualified personnel, inadequate standards in training, understaffed and underfunded supervision of adoptions and fostering, cross border adoption practices, and outmoded institutional care at all levels were among the criticisms directed at the postwar Albertan child welfare system.[4]

Concerned about the discontent among provincial social workers, the Edmonton chapter of the IODE approached Whitton in June 1945 to advise them about the possibilities of a survey. Whitton insisted that government co-operation was imperative for success, but given the suspicions of Manning and Dr. W.W. Cross, Minister of Health and Welfare, about the CWC, it would be unwise to expect it. She felt the council might "be prejudiced before it started."[5] Instead, she suggested a neutral, Laura Holland, to direct such a study because Holland had enjoyed good relations when she was the fieldworker involved in setting up a Family Bureau and Community Chest in Edmonton in 1939. However, the sixty-one-year-old Holland declined, fearing such a survey would inevitably lead to confrontation with the government. In September 1945, when Mrs. R.C. ("Daisy") Marshall, president of the Edmonton chapter, approached her, Whitton too refused. She was unwilling to proceed without government approval, which was not forthcoming, even after she met with Manning and Marshall in late 1945.

In September 1946, Whitton had a second interview with Manning in which she insisted that she would conduct a *study*, not a survey, although she did not elaborate precisely what the difference was. Whitton described her reception as "gracious, generous, and patient," but Manning, intransigent as ever, refused to participate. Thus, when Whitton finally agreed to go ahead on 8 January 1947, she was virtually admitting that her career had come to a standstill. The only alternative at the time was an offer to spend eight to ten months lecturing and engaging in public relations for the YWCA of Oklahoma City. She regarded the offer as "intriguing and flattering," but it did not offer either permanence or prestige.[6] The kind of position she wanted, but could not get, was one with the Social Commission on the Traffic in Women and Child Welfare for the United Nations. Professor Hilda Neatby of the history department of the University of Saskatchewan, convenor of the Committee for International Relations for the UN and president of the Federation of University Women, had put Whitton's name forward.[7] The Alberta study, on the other hand, was as much a political adventure as it was a professional engagement. To embark on it without the government's permission was hazardous, yet she knew that it would receive national publicity and that it might force Manning's Social Credit government into making reforms. It was a gamble, but Whitton's bleak career prospects justified it.[8]

Whitton had kept up her connections. Among her technical staff familiar names appear once more: Ethel Dodds Parker, who had been the acting director and had served Whitton on the CWC from 1933 to 1936, was the assistant director of the survey, and Robert E. Mills and Kathleen Gorrie, who had worked with Whitton during her SSCC days over twenty-seven years earlier, were consultants. Reverend J.A. MacDonald of the Catholic Charities of Ottawa responded to her request for his services as did Marjorie Moore, a McMaster graduate who had been involved with the SSCC before working with Frank Stapleford of the Neighbourhood Workers Association of Toronto and becoming director of the Family Welfare Bureau of Greater Winnipeg in 1938.

American consultants included Robert W. Beasley of the Bureau of Public Assistance of the Federal Security Agency and Raymond M. Hilliarde of the Illinois Public Aid Commission, who surveyed the plight of the aged in Alberta. Input on an *ad hoc* basis was given by such associates as Zella Collins, lecturer at the U.B.C. School of Social Work, and Elsie Lawson, then with the Dependents' Allowance Board of the federal government.

Within two days of her arrival in Alberta, Whitton began to advertise the study in public addresses whose content made it quite obvious that she was just as "prejudiced" as the CWC would have been. Indeed, the conclusions she would reach were already apparent. Although Whitton clearly intended to provoke a confrontation to ensure that reforms would occur, she had interviews with Manning and Cross on 15 and 23 of January. On 8 April 1947, she issued her initial findings at a luncheon of the Men and Women's Canadian Clubs at the Palliser Hotel, Calgary. This was followed on 21 April by the first news release, "Some Wrongs That Need Righting," which contained a blistering attack on Alberta's services for children, the aged, and the mentally handicapped. A series of addresses, interviews, and the July summary of the report quickly followed. In May, the *Calgary Herald* published its own series on "Children In Iron Cages." These articles, especially the one on the Edmonton detention home where boys, confined in a "stinking Edmonton jail" for up to two weeks, suffered from "prison pallor," provoked a public outcry. *Time* magazine, in a piece on Alberta in its 14 August issue, pointed out that Whitton was ready to fight the government, that she was already "fighting to win," and that she had spent the last months "planning indignation meetings all over Alberta" to publicize her findings. *Time* described the Alberta child care system as a "creaking adoption mill." All of these items insured a sensational coverage for the IODE report, which had cost $10,920. By the time *Welfare in Alberta* was finally released in late August, news reporters had already established the case against the government and restored Whitton's reputation as "Canada's First Lady of Social Service Work."[9]

The adverse press coverage forced the Alberta government to authorize a royal commission into child welfare, which opened its hearings on 13 August and then adjourned until the fall in order to accommodate testimonials and briefs. Satisfied, Whitton returned to spend the rest of the summer at the lake and to complete the IODE report before she returned for the hearings, which were resumed on 24 November 1947. She had wanted nothing less than such an inquiry to vindicate her study. The difficulties that would be involved in achieving such a vindication would not be easy to overcome, as was explained by a sympathetic Catholic priest, Patrick O'Byrne of Claresholm, who observed that many Albertans, including Judge "Billy" Macdonald, one of the commissioners, saw Whitton to be "on a political venture" and that the IODE's case must establish "the non-political nature of the crusade for welfare standards."[10]

The charges Whitton made against the Alberta government were damning. They included an indictment of foster care with its inadequate supervisory provisions and pre-placement matching procedures. She charged that Hill handled adoptions on an *ad hoc* basis. The Department of Health and Welfare was "tainted with authoritarianism" and "water tight secrecy." Not only was its staff ill-qualified to discharge its responsibilities, many had obtained their positions as a result of personal appointments arranged by Dr. Cross. Delinquent children were ill-treated in detention homes, shipped off to other provinces, or indentured as cheap labour to farmers, and dependent children were subjected to appalling conditions in inadequate shelters. Children were removed from families on grounds of poverty of the parents alone, and citizen participation in the social services was discouraged. "Bartering" illegitimate babies before their birth was common practice, and child welfare officials pressured mothers at their most vulnerable point, immediately after delivery, to give up their babies for adoption. Children's institutions were underfunded and understaffed, and the child welfare branch exercised extraordinary discretionary powers over neglected and dependent children. Scientific methods in community and family welfare and casework were discouraged, with next to no co-ordination between private agencies and government. There were few trained social workers in the whole province and none in the child welfare branch. Placement of adoptable children outside of Canada was common, and the adequacy of these adoptive parents or homes was in considerable doubt.

In a letter to the State Child Welfare Division of Montana during the first week of her study, Whitton called child placement practices a "fast and loose adoption traffic, largely carried on by one official and notorious in Western Canada." Whitton wrote many other similar letters to ascertain the extent of the practices in order to support her claims that the bootlegging of babies across borders had "reached considerable proportions."[11] She claimed elsewhere that the Alberta Child Welfare Division placed children from "Anchorage to Guatemala"

> with wealth rather than any other human consideration apparently the determining factor. . . . If these children promise growth into sturdy, useful citizenship, Canada and Alberta needs them and they have a right to life in their own country. If there be a question of the necessity of their suitability for adoption it is a dastardly wrong to the children, the adopting parents and a friendly neighboring state to export them.[12]

She called this the "trafficking" of children.

During the time she was in Alberta and in the months between the conclusion of the study and the November hearings of the royal commission, Whitton engaged in a scrupulous investigation into the extent of cross-border placements.

Her interest in this matter had been fired during her last years with the League of Nations when, along with Katharine Lenroot and Robert Mills, she had been involved in League reports on the Placement of Children in Family Homes, but her interest had its origins in her juvenile immigration survey of the 1920s. Writing to child welfare agencies and welfare departments in the United States, she asked for details of exchanges between them and the Edmonton department. The replies were mixed and the rhetoric she used to embellish the numbers was excessive, but she did collect sufficient data to support her claims about the "export" of babies. For example, in the House of Commons on 28 April 1947, Arthur L. Smith of Calgary West asked about the number of passports issued to Canadian-born children on application by the superintendent of child welfare in Alberta. There had been sixty-four in 1946 and eleven in 1947.[13] Possibly Whitton's investigation accounts for the smaller figure that year.

Of all the officials involved in Alberta's child welfare system, Whitton most detested Charles Hill. An English immigrant, but not of the "class" that Whitton admired, he was in her mind the epitome of all that was wrong in Alberta Child Welfare. In January 1948, she asserted that Hill's basic philosophy was that all healthy babies of healthy mothers are equal and similar in capacity. Whitton rejected the idea that the baby of a "healthy moron" had as much chance of becoming an intellectual leader as that of the most intelligent woman in the land even if they were given the same environment. When he was asked about matters of heredity, Hill replied that it was "rot" and that he did not pay any attention to "fads and pet theories and new discoveries about babies." All that mattered was love, and all he did was look foster parents over and decide on the spot if they were capable of loving the child. As for matching personalities or socio-economic background, Hill regarded this as "Hooey."

But just as all this publicity was giving new life to her career, disaster struck. During the last weeks of November and the first week of December, Margaret Grier, who had undergone surgery during the summer, fell seriously ill with "abdominal symptoms" that compelled her in September to take leave from work as assistant to the Minister of Labour dealing with women workers and welfare services. A second abdominal operation on 14 October weakened all her resistance, and "the malignancy raced away." Whitton afterwards claimed that she returned to Alberta to attend the commission sessions because Grier's doctor insisted that "given the importance of the case," had she remained, Grier would have become aware that her condition was critical. However, it is even more likely that Grier was well aware of her condition and that she insisted Whitton return nevertheless. No one would have been more sensitive than Grier to the significance of the Alberta defence in restoring Whitton's career.[14] Even so, it is still surprising that Whitton *did* agree to leave, and nothing could show more clearly how important the Alberta report was to her at this time.

Margaret Grier died on 9 December 1947 at the age of fifty-five. Whitton had left Alberta for Ottawa the day before, but she did not arrive in time to see her friend before her death. There was no more painful incident in Whitton's life than this absence and none which had more psychological repercussions. Remorse and guilt pervaded her actions and words for several years. In the first week of January 1948, she wrote to Father J.A. MacDonald, who had reviewed Alberta's Catholic Welfare Services for the IODE, that the commission findings had to be especially "good," "ever to justify Margaret being left to die with recent acquaintances while I was out here and to suffer all summer with me neglectful as I worked on this."[15]

About the same time she wrote to Fred Hoehler of the Community Fund of Chicago: "It means the re-orientation of my whole life and yet I have had to come right out here again. I have been on the stand for over two weeks and go on again Monday. I am more tired than I have ever been and hope never to hear the words 'cause of the child again,' " and to Mrs. G. Sheane of the Calgary Canadian Women's Club she wrote two weeks later:

> It is she who suffered most from this particular work of mine. . . . She faced the final crossing over without me when we had never taken but one holiday apart in our thirty years of life together. It will have to be a great good for the children of Alberta that ultimately results to compensate for that in the final days here of a woman as fine as Margaret Grier.[16]

In perhaps the most telling comment, Whitton told her friend Elsie Castendyck of the U.S. Children's Bureau that "Margaret's going has taken half of my life across with her."[17] Charlotte's guilt was certainly not assuaged by a letter she received months later. Charlotte had asked for the details from Grace Towers, a friend who had shared Margaret's last moments. With little tact and a certain relish, Towers informed her how she felt for Charlotte "each step of this dreary summer and foresee what the weeks hold for you in memories." She continued that Margaret had received holy communion at 4 a.m. and had said "from the depths of her great weakness, 'Comfort my Charlotte, Grace, she'll need it, oh how she'll need it.' "

> I didn't reply but pressed her hand without admitting that I fully understood but she knew. . . . Rest assured I will never bring up anything unless you ask me first. I think one of the most intolerable things for you is to have to ask these most personal things from a third person, these things which should have been your right.[18]

Buried in the Whitton family plot in Renfrew beside Whitton's grandmother and father, Grier was joined within three years by Whitton's mother. A sturdy but graceful Celtic Cross was erected over her grave with the following inscription:

Rose Margaret Grier
1892-1947
Beloved Daughter of
Robert and Rose Grier
and dear friend to
Charlotte Whitton

Beside the last words, Charlotte left the space to record her own birth and death for she intended that they would be buried side by side. This moving public statement of love is echoed in the empathy expressed in a letter written after Margaret's death by Laura Holland. She gently urged Charlotte to transform her sorrow into creative channels. "Holly" was afraid that Charlotte was brooding too long and that grief was paralyzing her.

> I know how 'alone' you must feel and that no one would ever make up for the loss of Margaret's companionship—but Charlotte dear, don't try to run away from it always—for it can bring no comfort and peace—one must try to live with it. I mean *live* and grow and be grateful that for so many years you were surrounded by such love and companionship. . . . You were given the blessing of such a friendship in your formative years and perhaps where you needed it most; to build up your ideas, to strengthen your courage, to comfort you in disappointment and so are more fortunate than most. . . . she loved you and still loves you. . . . I just don't want your intensity of feeling to burn you up—love should fan the fire not extinguish it.[19]

Even when she travelled to England in 1949 with Holland to stay with Marjorie Crowther, Whitton wrote to Ethel Dodds Parker that while the two women proved to be "the best of companions," "You cannot share a life as closely and with as lovely a person as Margaret and not be forever wandering in the hope of finding again somewhere the grace of a day that is dead."[20] Whitton never sought or found a substitute for Grier, and she spent almost the same number of years alone as they had had together. When her mother died in July 1951, some fifteen years after Whitton's father, Hilda Laird wrote, "You have succeeded in an unusual degree in keeping Margaret's personality as a vital influence about you in your home. You will preserve much of your mother's personality and influence in the same way."[21] Charlotte tended the graves of her parents, grandmother, and beloved friend all together in Renfrew until her own death, and she cherished a lock of Margaret's hair as a constant reminder of the grace that had gone out of her life.

Whitton saw her actions at the time of Grier's death as an abandonment of her friend in the time of her greatest need. She expressed this belief most tellingly in a metapsychological correspondence with Margaret's older sister, Sister Dora, an Anglican nun with the Order of St. John the Divine in Aurora, Ontario.[22] Some of the correspondence such as speaking of "Mardie" as if she were alive and Whitton believing fervently that they would be re-united after having a dream foretelling it now seems morbid. It was not until Dora's death in 1966 that the last things between Grier and Whitton were finally put to rest. In the meantime, Whitton transferred some of her emotional needs to Margaret's sister.

The romantic and almost spiritual perception of her relationship with Grier was manifested in the memorials Whitton chose: beautiful and delicate ecclesiastical vestments—a chasuble, maniple, and stole of gold thread, damasque, silk, velvet, and embroidered tudor roses which even then would not befit "one of the most wonderful women who ever lived."[23] Whitton wanted the religious order which she commissioned to make the robes to take great care in their creation, insisting that they "be the most perfect and exquisite piece of work which the Sisterhood has ever made." The vestments and the dedication assumed the proportions of a "holy purpose."[24]

When the sisterhood of St. John the Divine could not complete the vestments by All Hallows Eve, 1948, owing to other commitments, she sought the services of a seamstress in Toronto.[25] The vestments were to be endowed in perpetuity and dedicated at St. Alban's, her parish church, on 31 October. After paying $175 for the materials, she was further dismayed when it became increasingly obvious that the seamstress would not have them completed. Disappointed and angry, Whitton accused her of being profligate with her money, of spending it on "flipperies" during a visit to New York to buy more materials. Embarrassed, she was compelled to cancel the event. After ordering substitutes from England, she wrote to the seamstress expressing her humiliation at the cancellation:

> Under such circumstances I should never be able to associate these vestments with anything but pain, regret and shame; they could never serve the holy purpose for which they were planned. The unpleasantness and uncertainty which has already attended their preparation has done much to ruin them for a memory to my Margaret, and this is the crowning humiliation and development.[26]

The original vestments were given over to the chapel of Trinity College, Toronto, at Easter 1951, while the second set was ultimately dedicated at St. Albans.

These actions did not reduce Whitton's feelings of guilt. She arranged for other memorials: furniture to the chapel in the Education building at the Ottawa Civic Hospital and a flower pastel painting to St. Hilda's College where Grier had done social work courses. Underneath the painting, a plaque read,

"Flowers of her own brightness recall Margaret Grier, B.A., 1915." Whitton's presentation speech recalled Grier, "whom we all loved and with the hope that something of her graciousness, love of beauty and equanimity of spirit may be evidence and bring peace to all who pause beneath this bit of autumn glory."[27] Every time she summered at McGregor Lake after Grier's passing, she remembered Margaret crying out in pleasure, "Here is our valley!" Almost ten years later, Whitton presented a stained window to St. John's Church, Trenton, Ontario, in memory of Margaret's grandfather, Reverend John Grier, the first priest and missionary of "The Carrying Place."[28] She also asked that all requests from St. Hilda's that ordinarily would have come to Margaret come now to her because that was what Margaret "would have wished."[29]

Whitton's grief and loneliness may not have been qualitatively different from those of anybody who has shared the joys and hardships of life with a parent, a sibling, a lover, a spouse, or a friend. But her grief was exacerbated by her absence when Margaret died and the eruption of a highly publicized controversy with the Alberta government within a week of the funeral. The normal processes of mourning and the necessary emotional rituals of bereavement were displaced as she became immersed in the urgent and alarming necessity of answering criminal charges. When the 27 December issue of *New Liberty* containing the article "Babies for Export" hit the newspaper stands in Edmonton on 15 December, the government charged the publisher, Jack Kent Cooke of Toronto, and the author, Harold Dingman of Ottawa, with contempt and "conspiracy to commit an indictable offence," that is, defamatory libel. Whitton was included in the charges because the article was based on information she had supplied Dingman. Dazed and griefstricken, Whitton knew that her reputation was in grave jeopardy. Scarcely able to sleep or eat, she became obsessed with the forthcoming trial, which she was to describe to friends as a "persecution" and a "queer and fantastic performance."[30]

Subsequently, indignation replaced Whitton's grief; she projected her feelings of guilt about Grier's death onto the Alberta government. A curious martyr complex resulted, compounded by Whitton's most common form of emotional release—aggression. Her anger with herself was now re-directed to this *cause célèbre*. During the first half of 1948, she mustered all her psychological resources for her defence. She claimed afterwards that the inflammatory nature of the article had escaped her notice because she had received the galley proofs while she was preoccupied with Grier's admission for the emergency operation in October.[31] She did not finally read them until she was on the train trip going west in late November. Because she was urged to hurry, certain things had slipped through. Some of this was probably true, but there can be no question that the tone and content of the article were precisely what Whitton intended. However, she had not anticipated such extreme a response as a charge of conspiracy.

The opening paragraph of "Babies for Export" illustrates why the Alberta government was outraged.

> One of the blackest and ugliest chapters in the development of modern governments has been written against the Province of Alberta. It is the unparalleled story of a government trafficking in illegitimate babies, exporting them to foreign homes and the further story of unjustifiably harsh and delinquent care of Alberta's very young and very old. At these extremes of life bureaucracy and tyranny rule.[32]

The article continued that "ten per cent of Alberta children born out of wedlock were being shipped out of the country," that "nine tenths remaining in Alberta in doubtful care," that there was "strong suspicion of child labour and exploitation," and that there was "open evidence of cheap commercialized boarding houses" for children. The article was accompanied by sensationalized drawings of children being "farmed out" and babies being "surrendered." Alberta was described as "one of the sorriest areas of human frailty any where," where the Child Welfare Commission held and exercised powers without parallel in any country except Hitler's Germany. Child caring services in Alberta were based solely on their cheapness, which forced unmarried girls to sell "their winter clothing and cherished possessions" in an effort to keep their infants. Adopted infants came from mothers who were later sterilized as "unstable sex morons"; while the "cream of the crop" went onto the export market. Twins were "created" by the Welfare Commission in cases where twins were requested: "In one case two baby boys were born within a few days of each other and were officially talked about as twins, although they were extremely different in temperament and appearance." The aged and the crippled, it also said, were exploited in commercialized boarding houses while "wistful little mites" were crowded into boarding homes or placed on lonely farms in "some of the drought land toward the south-western portions of the province." Moreover "An interesting 'Time Sheet' could have been kept practically any week of the Study, revealing a steady stream of girls, usually in taxies, coming to . . . surely the most unique Child Welfare offices in Canada, where hundreds of pictures of adopted babies, arranged in decorative design, and visible from the street, are spread over the walls of the offices of the Superintendent of Welfare."

Described by Justice W.R. Howson of the royal commission as "one of the most scurrilous" he had ever read, the provocative *New Liberty* article was only the culmination of a year of anti-government propaganda by Whitton. For instance, the *Winnipeg Free Press* had allowed her to write accounts without her name being attached, and it had also published her point of view in an August 1947 pamphlet reprinted from its editorial pages. The pamphlet included the comment that "members of the Social Credit Party never weary of posing as the prophets of a new social order in which justice and prosperity will rule with unchallenged sway."[33] Angry exchanges between the maverick from the Ottawa Valley and her Prairie antagonist, Dr. W.W. Cross, were well publicized. His much-quoted description of her as "a human talking machine" whose criticisms would make no difference to the government was matched by Whitton's retort that even Hitler's boasted "1,000 year Reich came to an end."[34]

Even before the publication of "Babies for Export," Manning's suspicions of Whitton's motives were evident in his replies to Pearl Johnston, an ex-resident of Alberta then residing in Ontario, and to Annie Kennedy, R.N. On 3 December 1947, he wrote that

> This Miss Whitton, who sets herself up as an expert on social and child welfare work has, for a number of years since she was retired from the Canadian Welfare Council, been making a practice of placing her services at the disposal of different organizations who may be interested in welfare work and all of her reports which I have seen are inclined to condemn the work being done by the Provincial Governments and other public bodies. . . . Our people here are not much concerned with these statements as they fully realize they are coming from an unreliable source and are being made for *political* reasons.

And he drew to Miss Kennedy's attention that Whitton's study was "not just a criticism of a government, but an unwarranted denunciation of all the people of this Province." He was concerned lest adoptive parents, foster parents, and other citizens, be filled with "fears and misgivings" about child welfare in Alberta.[35]

Determined that Whitton should answer for her criticism, the government called the RCMP in to charge the three on grounds of conspiracy, thus circumventing the requirement that libel be tried in the province of residence. The charge became "conspiracy to commit an indictable offence," to wit, criminal libel against Charles Hill and the child welfare commission consisting of Hill, A.H. Miller, the deputy minister of welfare, Judge C.F. Willis of the Edmonton and Northern District Court, and Miss Clara Frizzell, a member of the staff of the Child Welfare Branch. *Time* magazine reported the event on 29 December 1947 and followed it up in its 16 February issue. It claimed that Alberta lawyers had "pulled a slick legal trick out of their sleeves."

An order by the commission against the distribution of the *New Liberty* was withdrawn soon after it was issued, but Whitton knew it was inevitable that she would be charged. Her counsel was George Steer, K.C., of Edmonton, who was the counsel for the IODE before the commission of inquiry. Queen's University was well represented for the pending trial with Steer and Whitton and the other counsel, Stanley McCuaig, also of Edmonton, all graduates.[36] She was not summonsed until 27 January 1948, and after four days of hearings, she was committed for trial in the Supreme Court of Alberta at its next sitting on 2 February. This date was postponed until 5 April with each conspirator released on bail of $1,000. Whitton claimed: "My own fixed determination to accept alternative detention in the common gaol failed in face of counsel's adamant refusal to concur therein."[37]

Philip Fisher resigned as president of the CWC when the council passed a resolution to support Whitton. As director and manager of Southam Press, he found himself in an embarrassing situation for his press had publicized Whitton's work and consistently attacked the Social Credit government.[38] The press also saw the conspiracy charges as a threat to basic freedoms. *Time* joined in the attack, and John Diefenbaker let his dismay be known in the House of Commons. Every time a breach in social welfare standards occurred in Alberta, the press drew it to the public's attention. For example in the first weeks of January, the *Albertan*, the *Globe and Mail*, and the *Calgary Herald* criticized Frank Drayton, the superintendent of civic relief in Edmonton, accusing him of approving "whippings" as deterrents for delinquent youths.[39] In the last week of January, four deaths in the Baptist Haven for the Elderly at Medicine Hat were publicized as yet another example of negligent welfare supervision,[40] and on 1 April, the "Conrad Child Murder Case" heightened the nation's interest in child welfare in Alberta.[41] David Conrad, aged two-and-a-half, had been beaten to death by his *adoptive* mother. The lax handling of the adoption embarrassed the Alberta government, and George Steer notified the commission that the Conrad case must become part of its considerations after the trial of Mrs. Conrad on 21 June.

The degree of support Whitton received during the first months of 1948 was extraordinary. She was overwhelmed by spirited letters from social agencies and women's groups across the country and from individuals who had worked with her during her lengthy social welfare career. These champions of her cause also informed the government of their concern about the pending trial and their full endorsement of Whitton's work. Whitton was gratified that she had not been forgotten.

Her old rival Harry Cassidy came to her defence and wanted to testify before the commission of enquiry, but Whitton decided against it. She felt that Cassidy was too associated with the dominion government and that his "enthusiasm" for his field might be "construed as impatience or even contempt for some of the Commission." His views about Alberta in *Public Health and Welfare Organization* (1945) had provoked "violent reaction" from Dr. Cross in September 1946.[42]

The Canadian press, including the *Calgary Herald*, and the *Albertan*, were aghast at the implications of the conspiracy charge, and Raymond Hilliarde informed Whitton that the American press was no less so. The *Chicago Sun*, for example, included items on the incident and the progress of the defence on 20, 28, 29, 30, and 31 January. This coverage continued into February, and the matter had been the subject of an editorial of 23 January because of "its significance for free people under allegedly free governments."[43]

During January, Whitton prepared two major articles for her defence which explained what she had intended in her extravagant claim that the Alberta government resembled Nazi Germany and the U.S.S.R. "Legislation on Unmarried Parenthood . . . in the USSR" and "Provisions of Guardianship . . . in Pre-Nazi Germany" were sent to Elsie Castendyck at the U.S. Children's Bureau where they were carefully examined by Anna Kalet Smith, the USCB's expert in European matters. Smith provided "corrections, revisions and additions to the memoranda."[44] Along with *The Dawn* and the Montreal lectures, they demonstrate what Whitton was capable of when her energies were focused. Having collected the data during her years with the League of Nations, she still had the information for these articles at her fingertips. During January and February she also engaged in an exhaustive analysis of the text of the *New Liberty* article as well as in writing letters seeking support and evidence for her many sweeping claims in the IODE report and "Babies For Export."

Claiming police harassment Whitton gained even more sympathy. The police had visited her home in Ottawa seeking documents to implicate her further while, somewhat theatrically, she had sought "sanctuary" in the church. To support this claim, she made a phone call to Robert Mills's wife, advising her to get rid of any evidence which might be used against her and which might implicate her husband, who had been an important member of the IODE study team which had provided most of the background to the *New Liberty* article.[45] In April, Whitton was also informed by a friend that the RCMP had been checking her handwriting with documents she had submitted to the National Employment Commission.[46] During these months, Whitton asserted that "one is upheld by the knowledge that one is right" and frequently quoted the words of a hymn

> Age by age the Pilgrim Church has trod,
> the path of pain, of splendid pain,
> That leads to God.[47]

In her highly strung state Whitton saw in the charges persecution, martyrdom, and ultimately justification for her absence at Margaret's death. All the while, she used the press and public encouragement to her own advantage. She knew that a conviction would incense the nation, already in uproar, while acquittal would both have political import and provide a personal vindication.

Although many ordinary Albertans were appalled at what they thought was a rash course on the part of the government, others saw the *New Liberty* article as a condemnation of everything Albertan and just another example of central Canadian contempt for their Social Credit government. A prominent local pastor, the Reverend John Quincy Adams, was quick to react to the furore and wrote a lengthy admonition to Premier Manning on 23 January.

It is my opinion, . . . whoever it is that conceived and launched the libel charges against Dr. Charlotte Whitton sure pulled a political 'bone-head.' Almost the actual totality of the population of this province do not read 'The New Liberty Magazine,' and would never have seen or heard of the article, and (note it) the folks who do read it, would have read it merely as an entertainment and would never have thought any more of it, thinking it is out of their realm.

But folks do have full confidence in the IODE, it seems to me, and in Dr. Whitton and from humanitarian instinct they unconsciously swing whole-hearted to a genuine belief in her. I am of the opinion that regardless of how the case may go, folks will continue to say, 'We know that woman did not lie and we also know politics can sometimes become dirty.' And if the Woman should be 'railroaded' to being condemned, then you will find, I would estimate in a period of two years if not sooner, public opinion will crystallize hopelessly against you. It is kind of a dangerous thing to fool around a Woman,—and especially Women and Children. And to go after the two men, writer and publisher, or either of them, will inevitably bring in the Women and Children and this thing will become a national thing; for the IODE is dominion-wide, and you will find writers everywhere will and can easily swing into a public and general (and also hot) campaign in behalf of their fellow writer and, especially when so fine a cause as Women and Children afford the foundation.[48]

This opinion was endorsed by a reporter on the *Hamilton Spectator* when he wrote to Whitton on 25 February to tell her of the paper's support and to say that Alberta had made "a tactical mistake . . . given your involvement with child welfare . . . no one would challenge either your motives or your honesty." The Calgary Women's Club, also convinced that whatever she did was "for the public good," supported her too.[49] Whitton saw herself as a martyr in the service of the nation, and apparently this characterization appealed to other women also.

The prospective conspiracy trial incited public protests about freedom of the press because it bore an ominous resemblance to the infamous "Gag Act" of 1937, the Alberta "Accurate News and Information Act," which had been declared *ultra vires* in 1938. In other words, fellow Canadians suspected Alberta of an autocratic tendency to ignore democratic rights. Neither had the nature of the charges escaped the attention of the press as far afield as Britain. On 7 July 1948, *The Times* noted Alberta's previous involvement with repressive legislation and said the province seemed to have a "scheme" in which "nobody should be permitted to criticize," in short, a "muzzling of the press."[50] What is more the case proved to be so indefensible that the attorney-general's department abandoned it and declared a "stay" of proceedings on 12 April.

The *London Free Press*, 14 May 1948, congratulated Whitton on the victory over injustice, and Beatrice Taylor in "Better Than Wisdom" elaborated the Joan of Arc analogy.

> Charlotte Whitton, CBE, DCL., LLD., who has been Canada's Joan of Arc doing staunch battle in the cause of freedom, has emerged from the fiery ordeal of a conspiracy charge wearing, not only her discharge, but her wonted high courage and devestating wit.

When she spoke before the London Canadian Women's Club, they "rediscovered a little woman with tiny feet in Cinderella slippers, an enormous mind, an illumined rhetoric." Despite her common sense, Whitton must have relished the florid praise, and she kept her public image alive speaking before social agencies and women's groups during the months she waited for the Alberta Royal Commission's conclusions. Finally, she took the summer off at McGregor Lake wondering whether the recent months had damaged her reputation or whether the foolhardiness of the Alberta government had enhanced it.

The commission's findings were released on 3 December 1948, signed by the chairman, W.R. Howson, chief justice of the Supreme Court of Alberta, J.W. MacDonald, chief judge of the District of Southern Alberta, and E.B. Fair, judge of the District of Southern Alberta and local judge of the Supreme Court.[51] Whitton was elated because the report generally vindicated her work in Alberta, restored her reputation, and agreed with many of the major conclusions of the IODE study.

This vindication of her integrity was imperative "to justify Margaret being left . . . to suffer all summer." With public figure and private woman together she regained her "sense of direction" and went back to child welfare. Congratulated and applauded, Whitton left Alberta triumphant. Now a national celebrity, she would never again be content with anything less. Her need for love and reassurance, previously provided in abundance by Margaret, now would be satisfied only by public acclaim. Ottawa civic politics provided the arena.

8

A WOMAN NOT A LADY

"Whatever my sex, I'm no lady."

WHITTON, 1954.

Professor Gordon's warning to her favorite student at the start of her professional life had been perceptive. "Lottie," she said, "there are two currencies in life—popularity and principles. One is spurious coin." It was a prediction for Whitton's political years. From 1950 to the mid-1960's, when she evoked adulation more often than hostility, she clung tenaciously to principles in what appeared to some to be "a two dimensional point of view—her side and the wrong side."[1] During these years on the Ottawa municipal scene, Whitton was busier than ever as the press recorded her innumerable aphorisms and published her many columns. She was heard on radio and seen on television. She spoke on politics, women, morality, liquor, bilingualism, aging, youth, medicare, and the National Capital Commission, and she visited the Middle East, Japan, Russia, and the Vatican on public relations tours.

At the conclusion of all of this frenetic activity, Whitton evaluated her life in municipal politics with candor. In a 1965 interview she was asked whether she preferred being a "television personality" to holding civic office. Her reply was thoughtful: "My 'Dear Charlotte' program is not my life nor is it a position. It carries with it little sense of duty or vocation. . . . My T.V. 'stint' is only incidental, an interesting and enjoyable opportunity to keep in touch with people and current problems." Conceding that her viewers were primarily interested in what she had to say because of her career as mayor, she continued: "You have to admit I had had some thirty good years in the life of Canada and in nine of its ten provinces, and had served several times as Canadian representative in international affairs. All in all, I think I was better known therein, if not as widely as in later years as Mayor of Ottawa."[2] Certainly she would rather have been remembered for her child welfare work than for any other accomplishment. Nevertheless, it is as the controversial mayor of Ottawa that Whitton is best known.

Her stints as a syndicated columnist for the Ottawa *Evening Citizen* brought her regularly to local attention. Whitton's journalism career started with the "Offshore" series in 1949 when she wrote about her extended summer trip to England, Germany, and Scandinavia. This was followed in 1950 and 1951 by her "A Woman On the Line" series for the Thomson Dailies. At the same time she continued to write for the Ottawa *Citizen*'s "Every Other Day" and for the Halifax *Chronicle-Herald*. These ventures provided a steady income which alleviated her financial anxieties.

Although columns such as "Half Bond, Half Free," "Women in Government, 1950," and "Voting in Britain—The Women," addressed feminist issues, Whitton also wrote about child desertion, old age, rent controls, and housing. She was priggish on public morality, didactic about public responsibility, still an enthusiastic schoolgirl about Royalty, and florid about nature. Without a talent for pungent social commentary and given to a rather tedious erudition, her writing was nevertheless popular because it usually tapped public concerns. She thrived on the attention that she received as a columnist and broadcaster. Often she played to her public as a comedian, sometimes to the point of melodrama, or as a tragedian, sometimes to the point of histrionics. Gordon had accurately sensed this exhibitionist tendency in the young Whitton, and it came to dominate her latter years.

In light of her constant admonitions regarding women and public life, it was not surprising that the Ottawa Council of Women insisted that she should practise what she preached and stand for controller in the 1950 civic elections. Whitton agreed to accept a nomination "on behalf of the women of Ottawa," and a campaign committee was established in October.[3] Lacking a profession to which she could easily return if defeated, Whitton absolutely refused to be responsible for the cost of the campaign.

> I outlined very clearly the conditions on which I would become a candidate for the Board on behalf of the women of Ottawa. One of the explicit points on which I insisted from the beginning was that under no conceivable circumstances would I pay for the responsibility of running for office. Apart from the principal involved, I pointed out that upon election to office I would have to forego, at once, large sources of earning from outside speaking and special writing assignments to devote myself to the City's business. I would lose, not gain, financially from membership on the Board of Control.

When the surprised women protested this obstinancy, insisting that she contribute up to $1,500, an outraged Whitton fulminated that "even the bequests of my dear friend have come under discussion, an intolerable intrusion upon one's private life."[4]

On this point Whitton demonstrated her customary adroitness. Given the prejudice against women in public office, she realized that she could become the first female on Ottawa's board of control only if "woman power," which she believed was lying dormant, could be mobilized. To be successful, a woman's campaign had to be devoted totally to the cause. And whole-hearted support was more likely when women had committed money.

A variety of clubs and organizations contributed to the campaign: the IODE, the Canadian Women's Press Club, Ottawa West and South PCs, the Soroptomist Club of Ottawa, the Queen's Alumnae, the Business and Professional Women, the Canadian Club, the WCTU, University Women, and the Women's Historical Society. It was an impressive display of support. The *Journal* of 31 October commented, "Miss Whitton in effect told the women to get behind the campaign and push, or go back to their vacuum cleaners and mops." And this astute tactic paid off. At a stormy meeting, the Ottawa Council of Women and affiliated women's groups such as the Historical Society and the University Women agreed to her conditions. An all female committee with Edna Dorman and Jennie Armstrong as chairman and vice-chairman devoted themselves zealously to getting their candidate elected. Mrs. Dorman's testimony over CFRA radio in November reminded the public of the honorary degree their candidate had received from Queen's as its most distinguished woman graduate, "who has made a place for herself not only in Canada but also throughout this continent in the organizing of social service work to the greater benefit of those who are in need."[5] An interesting sidelight, although one that was easily resolved, was the matter of her religion. Probably because of the visibility of her Roman Catholic sister and brother-in-law, Kathleen and Frank Ryan, and of her mother, whose charitable activities in Ottawa were well known, some thought Whitton was Catholic too. Although it went against the grain, Whitton made her Anglicanism public. This compromise was important in the English-speaking Ottawa of the 1950s.

As Whitton had insisted, she found that civic politics was an appropriate arena for married women. Twenty-three of the original twenty-six member campaign committee, known as "the thread and needle brigade" to signify that Ottawa's pants needed patching, were married women.[6] The domestic analogy dominated the campaign, publicizing Whitton as a candidate who would run the city on a "housekeeping basis." She declined to own up to her fifty-four years and "came out in the open to admit to around fifty years."[7] Whitton appeared confident, but she clearly feared the public's stereotype of an older spinster.

Neither Whitton nor her committee members saw any irony in using their husband's Christian names when they campaigned and scrutineered—or even in private correspondence. Apart from social custom, this usage provided a public demonstration that the women who supported Whitton were respectable, conservative, and often married to influential men—which was bound to attract male voters. A list of fifty-seven key names on the 1952 committee includes only sixteen single women and no more than half a dozen married women's Christian names. Even her sister was listed as Mrs. Frank Ryan. Whitton knew that marital status carried considerable weight, and she found it perfectly compatible with her views that, as part of the secular unmarried, she could provide leadership. Nor did she find anything wrong with her own use of what is now seen as sexist terminology, such as "atta girls," "what about it girls"; she referred to the "boys" in the same way.

After solemnly promising "I *will*—promise to love, honour and obey—the most binding, most important words a woman can say" in the nomination speech before a predominantly female audience, Whitton's first formal pledge was for a new mental institution for Ottawa to relieve the Nichols Street jail, where patients were housed before they went to Brockville. Following the claim that she was "as good a man as anyone on the Board right now," she pledged herself to better and cheaper housing. Municipal government was like "running a home"; it required "good planning, good partnership, and not spending above what you make."

The following headlines were positive images.

> *Men, Bachelor Girl Charlotte (Phone 3-8392) Bakes a Tasty Cake and Can Fix Gadgets Too.*
>
> *Civic minded Charlotte Can Cook up more than a Speech.*
>
> *Charlotte rolls Sleeves for Cake Not Elections.*

The last one was accompanied by a cosy picture of the candidate baking at her kitchen stove with the remark that "manless though she may be, she can sling the skillet as skillfully as a *bon mot*."[8] "Manless" and "bachelor girl" established her single status, but they also emphasized her femininity.

Whitton did cook well; she also fraternized at married women's clubs and agreed to increase day care nurseries. She vowed too that the next year "win, lose or draw," she would rectify a voting inequity which disenfranchised women in hospital labour wards at election times. The *Ottawa Citizen* of 28 November quickly spread the news that "Whitton's Stork Stop Franchise Would Bring Ballot to Bedside" and quoted her as saying: "Women who are helping Canada by having babies should not be deprived of the privilege of voting next Monday. I'll do something about it." A woman needed women's votes to get into the male sanctuary of Ottawa's board of control, so Whitton refrained from references to "bonussed breeding," the complacency of women's clubs, or the single citizen subsidizing day care for working mothers.

Accompanying the "homey" publicity were comments on her executive ability and experience. On 21 October, the *Journal*, in "Alderman Charlotte Whitton—Why Not?" reiterated her views that it was not only prejudice that restricted public office to men but also the unwillingness of women to "mix in the hurly burly of politics, and reluctance to run the risk of defeat." An "unsolicited testimonial" from Frederick C. Blair in the *Citizen* on 21 November strengthened her candidacy. While she was director of the Canadian Welfare Council, Whitton had enjoyed a mutually respectful colleagueship with Blair, who was then deputy minister of immigration, and they had co-operated on the juvenile immigration question in the 1920s.

However, the strongest testimonial came from an admiring male reporter, Holland Cox. Cox wrote "The Whitton Story" for the *Evening Citizen* on 18 and 20 November. In descriptions that were intimate and persuasive, Cox's mini-biography proclaimed that Whitton was "one of the most amazing personalities this city, and indeed this country, of ours has ever known." He described Whitton's personal qualities in terms that would convince the electorate she was a very personable candidate.

> Charlotte is a bare five feet one and a half inches tall, and her biggest struggle she conﬁdes sadly, is to keep her weight at 130 instead of the 140 to which it climbs on the slightest provocation—which is food, for she's a dandy cook and likes what she cooks. . . . Her hair is black except for a streak of white which has been there since youth, and she keeps to a close shingle—"less trouble in the wind." Her hands and feet are very small, but it is her hazel eyes—alive, changing color with every emotion—that are her most attractive feature. They dance and sparkle with amusement, grow fierce at mention of injustice, tender and sympathetic when she comes in contact with misfortune and unhappiness.

The article dealt at length with Margaret Grier and the loss Whitton had sustained at her death. In that time she could be certain the electorate would not misconstrue the nature of their relationship. Cox noted the years they had spent since sharing accommodations at the "Kats" house in Toronto, and having commented on the complementary differences of their natures, he observed:

> Three years ago this companionship was shattered by the death of that luminous personality who for nearly 30 years had been [her companion]. There are those in Ottawa who say that Charlotte's plunge into the municipal arena is just part of her determination to fill a life made suddenly so lonely. But this is not so. Whenever Charlotte can fight a good battle for a cause she believes in there she will be found.

In the second chapter of the "Whitton Story," Cox noted that Whitton's candor could be devastating and that she was not afraid to threaten the *status quo*.

> Her intellect is as keen and tenacious as a terrier on guard at a badger hole. She hits with one decisive blow after another and this would be the reason why she is suspected at times of arousing male antagonism for she has that abomination in a woman, a logical mind.

Such positive reporting from an influential pressman did Whitton's campaign more good than a dozen laudatory comments from her "petticoat brigade."

In December 1950, with 38,405 votes Whitton became the first woman to the capitol's board of control and took up her appointment in the new year under a new mayor, Grenville W. Goodwin who replaced Mayor Edouard Bourque. Whitton quickly became the most vocal, militant, and irascible civic politician Ottawa had ever known. She spoke about her "pet scheme"— low-priced housing—but by February 1951, she was opposing the Carling and Merivale Road Mothers' Committees, who accused her of "pigeon holing" a brief for more day nurseries. Denying the accusation, she cited religious and educational complications, but she did not assert that (with only one) Ottawa was oversupplied with day nurseries. Within six months, her real views were printed, the same views she had always espoused. In *Every Other Day* she commented on day care, saying it was necessary for those who " *must* earn" outside their own home now that maiden aunts were all earning and "the grandmothers are at bingo games."

> There is also the woman who much prefers to work outside her own home, though with little or no economic need. She wants some other woman to do for her children what she would rather not do herself. . . . What is of more value to a state, a spinster may sententiously enquire than fully and faithfully to discharge the vocation you choose?[9]

And of the increase in the demand for baby-sitting, she was contemptuous:

> Well if women are going to leave their homes and families for, profit, patriotism, or what have you, of course other women, younger, older, less fit or less inclined to do the same thing are going to have to take over and superintend the children . . . whom these women leave behind them.[10]

As controller, Whitton prepared a paper for discussion at the Canadian Conference of Mayors and Municipalities meeting in London on 12 June.[11] As chairman of the seminar on welfare services, she was in a position to air some of the ideas she developed during her tenure with the Canadian Welfare Council and amplified in the *Dawn of Ampler Life*. Noting the "mounting welfare obligations of municipal government," Whitton called for thorough examination of the problems associated with welfare payments and services. Whitton saw welfare provision as falling under either income maintenance or welfare service, with the former largely a public liability and the latter best left to philanthropy.

The rise of social insurance schemes tied to industrial occupation represented for Whitton income maintenance plans rather than welfare services. Other more general forms of insurance—mothers' and old age allowances, for example—were also income maintenance measures. In Whitton's view, social insurance schemes left all workers except those who were insurable wage-earners without benefit and created a tremendous future public liability. In Canada, the commitment to income maintenance had taken the form of "a *general redistribution of wealth*" by means of a bonus or allowance to all eligible recipients "regardless of any existing social or economic factor, in the individual case." The essence of Whitton's argument was that such payments were made solely on fiscal grounds without any consideration of social or welfare concerns. She did not believe such transfer payments would help provinces or municipalities to provide health, welfare, or remedial services of any kind.

Citing the 1948 National Health Service Plan, Whitton called for a tripartite organization of welfare services: the federal government should be the major source of funds to ensure minimum comparable standards nationally, provinces should be recognized as the fundamental welfare authority, and municipalities should be the effective administrators of essential services. While she acknowledged the priority of publicly financed agencies, Whitton's support for locally provided welfare service is clear in her argument for enlarged units for isolated areas and co-operation with privately financed welfare services such as the VON and the children's aid societies.

Harkening back to her long-held opinions on relief, Whitton claimed that more than increased funding for welfare services was required. Sound administrative procedures and improved control of expenditures were essential to prevent rising costs and "crushing increases in provincial and Dominion taxation" for welfare services. As in the Great Depression, the level of government with the least financial resources and most responsive to pressure from citizens had to be assisted on both counts by senior governments.

When the Board of Control was in recess in the summer of 1951, Mrs. Whitton died. Charlotte's *Every Other Day* column included a tribute to her mother which was so moving that it inspired a personal letter from Harry Stevenson Southam, publisher of the *Citizen* and vice-president of Southam Company, written from his home "Southdene."[12]

My dear Charlotte,

I hope many thousands of Evening Citizen subscribers, indeed, all of them, have read and re-read in Thursday' issue your Every Other Day column, "My Mother."

Of your many, very many, outstanding contributions to my favorite paper, this one, in my considered opinion is easily the best judged from any point of view. It is of course, steeped in human interest. It is comprehensively encouraging and comforting and perhaps now and always its most needed content; and finally, it is tenderly constructive, helpful, inspiring, and its healing effect will be deep and widespread.

What a mother! What courage! What selfless adherence to the second great commandment . . . The beautiful and discerning tribute to a wonderful mother, expressed with such love, humility and conviction, is the more comforting and inspiring coming as it does from a daughter whose life is so completely devoted to the service of mankind as to constitute an enduring memorial to the loved one who has passed on.

It is a privilege to know you. I send you my warmest love.

While mother and daughter had become very close in later years, within the month Whitton's mourning period was cut short by the unexpected death of Mayor Grenville Goodwin. Although she promptly claimed the position of acting mayor, the "change to petticoat government" was not smooth. Despite the *Journal's* claim in the first week of September that "to the world outside of city council Charlotte Whitton [was] Ottawa's mayor," the male board of control insisted that she was, at best, only "acting" mayor. The controllers favoured Leonard Coulter for the position, while for his part, Coulter claimed that he would become "acting mayor" only at their insistence. In fact, Coulter was in a difficult predicament. In the 1950 election, Whitton had polled 38,405 votes to Coulter's 31,071 (Mayor Goodwin's total was only 28,698). Coulter had been elected acting mayor in 1949 when Mayor Bourque was ill because he had polled the largest vote among the controllers. Given the precedent he had established, Coulter could hardly challenge Whitton's claim, and when he stepped down in favour of Whitton, the other controllers agreed to bide their time until the next election in December 1952.[13]

Telegrams of congratulation poured in from across the country, including one from Dr. R.C. Wallace, retiring principal of Queen's University, who noted that Whitton was the first Queen's graduate of either sex to become a mayor of any municipality over 40,000. In fact Ottawa's population was much greater, approximately 204,375.

1. Matilda Carr Whitton, Charlotte's strong-willed grandmother, c. 1900.   2. Charlotte's mother, Elizabeth Langin Whitton, was tormented by her marriage out of her Roman Catholic faith. Charlotte's decision to remain an Anglican when her mother returned to "Mary's altars" was an early indication of her strong commitment to her principles.   3. John Edward Whitton, who catered for lumber companies in Northern Ontario during much of Charlotte's childhood, late in life.   4. Charlotte, far right, with her mother, grandmother, brothers John Bartholomeau (b. 1899) and Stephen (b. 1905), and sister Kathleen (b. 1904).

Who is it?

She rules the roost where a majority of men rule Canada. Turn to page 46 to see who this young lady grew up to be.

5. Who Is It? A picture of five-year-old Charlotte published in *Maclean's* in 1956.   **6.** A frisky tomboy as well as a good student, Charlotte excelled in sports. In 1909 she was a member of the Renfrew Collegiate Institute's basketball team.   **7.** Bill King, Charlotte's university romance, finally abandoned his pursuit in 1924.

8. Whitton (centre) continued to be involved in sports at Queen's, but her major extracurricular activities were the women's society Levana and the Queen's *Journal*. **9.** Elizabeth MacCallum (c. 1918), joined the Department of External Affairs in 1942 and in 1954 became the first woman head of a Canadian mission. **10.** A picnic in Algonquin Park in 1919. Charlotte, her brother J.B., and classmate Mo are on the far left; Professor Wilhelmina Gordon is visible at extreme right.

11. Emily Murphy (Janey Canuck), the first woman magistrate in the British Empire, promoted Whitton's career in social service.　**12.** Helen Reid, director of the Social Service Department at McGill, was also a mentor to Whitton and gave her wise career counsel.　**13.** Julia Lathrop, the first chief of the U.S. Children's Bureau, helped Whitton obtain the position of assessor with the League of Nations.　**14.** Grace Abbott, the second chief of the U.S. Children's Bureau.

15. Katherine Lenroot, Abbott's successor was another important American contact for Whitton. **16.** Margaret Grier in 1926. She and Whitton met in the Kats house, Toronto, moved to Ottawa in 1922, and made their home together until Margaret's death in 1947. **17.** In 1926 Whitton and Grier leased this house on Rideau Terrace near Government House. **18.** In this 1934 League of Nation's picture, Whitton is in the back row, right. She was awarded the CBE in the New Year's Honour's List in the same year.

19. A formal portrait of Whitton in 1935. After the defeat of R.B. Bennett's government that year, Whitton's career entered a critical phase. **20.** Harry Cassidy, c. 1940. By this time, Whitton regarded this leading proponent of social reform and his colleague, Leonard Marsh, as both rivals and adversaries. He was not the last to mutter, "Damn that woman!" **21.** Her disappointments of the early 1940s behind her, Whitton restored her reputation as a leader in child welfare. Here she arrives at court with the IODE president during her 1948 libel trial following the "Babies for Export" scandal. **22.** Canada's first woman mayor, Whitton poses happily at her desk in 1951.

23. When she greeted the Queen and the Duke of Edinburgh in 1964, Whitton did not wear the ostentatious robes of office for which she was often ridiculed. She is wearing the mayoral chain whose detail is clear in the formal portrait inset. Premier John Robarts is behind her.   **24.** Whitton in 1955 with Margaret Aiken, M.P., Cairine Wilson, the first woman appointed to the Senate, and Ellen Fairclough, two years later to become Canada's first woman cabinet minister in the 1957 Diefenbaker government, at the unveiling of a bust of the first woman M.P., Agnes Macphail. **25.** Whitton and Grier escaped the heat of Ottawa's summer at their nearby cottage on McGregor Lake, and after her friend's death Whitton continued to seek refuge there.

26

27

28

29

"I shall return."

26. By the early 1960s, Whitton's aggressive public stance had made her a caricature of the spinster stereotype in many eyes. This *Maclean's* cartoon is one of the kinder renditions. **27.** Pat Bald Eagle makes Whitton an Honorary Piegan Princess at Dominion Day celebrations in Fort Macleod, 1961. **28.** Whitton wore her formal robes at her last official greeting of a member of the Royal Family, the Queen Mother, in 1962. **29.** Two years after her defeat in the 1964 mayoralty campaign Whitton did return as an alderman and served for five more years.

Preparations were begun for the visits of the Lord Mayor of London in September and of Princess Elizabeth on 3 and 4 October. For the royal visit Whitton prepared a banquet menu that consisted of ten different courses representing the ten provinces. On the day of the visit, she further surprised the board by rescuing the historic mayoralty chair from an attic and ordering that the "throne-like, carved wooden seat" be restored for board meetings. This was the first indication of a preoccupation with ceremonial and status which earned her mayoralties the title of "Queen Charlotte's Reign." She was already planning a new Civic Hall, and within a year, the controllers and their mayor would be dressing in ostentatious robes of office which cost $1,729.51 and provoked heated debate on various occasions after their introduction.[14]

Overwhelmed by this direct encounter with the heir to the throne, Whitton told the prime minister, Louis St. Laurent, that she was "so excited" on that morning that she "couldn't have been more so if she had been getting married." She had sat up into the early hours of the morning rehearsing her speech for the presentation of the keys to the city. Two weeks after this excitement, she gave her inauguration speech as acting mayor. On 15 October 1951, the day of the speech, the *Ottawa Citizen* reported that "While men groaned and women gloated, Charlotte Whitton took up the municipal reins." As she promptly got rid of the official limousine of office along with its chauffeur, she snorted, "I've never had a man or a Cadillac in my life."[15]

In May, Whitton gave a much publicized and highly moralistic address to Queen's graduates. In "Flunking the Finals," Whitton insisted that the purpose of education was to form character: "It is in the quality of character that the virtue of faithfulness finds life, nurture and growth, and from it comes the whole basis of an ordered community living." She criticized modern trends which persuaded youth that life could be "cajoled and cozened" and that graduates need not meet their responsibilities. Since taxpayers contributed 48 per cent of tuition costs, she insisted that the graduates were morally responsible to society as a whole. Evading "the real trenches and posts of danger to democracy," they sought lucrative positions and personal aggrandizement. This escape into pragmatism led to a "plundering" of the "resources of the State." Its focus reaffirmed the old verities of her own generation.[16]

In November, 1952, the mayor celebrated the anniversary of her inauguration with an address in which she reminded the local council of women of some facts about female representation in municipal, provincial, and federal government. Although a 1916 plebiscite had enfranchised women in the city of Ottawa, it was thirty-six years before the city had its first woman mayor and only by accident then. Moreover, there were still only three women in the federal houses, one woman held a portfolio in B.C., and three others were in the B.C. chamber. There were the same number in Alberta, but no more women representatives eastwards. In all, there were no more than sixty women in municipal elective office although there were others in local government. "I am frequently called *that woman*," she laughed, and then listed her accomplishments over the last year. They were impressive. She had lowered the general tax rate by .07 mills; carefully studied estimates for sewers, sidewalks, and waterworks before borrowing funds; introduced some equity into water charges as well as a just and provincially supervised assessment rate; initiated better working conditions for civic employees and lifted the discrimination against women employees that insisted they retire at age sixty; improved nursing services to the aged and infirm and provided care for the chronic patients; improved housing conditions, implemented a more efficient milk supply, and established a provincial mental health clinic at Ottawa Civic hospital.[17]

With the motto "One Good Term Deserves Another," Whitton's nomination speech for 1952 elaborated the theme. Seeing political life as another vocation, a new stewardship, Whitton reminded her audience that two years before she had "plighted" her vows "to serve this city under God." "Give me your good faith again," she asked, "and I will pledge with mine. . . . Now I offer to your judgment of my fidelity and devotion to your service." She dismissed her problems with other controllers by suggesting that their opposition in council resulted from a perception that she was usurping male prerogatives.[18]

Within a few weeks Whitton was putting together a campaign organization that would re-elect her as mayor. Her all-woman committee used a darning needle as a motif to indicate that the job of patching Ottawa was bigger than ever. Their candidate, paraphrasing Virginia Woolf, pleaded with the electorate to give her "a term of her own." She made herself highly visible during the weeks before the December election, and her speeches to the service clubs reaffirmed her reputation for wit and perspecuity.

Her nomination speech a year before had resounded the words, "I will," and in 1952, she took up this theme again.

> An unmarried woman, my mother and the friend who shared my life both gone, I promise to devote to this city all that I have within me to give of strength and devotion to her service . . . and let us remember, too, that courtesy is not the least of the elements of good government and that it is a virtue within the gift alike of prince and pauper.[19]

The implication of a freedom newly acquired since her mother's death is curious for there is nothing to suggest that her filial responsibilities had ever circumscribed her ambitions and Margaret had certainly supported them. At worse, her relationship with Margaret had inhibited her movements out of Ottawa and perhaps Canada, but they certainly would not have inhibited earlier civic involvement. Now, Whitton was drawing attention to her single status to emphasize that it provided her with more autonomy than her married associates, male or female, with the implication that as part of the "secular unmarried" her devotion to the city would not be surpassed. On this ground Whitton was correct, for despite problems in her *style* of administration, there is no doubt about Mayor Whitton's devotion to her city.

As she had done the year before, on election day Whitton attended 8 o'clock service at St. Alban's. When victory was finally hers, she gave her female campaigners a horseshoe pin with the initials "CW." But having received the mandate she deemed necessary to legitimize her mayoralty, Whitton made it clear that she would no longer "chat" before "mixed grills of Ladies Days and Ladies Nights or Wives-and-what-have-you-females at the convention." From now on, since she understood clearly that to win re-election in two years time she would need the male vote, she would only address "bi-sexual meetings."[20] While the *Ottawa Journal* disagreed with some of her ideas, it reflected public opinion as it praised the mayor. Its editorial on 7 January 1953 acknowledged "the scope of her practical and versatile mind, the breadth of her understanding, the brilliance of her far-ranging vision of this city, its people and its problems."

Hosting Princess Elizabeth in 1951 had been the most memorable event in Whitton's public life; however, in 1953 even this was surpassed when she was invited to attend the coronation of the new Queen, to sit among the dignitaries of the Empire and Commonwealth and the nobility of Great Britain in Westminster Abbey. In an atmosphere of feverish anticipation, she insisted that she must be attired appropriately. As the Canadian equivalent of the Lord Mayor of London, she must wear robes of office. These she duly ordered—silks and satins of crimson and black, fur facings and cuffs, gold lace trim and lace neckpiece, a tricorne hat, and a heavy gold chain.[21] In her splendour, she paraded herself and the similarly berobed controllers on a barge along the Rideau Canal so that the astonished public might exclaim at the exhibition. This was Whitton's *tour-de-force* as a publicity stunt. The analogy with Cleopatra's procession on the Nile was obvious, and the press enjoyed making it. Indeed, as recently as 1984 the *Globe and Mail* reported that "the barge concept was so dear to Whitton's heart" that she had suggested one be presented on behalf of the people of Canada to the Queen for her coronation but that the proposed gift was rejected.[22] Her costuming reminded onlookers of her social status and official standing just as her ribbons and medals reminded them of her accomplishments.

During her coronation visit to Britain she wrote a series of fifteen articles for the *Ottawa Journal*, among them a description of Canterbury Cathedral on Whitsun, historical pieces about the monarchy, details of the symbolism behind the coronation and the trappings associated with royalty, and an account of the general assembly of the Church of Scotland in St. Giles Cathedral. She assured her readers that the Queen was "all that we envisage as womanliness and charm."[23] On the morning of the coronation, she was especially effusive:

In . . . the slight and beautiful young queen, re-dedicating her life again in the service of her people flows the blood of Cedric, the Saxon. . . . Down that long vista of history, riding with Her Majesty to her crowning shines the bright "cynehelm," an iron crown of Ine, the early able King of Wessex.[24]

Recalling the ceremony, maximizing once again the sense of consecration and service with which she so identified, Whitton described the young queen as

a priestess in a plain white habit offering herself for the Annointing. This was the setting a part of her life in consecration to the service of all those states which had chosen her head in all the quarters of the earth.[25]

She remembered her response to the experience: it was "as if the very countryside, the rivers, lakes and hills, had taken unto themselves of the haunting mysticism that clings to the very symbol of the Crown."[26]

All this solemnity disappeared on her return to Ottawa, where she immediately became embroiled in disputes over the extension of liquor outlets and the licensing of hotel dining areas and restaurants which were presently not yet licensed. This grievance received much attention throughout her mayoralties, although she had never before given particular evidence of such teetotal zeal. Since the women of Ottawa were generally opposed to liberalizing liquor legislation, Whitton evidently saw herself as a representative of such a constituency. She always had support of WCTU women although she was not a member herself. For example, the president of the Frances Welland, Westmount-Montreal branch congratulated her after a luncheon for the Queen Mother in the next year, saying, "We commend you highly for serving non-alcoholic beverages at the luncheon for our beloved dowager queen. It is an encouragement to the WCTU to see women of your calibre and strength of character holding such high office."[27]

Early in 1954, she began her preparations for re-election. In the spring, she addressed the local council of women with a "Report from a Threatened Front," which briefly outlined her accomplishments since 1951. She pointed out that the bonds the council had set aside for her campaigns had not been touched and that election costs had been remarkably low owing to the enthusiasm of volunteers. Expenses, radio, and advertising for the two campaigns had not exceeded $3,000. Moreover, she was confident that the requests for increased dominion grants to Ottawa as the national capital would be forthcoming. City land sales had increased revenues and developed real estate in the city, and a housing committee was now operating a pilot scheme of low-rental housing. Already 158 occupied units were being efficiently managed and 316 more were underway. Some of these were blocks of apartments for elderly couples, including partners other than married couples. A slum clearance scheme was underway, and the city had taken over rental decontrol from the province because of perceived hardships under the old system. Whitton argued that landlords must not be permitted to "charge anything they want." Traffic, new bridges, a mental hygiene clinic, upgraded hospital facilities, a nursing school, and recreational services had all been part of the board's mandate under her mayoralty.

But during fall the mayor's confidence was somewhat shaken after a council session "rowdier, more bitter, less dignified" than any before. In mid-October, on the night that Whitton was to attend a reception at the prime minister's residence for Viscount Swinton, the British secretary of state for Commonwealth Relations, a by-law regarding the wearing of the official robes was to be debated. When should they be worn; how should they be worn; and by whom should they be worn? The argument that ensued made Whitton look ridiculous; her council members answered almost unanimously, "Never!" Some suggested they be put "back to the moth balls," while others declared that the robes had become "a laughing stock." Contemptuously, Alderman Henry Parslow asserted that "We probably wouldn't have to wear them at an Irish Wake—but that's about all." Whitton attempted to dismiss the incident by quipping that "Every time they see me wearing a pretty dress they know I have an engagement and they do their best to delay me." But the meeting did not adjourn until 12:50 A.M. and she did not keep her date.[28]

The next weeks were fraught with uncertainty for Whitton refused to commit herself to a re-election campaign. Even the press were unsure whether she was merely making a political gesture or whether her ambivalence was genuine.[29] Keeping coy about her intentions, Whitton did not address her committee until the first week of November, only a month before the election. The *Journal* commented that her tea was attended by five hundred women and "ten brave men . . . one man who arrived early scanned the eager faces of the women— and lacking courage, departed."

> The tea was perhaps the gayest gathering seen in Ottawa for many a moon. . . . A few of the more ardent kissed the Mayor's cheek, and vigorous handshakes spread like wildfire the length of the hall.

Whitton demonstrated again the subtle psychological relationship she perceived between single status and service, commenting that "as a spinster nearing sixty," she was "wedded to this city." The *Journal* headline read, "Charlotte Feels Wed to Ottawa Sees No Grounds Yet For Divorce." Of course, Whitton ran. She conducted a short, emotionally charged campaign. Her nomination address on 26 November answered criticism about disturbances at city council.

> Practically all members of the Board of Control and, with but two exceptions, all members of the Council, whatever our differences, clashes or controversies,

have sought, with single mind, to further the City's interests. Where there is life and growth, there is bound to be action and struggle but may I stress that in nearly 2,500 items of report from 250 meetings of the Board of Control to Council in two years, in less than 25 items has there been any recorded dissent among members of the Board, and remarkably few recorded divisions in council. Honest conflict is healthier than drift, no matter how dignified.

Council minutes support these observations. If it were not reported in the press, a disinterested reader could not isolate many of the controversial incidents in them. On a radio broadcast for CBOT, she said, "I have made mistakes; they have not been of intent. I have my faults; my defects are those of my qualities. I have attempted much; I think I have accomplished much."[30]

By delaying her decision and by using innuendo, charges, and countercharges, she consolidated her position. On 6 December she was re-elected by a "groundswell," with pluralities in eight of the nine wards (the exception being the French-speaking Ward 2 in Lower Town) and a majority in wards four to nine, west and north of the Rideau river and canal.

Between 1950 and 1956 many of Whitton's closest friends and family died, grimly reminding her of her own mortality. Whitton was haunted not by fear of death but by the possibility of becoming socially useless. Her silent prayer throughout her life had been simple enough: "Lord give me work while my life shall last and life till my work be done." She was also known to quote from Han Su-yin's novel, *Love is a Many Splendoured Thing*:

> Everyone wanted security, security no longer a word but a duty. . . . I found people smaller and meaner, shrunk in a fixed search for security. Deep-buried in this word lay the talent of the slothful servant unadventured on the dangerous seas of life. For this strange end, men planned with single hearted passion, pensions and retirement, at twenty dreaming of 65, in youth, aspiring to safe senility. For the security of death they forsook living.[31]

Whitton asserted she would die with her "boots on."

One incident that gratified Whitton came as a reminder that her contributions to social welfare were far from forgotten. During 1955, the year of the Princess Royal's visit to Ottawa, a group of Vancouver social workers lauded her as the most important figure in B.C. social welfare history. When the school of social work at the University of British Columbia celebrated its 25th anniversary, a skit retold Whitton's story. To the piano tune of "Charlie is m'darling" a chorus boisterously included the following verse:

> Charlotte came to our town, to our town, to our town

Charlotte came to our town, in 1928
She said we had no agencies, no workers, no school,
She said we'd better grow our own and Charlotte was no fool.

Reminding the audience that "Charlie" was now installed at City Hall, the narrator quipped: "To the male citizens of Ottawa must go the credit for *the* sociological discovery of this century, to wit: They found that there is a whole sex made up entirely of women."

Reading from her forty-two page inauguration speech in the first week of January 1955, Mayor Whitton promised the city a twenty-million-dollar public works programme that would include bridges, waterworks, street repairs, sewage, a new city hall, improved transit services, schools and recreation facilities, and a confederation hall for the arts.[32] All of this was to be financed partially through agreements with the federal government. By the end of her term, she had increased the federal grant to the national capital from $400,000 to $3,500,000. In addition, she requested a survey of the Social Service Department of the city by the Canadian Welfare Council. The survey was conducted on the model Whitton had established herself when she was director of the CWC, and its recommendations that the department ought not to be entirely made up of qualified social workers although they should be in key positions, with less qualified employees working under them, reflected many of her own attitudes made years before.[33]

Nevertheless, her suspicion, talk of conspiracies and being misquoted, denials, and recriminations were creating a "cloak and dagger atmosphere" in City Hall. Although the goings on were newsworthy, they ultimately eroded Whitton's credibility and began to tire the public and the press. As early as May, Controller Paul Tardif wearily suggested that the mayor's repeated threats of resignation were "dramatics" that provided "a smoke screen" for the very real discord among the controllers, which she had provoked and was no longer able to control. In fact, City Hall was even more fractious than press reports conveyed. There had been early retirements of disgusted senior civic employees, including A.H. Ritchie, the civic financial commissioner, over the mayor's opposition to increased expenditure in the high schools. She objected to the inclusion of "frills"—auditoriums, gymnasiums, and cafeterias—which caused expenditures to soar and tarnished her boasted frugality. Alderman Wilbert Hamilton was blunt. He advised the mayor to resign before more officials quit, adding, "Her Worship the Mayor is not always right. Only God is always right."

In February 1956, Whitton submitted a personal statement on municipal government to the Royal Commission on Canada's Economic Prospects that called for a re-examination of "local government in the light of modern community administration, as well as its financial needs and re-adjustments in taxing powers or grants-in-aid."[34] Whitton maintained that taxes were not the essential issue and indeed that they often acted as an opiate, dulling thinking about the central problems of municipal government. She called for specialized levies on those who gained most from specialized services, improved and equalized assessment practices supported by technical assistance and inspection from the provinces, and a realistic business-tax structure.

Among Whitton's suggestions were longer terms for financing major permanent works such as sewers and provincially established minimum and maximum mill rates for communities. She complained that while senior governments denied their employees the right to strike, municipalities were forced to negotiate with their employees, which severely limited their control over expenditures. Another old theme also featured prominently in her submission—namely, that federal and provincial grants-in-aid were often made without recognition of the conditions of local communities. By requiring a minimum standard beyond community resources, such grants simply increased the financial problems of municipalities.

In essence, Whitton was calling for classification and investigation of specific municipal needs instead of indiscriminate grants from senior governments. She recommended user fees for special services to halt the use of general revenue for the benefit of a few. Since municipalities were closest to their voters, they needed both courageous leaders and provincial support to ensure honest behaviour in the face of community pressure. At the same time, senior governments had to be sensitive to local social and economic conditions and to forecast the results of their policies on municipally supplied services.

Not even the opening of the new and splendid Civic Hall on Green Island by Princess Margaret in August 1956 could silence the growing criticism of Whitton's tenure. Perhaps Ottawans, who now have a justifiable pride in their civic building set in the lush green of sweeping lawns and bejewelled with sparkling water, felt that it was too obviously an extension of their mayor's ego—an edifice where she would be paid court, ultimately a monument to herself. It was scarcely built for the citizens' convenience since it is not downtown and is difficult to reach. Whitton had dismissed this "problem" of access as inconsequential. To the question, "Why do people go to City Hall?" she answered "to pay taxes and fines." To lessen public inconvenience, the police department stayed downtown, and she established agreements with the banks to accept tax payments! Civic Hall was close to her own home and she was able to walk there each day.[35]

Grumblings were heard. By now the *Ottawa Journal* was describing her as "domineering" and a "bad actor" when crossed and saying that "in name calling her sex gives her an advantage of which she makes use, perhaps unconsciously." The *Citizen* had to agree that "what she thinks of as dedication to a great purpose her enemies denounce as a flat refusal to accept the possibility that she might ever be wrong." Finally, the *Citizen* concluded that "Those who disagree with her shudder at the thought of another two years of turmoil, namecalling, and disputation." By October, her campaign committee refused to lead a "draft" as it had done in the previous election. "If the people of Ottawa are interested enough in their welfare as we see it, it's up to them to ask her to run again," said Jennie Armstrong, the committee president. The people of Ottawa did not. Whitton always liked to be on the winning side, and a draft would have been a sure sign of strong support. In its absence she realized that she had overstayed her time; she had tested the loyalties of her supporters too often.[36]

When it was clear that Whitton would not run for a fourth term, the usual rumors began to circulate, rumors which frequently originated with Whitton herself. It was predicted that she would become John Diefenbaker's "right hand man" on the Conservative front benches. If not that, then she would replace the retiring George Dunbar of Ottawa South in the Ontario cabinet as minister of municipal affairs.[37] If that alternative failed too, it was suggested that she would join a United Nations agency or be invited into a U.S. social foundation. The *Citizen*, for one, regretted Whitton's decision to retire. Despite "her volcanic reaction to criticism," an editorial pointed out that it was "hard, if not downright impossible" to imagine her "in complete retreat." Whitton, however, had no intention of retreating and she was already planning her future. On 27 December 1956, the *Journal* announced that Mayor Whitton had "bow[ed] out."[38] It also noted that in many ways she was a victim of her volatile temperament. She demonstrated

> a kind of intellectual arrogance, a contempt for those of lesser minds —an attitude which has made co-operation difficult and cost her the support of some of those who did not fail to realize her outstanding qualities. Her faults have been faults of temperament and not of ignorance, for she is an extraordinarily knowledgeable woman.

It was not only the apparent disaffection of the public and the lack of enthusiasm for her candidacy on the part of her women's committee which persuaded Whitton not to run in 1956. It was a propitious time to leave civic politics: a federal election was on the horizon, and 1957 would be the year to seek a nomination. Soon after the announcement of her retirement, Whitton gave a speech at the Conservative Party leadership convention, which some claimed merely demonstrated again her talent for "pontification." To the audience it was obvious that in her address of welcome, which supported Diefenbaker, "she was killing two birds with the one stone—polishing up her own little shining political axe in preparation for a fresh venture into politics."[39]

Whitton's federal ambitions were well known; she had bided her time during the long years of Liberal power while she was making her own political affiliation a matter of record. The only time she had supported a losing side was on the baby bonus issue. The press speculated on the Party possibilities—would she be appointed to a position such as National Women's organizer or would she seek a federal riding, Ottawa West or South Renfrew, for example, now that a prediction of a Conservative victory was circulating?

Without sufficient preparation, Whitton tried for the P.C. nomination in Carleton County in the spring of 1957. Along with G. Russell Boucher, who had resigned to accommodate George Drew when he became party leader, Whitton was resoundingly defeated by the national director of the Conservative Party, Richard A. Bell. Her expectations had been extravagant. Although "relatively unknown outside Ottawa and with no notable successes to his record," Bell defeated Boucher two to one and had six times as many votes as Whitton.[40] One of her own supporters told her that both Bell and Boucher had worked on delegates for over two months before the convention to get their votes and that he felt that if she "had been canvassing as they did," she certainly would have "gone over the top."[41] That, however, was probably wishful thinking.

Disgruntled and disaffected Whitton publicized her feelings in a *Maclean's* article in May, and she informed one of her supporters that it would become obvious to all who read the article

> how very unsatisfactory I found my relations with the Conservative Party. I did a great deal to influence Mr. Diefenbaker's choice as a leader, and quite frankly, I had hoped I would be able to take an active and responsible part in this important campaign, either as a candidate in a seat that offered some possibility of carrying, or as an officer of the Conservative Association nationally.[42]

Whitton may have felt deeply rejected, but she had not been an active campaigner during the period of opposition, and Diefenbaker had not recognized her a king-maker.

Still determined to try for a seat, Whitton mustered all her resources, and by December 1957, she decided to seek the nomination for Ottawa West, a riding that had been Liberal for thirty-seven years and whose encumbent, George McIllraith, had held the seat since 1940. It was a formidable undertaking.

While planning her strategy, Whitton kept in touch with her prospective constituency by engaging in political punditry and folksy local pleasantries in her "On Thinking It Over" column in the *Citizen* and in broadcasts on CFRA radio (owned by her brother-in-law).

Before actually getting to the hustings, however, she had to do battle within her party. Her opponent for the nomination was Osmond F. Howe, Q.C., whom she had accused in 1954 of being part of the "Get-Whitton campaign." The "woman question" had to be resolved if she were to get the nomination for without the woman's vote, she could not effectively challenge the party structures, which then barred women from voting at conventions except "by courtesy." The constitution of the Ottawa West and South Progressive Conservative Association limited all voting rights at a nominating convention to "male British subjects," "except as other groups having like objects [the Women's and the Young PC Association] 'may' be 'invited' to participate." That year those groups had even been barred from moving or seconding motions or voting at executive meetings. In the face of this discrimination, Whitton threatened to call her own convention—one consisting entirely of Women's and the Young PC Association members. The West Ottawa Women's PCA had agreed to this by January 1958, with Mrs. Arthur Pridmore, the president, stating that her group would hold its convention on 24 February. The threat persuaded the association that it must allow these groups to participate and to nominate their candidate—Charlotte Whitton.[43]

Whitton defeated Howe handily—1,666 votes to 350. The *Citizen* noted that the instant "Ozzie" [Howe] started speaking, "some of the ladies took out their needles and started knitting—this was the tip off that he was headed for the guillotine." Accompanied by thunderous applause from the audience at the Coliseum, Whitton triumphantly exclaimed, "Oh yes! This old girl has been around a long time and run up quite a mileage, but she's still going strong."[44] She disconcerted Labour Minister Michael Starr, the guest speaker at the convention, with her "blurted out proclamation of Cabinet ambitions."[45]

The campaign now began in earnest. During it she used the slogan "Going My Way?" which introduced her CFRA broadcasts of the same name. But McIllraith's previous majorities had always ranged around 7,000, and he was a popular incumbent. While the nation expected a Conservative victory, it was nevertheless stunned by the landslide announced on 1 April 1958. Tories everywhere were jubilant at their 208 seats to the Liberal's 47 and the CCF's 8. In Ottawa alone they had taken fifteen seats—but Whitton's was not one of them. It was not an ignominious defeat, and the race had been exciting to the end. The polls told what had happened on 31 March 1958: McIllraith, 18,431 votes, and Whitton, close behind, with an astounding 17,397. The CCF candidate, James Allen, received 737. It was claimed that the West Ottawa seat had been "the toughest constituency" in the country and the most expensive campaign in Eastern Canada, with McIllraith's expenditures at $11,989.48 and Whitton's $11,106.96. Sixteen years later, the Canada Election Act of 1974 set expenditures at 30 cents per voter on the preliminary list. Given the 44,767 names, the limit for both candidates would then have been $11,376. With such a strong showing, Whitton thought she deserved a reward from Diefenbaker, but it was not forthcoming. The New York *Herald Tribune* aptly summarized the problem when it observed:

> Her victory was the climax of a fractional fight within the party, in which the Conservative Men's organization tried to bypass Miss Whitton, but was foiled by her women's groups. For years the party's top brass has shuddered at the thought of having the voluble and independent-minded Miss Whitton in the House of Commons.

An astute observation: despite her loyalty, Whitton was a maverick who would not easily bend to party discipline, and she could not be depended upon to do so if something she perceived as "principle" was at stake.[46]

The *Citizen* predicted that "in any event there is a virtual assurance that Miss Whitton can have her pick of a number of federal positions" or that Diefenbaker would offer her a Senate seat. There were other possibilities, running again for the mayoralty at the end of 1958 or for the Ontario legislature. Only a month before the *Citizen* had wished her a happy 62nd birthday and said that if she lost the election she would be an ideal person for a post as dean of women at a university or head of a government social service department.[47]

Back at the Coliseum Whitton conceded her defeat:

> 'Friends, Romans, Countrymen, you come to bury Caesar.'
> 'No. No!' shouted the audience.
> 'Well,' replied the doughty Charlotte, 'I'm half Irish and only the Irish can make a good thing out of a wake.'[48]

Although she was disappointed, she did not anticipate that she was about to be buried by the Conservative Party.

She had a private grievance too. Despite her brother-in-law's radio station's support, tension erupted between Charlotte and her sister Kathleen because her sister had supported George McIllraith. Whitton saw this as nothing less than outright disloyalty, though the extent of her rancour was not publicly evident until some years later.[49]

Several months after the Conservatives took power, Whitton approached the prime minister regarding possible overseas posts in Mexico, Chile, Sweden, Switzerland, or Ireland. In a confidential memo, she suggested to Diefenbaker that the appointment of J.A. Chapdalaine as ambassador to Sweden had been a mistake because he was a Roman Catholic.[50] Chapdalaine could be "switched to Mexico easily—and Sweden made available," presumedly for a protestant such as herself.

> Any appointment here would be highly suitable in that Sweden has more women in Senate and Parliament than any other modern state; has led in welfare. Undersigned knows and is well known to Royal Swedish Social Board. Has visited and conferred with them.

The memo stated that she preferred Mexico in her rating of vacancies for ambassadorships, it being closest to Canada for consultation by phone or plane. In addition, Switzerland would do well in having a new ambassador to replace the present one, Edmond Turcotte, who "because of his anti-British, anti-Allied attitude during the war, should not be this country's Ambassador anywhere."

It is reported to be a real source of irritation, both to Calvinistic Switzerland, and certainly to the constant stream of Canadians, in and out of Geneva, for the almost continuous international committees, commissions and conferences, that this particular incumbent is the Canadian Ambassador. Note here—Turcotte was apparently a "familiar" in earlier Quebec politics with Claude Jodoin (Canadian Labor Congress) and there is suspicion of too close liaison between the two re the International Labour Organization (ILO) and related ILO labour matters.

While she argued that she could study and use Sweden's social insurance and welfare systems and adapt them to Canadian needs, with regard to Switzerland, she reminded the prime minister of her previous experience in Geneva seven times as assessor or delegate to the League and her appointments with Bennett and King. Charlotte Whitton would clearly have loved to return to Geneva as a consultant to the United Nations, but her requests went unheeded.

At first Whitton ignored Diefenbaker's snub, but finally she wrote to him in the summer of 1959, asking for "any assignment at home or abroad."

> I only ask that it be really useful and engage me to the full use of my capacity and that it be decided as soon as possible . . . to add to the glory of John Diefenbaker and thus of the Conservative Party . . . could not but add to the glory of God Himself in the end.[51]

She confessed to a "real hankering" for the opening of the ambassadorship to Ireland, saying that she was known "all across the country as characteristically Irish." Pointing out that part of her immediate family were Irish Roman Catholics, that for eight years in a row she had been invited to attend the Sons of Ireland banquet on St. Patrick's Day, that she attended CWL functions as well as "Northern" Irish churches and societies, that she had been engaged by the Irish Catholics of Montreal to study their charities, she offered as references the Bishop of Montreal, superiors of Irish sisterhoods, and all those prominent Catholic and Irish-Canadians she knew. She even included Frank Ryan's trotting-horse trade between Canada and Eire as a demonstration of her "Irishness." Such extravagance would have amused those who had read a 1943 article, "Britain's Throne, Symbol of Mankind's High Ideals," in which she noted that the Irish were ungrateful "to concessions made with little or no duress and apparently with little appreciation."[52] So much for Whitton's personal perspective on Cromwell and his merry men, the potato famine, and the Easter uprising! At the time her letter was written, bitterness ran deep because of the Irish Republic's decision to remain neutral during World War II. To all of this pleading for the Irish ambassadorship, she added and underlined a pathetic "PLEASE."

In January 1959 Whitton attacked the South and West Ottawa PC Association at its annual meeting where women were invited not as members but as "guests." Although she perceived Diefenbaker's lack of interest in her as a betrayal of her contributions, she continued to fight against the party's discriminatory practices. She was personally recognized as a member because she had sat on the executive the year before "by merit of her candidature as the official standard bearer in the past federal election," but the rest of the association was male.

At the annual meeting she read a letter from Diefenbaker making it clear that he opposed the discrimination, a message the "Old Guard" chose to ignore. The issue split the meeting wide open, and the fury among the women "guests" could not be contained. Whitton was shouted down fourteen times as she demanded that the association be opened to women, and another woman who stood to address the chair was reminded, "Please madam, you're a guest here." The suggestion that there be both a "mixed" association and a second one, all-male, was greeted by groans of disbelief and hisses of contempt. Charlotte Whitton sparred with Ozzie Howe throughout the meeting until he and the old guard conceded defeat.

Although there is nothing to suggest that Whitton ever considered journalism as a serious career, between 1957 and 1960, she wrote a tri-weekly series for the *Citizen*, "On Thinking It Over," which was broadcast on Sundays on CFRA. These columns were far more incisive than her previous ones, often more cynical, less patient, and less accommodating of popular views. Once more they drew attention to her favourite themes: women in the workforce, women in the Anglican Church, women's political involvement, and the decline of civilization. In 1957 she wrote "Where Do You Go Fair Lady?" advising girls to plan to work and warning them against only seeing a job "as getting something to do in the meantime," that is, before they married. Reasserting her belief in the special nature of women's work, she claimed that there were "three lines of work in which they may most richly and fully find the natural projection of women's most womanly attributes. These are in the care of the young, the ill, the ailing, handicapped and aging."[53]

In 1958, on the sixty-fifth anniversary of the founding of the Ottawa local council of women, she repeated her faith in "The Power of Woman" but also expressed her disappointment in the exercise of their franchise.

> The fears of the opponents of the emancipation of women have not materialized. They have not forsaken marriage, home and the family, nor have they recklessly taken over the life and government of the state. If anything, they have failed the faith and hope of those who fought for equal franchise, rather than justified the misgivings of their opponents. It may be as the Honorable Ellen Fairclough says, that we never carry the battle, that there is always too much fraternizing with the enemy.

She continued that men made millions of dollars every day on women's work in the form of gadgets, beauty products, and quick foods, that "by our millions, we are working for men again, just as our female forebears did in the days of household and manual crafts."[54]

Within a month, she wrote "How Could You Hamilton?" in response to a copy of a notice she had received advertizing two positions for "qualified social workers" for the United Services Fund. She noted that the position for director was "for a man with a Masters of Social Work" and that it held "excellent prospects" whereas the position for *assistant* to the director was for "a young woman, graduate of a school of social work or equivalent with interest and aptitude for social planning." The only honest part of the advertisement "was that for the second position no hope of prospects were held out." She decried the advertisement as something out of "the antidiluvian swamps," pointing out that this was a retrogressive step for Hamilton, the first city to have a woman controller, Nora Frances Henderson; the city that had produced the first woman cabinet minister, the Honourable Ellen Fairclough; and a city that presently had as deputy mayor Ada Pritchard.[55]

By far her most controversial piece was "Salvation by Sex" in June 1959 in which she criticized the recent Ottawa synod of the Anglican Church. She accused the synod of being anti-democratic when it denied women membership even though its laity had agreed that they be admitted to full voting status. Moreover, Ottawa lagged behind other dioceses on this matter. The opening statement, "Onward Christian soldiers marching as to war/with all Christian women barred behind the door" was intended to be provocative. Reaction came within a week and from no less than the archdeacon of Cornwall, who objected to hearing such views on CFRA. "I'm sorry," he wrote, "you saw fit to broadcast to all and sundry a domestic matter which concerns not even all Anglicans, but only our own Diocese." He corrected her on several points of church governance, argued that the Church was a theocracy and not a democracy, and placed the Church's position into the framework of its theology. On all counts he was quite right, but Whitton refused to recant views that also had right on their side.[56]

Even the Canadian Women's Press Club, which met in Ottawa in 1959, was obliquely criticized for its lack of journalistic assertiveness. Quoting from Vera Brittain's "Lady Into Woman," in which Brittain suggested that women were overly influenced by masculine perceptions and masculine prejudices about women's appropriate role, Whitton asked, "Is the hand that drives the pen— or taps the keys—too . . . well manicured, to bear the sword, or subtly thrust the rapier?"[57]

Answering a friend's accusation that she was always acting as a Cassandra in her columns, she wrote in "Prophets, Priests and Puritans" about "the sickness of the day" and the disappearance of responsible, even irresponsible criticism, into complacency, disillusionment, and pessimism. Lamenting the decay of society from within, the practice of thirty hours work for forty hours pay, "buying on tick," she dismissed the appalling surfeit of "superficial ethical illiterates" who, posing as prophets, utter cliches. Obviously no Keynesian in economic theory, she deplored the general acceptance of deficits in banks, the CNR, Trans-Canada Airlines, and governments. Finally, she witnessed to the truth as she knew it.

> It is so easy to be glib, to decry the good, to deny the divinity of God and discount any reasoned theology—queen of all sciences. But to do so is to discard therewith, in principle and practice, the basic moral values of decent living, and customs, of which religious conviction is the culture bed.[58]

Whitton was proud to act a Cassandra, and in this part she had more insight than when she played at Pollyanna.

Another eventful decade had passed as the turbulent sixties opened but the kind of appointment Whitton aspired to in government, with the United Nations, in the diplomatic service, or as a M.P. or senator had failed to eventuate. The fifties had begun with her entry into civic politics and being twice elected mayor. Sentiments that concluded the "Report of the State of the City" at the 1956 inaugural meeting reflected her view of the service she had rendered Ottawa.

> May I borrow from one of the Roman Emperors my closing words, should this "happen chance" to be my last Report to you? "Enough and more than enough will they render to my memory if they judge me to have been worthy of my ancestors, watchful of your interests, steadfast in danger and undaunted by the enmities encountered in the public service. These are the temples I would erect in your hearts, these are the fairest images and such as will best endure."[59]

In the fifties, she saw the mayoralty as a potential entry into federal politics or government service, not as a final stage in her career. By the sixties, Charlotte Whitton, now sixty-four, had fewer hopes for the future. She had reached an impasse and the only possibilities seemed to be in a return to the mayoralty, where she had enjoyed such absolute power. Therefore, her decision to return to civic politics can be seen, if not as a concession of defeat, at least as a sign of retreat. Nevertheless, there were risks involved, for in no way was she certain that she would succeed in regaining the position.

9

NO ANGEL BUT A GOOD MAYOR

*"Speak up gentlemen, I'm not opposed to
male participation in government."*

WHITTON, 1960.

By the end of the 1950s Whitton had not received any of the appointments that
she had hoped for, and the new year brought with it health problems, something to which she was not accustomed and which she was entirely unable to
tolerate. A vigorous and healthy woman, her only previous problems had been
bouts of poison ivy, which had never slowed her down; now she had to undergo
surgery for a twisted bowel and appendicitis. During her stay in hospital she
received hundreds of cards from friends and former constituents as well as
scores of bouquets including those from Lester Pearson, now leader of the
Liberal opposition, and the Diefenbakers. Her convalescence was slow and she
was still fatigued in March when she accepted an invitation to spend some
weeks with a friend in Tryon, South Carolina. Elizabeth Webster gave her
companionship and care, but Whitton remained restless.

Quite unable to endure enforced idleness, on her return to Ottawa Whitton
fell into the old familiar pattern of writing letters in which her feelings of social
uselessness expressed themselves as exasperation and moral rectitude. The
problem of extending liquor licences continued to exercise her, and she
accused the provincial government of "collaboration rather than control."
Alcohol was the root cause of much prostitution, crime, drugs, highway slaughter,
unwed motherhood, delinquency, child neglect, and family breakdown. Concerned that hotels were in fact offering little but liquor with some vice on the
side, she wrote in her *On Thinking It Over* column, "Indeed, there is a grave
suspicion that if 'ladies' are not also on the bill of fare, they may loiter not far

from the lobbies. Or there is likely a 'Sally in the Alley.'"[1] Moreover, she attacked singlemindedly a "Close-Up" programme which had dealt with divorce laws by interviewing a hired co-respondent.

June Callwood, already notorious among CBC viewers for her anti-monarchist remarks during the 1957 Royal Visit, was the interviewer for the programme "The Other Woman," in May 1960.[2] The show caused a national uproar because it was the first CBC venture into the territory of explicit sexual discussion and because it remained doubtful that the woman concerned, who earned $70 a week as a secretary and $100 a night as co-respondent, was genuine. The issue, nevertheless, was only a part of a growing social and media interest in the need to reform Canada's divorce laws which accepted only adultery as grounds for divorce and therefore sometimes led to the concoction of adulterous situations.

Knowing when the programme was scheduled for release, in April Whitton wrote urgently to Leslie Frost, the premier of Ontario and in May to John Diefenbaker. Calling the interview "indecent," "disgusting," and "decadent," she claimed that it was neither "culture nor Canadian." She was particularly repelled by that "revolting blunt question—Do you have intercourse?"[3] Within a week of the programme being aired, her column "Featuring—Lies for Sale" decried the "vicarious wallowing" the show offered, accusing it of being salacious and the woman of being a "phoney"—either a professional actress or a professional prostitute. If she did what she described, it was illegal; therefore, her place was in a criminal court and "certainly is not parading before the nation by grace and favor of the tax endowed CBC-TV." A little over a week passed before her column attacked the issue again, this time accusing the producers of "an imitative obsession with the U.S. social scene" by sensationalizing an area of human relations that did not belong in Canada which maintained "a reasonably settled pattern in family life" in which fewer than one marriage in five ended in divorce.[4]

Not content with protest, she inquired about the possibility of suing the corporation, and she implored the chairman of the board of broadcast governors to discipline its producers. Although there was plenty of criticism, not all Canadians agreed with Whitton. One female Ottawa resident congratulated the CBC for not allowing itself to be "intimidated by self appointed judges." "Would you," she asked Whitton, "prefer that this festering, odorous canker be carefully concealed to fester more and more because nice, sensitive souls, find it so objectionable?"[5]

There is no doubt that Charlotte Whitton was sincere in her rejection of changing mores regarding marriage and divorce. For the remaining years of her life she was to struggle with intellectual and spiritual difficulties, trying to uphold her values in a rapidly changing society. The following extract from "In Search of Oneself" summarizes the dilemma she faced.

I hold that neither the life of the individual nor of the race would appear to be part of any plan, or to have any meaning or purpose or to lead anywhere but to despair, death and chaos if we were not part of an unseen reality. We can obey or deny, or deceive, conscience. We are left with free will to deny or affirm God, and as we do so, we deny or affirm our duty to our fellow man who is also of God. . . . These are very simple truths but I guess just because they are such plain simple truths they are too hard to be tried in this modern progressive world.[6]

Though her attacks on "Close-Up" continued through the summer, they did not totally preoccupy Whitton during the months following her convalescence. By mid-June, she had written to Diefenbaker once more, pleading for an opportunity to serve her party and her country. While the *Toronto Daily Star* of 27 June 1960 said that Whitton "asked no quarter, gave none, and won more often than she lost," anyone who followed her careers would have seen the irony in such claims and understood that a comeback as mayor was the last resort, an acceptance of failure on a wider stage. In the light of her own ambitions, Whitton had not really "won more than she had lost."

In mid-November 1960 a "draft Whitton" committee announced that she was in the mayoralty race. Vowing to curb capital spending, she rose to the occasion with her customary rhetorical style: "I accept a draft which is a draft from the people. I have no cause but the people; no voting strength but theirs; no cause but the people which is my cause and with which I rest our common cause."[7] Her most formidable opponent was controller Sam Berger, a lawyer and an ex-RCAF wing commander.

This time she put up half of the $6,000 for her campaign cost and boasted about neither her personal frugality nor the enthusiasm of her volunteers. In a television appeal she underplayed her feminism and displayed her femininity. Frank Ryan's CFRA radio station prominently backed her and publicized an exposure of real estate transactions in which Berger had participated. While not illegal, they could well be taken as a conflict of interest. For those listening attentively to her nomination speech in November, her insistence that the preparations for the 1967 Centennial year start as soon as the mayor was elected, must have been striking. Anyone sensitive to Whitton's psychology might have suspected that she hoped to be mayor of the Capital during the celebrations, though they were still seven years off. She enthusiastically welcomed the challenge:

Few finer opportunities of usefulness could open before any Canadian today than that of Mayor of the Capital, as the people of Canada look forward to the 100th anniversary of the Confederation of their nation in 1967. No matter how extensive or vast those plans, their crowning events must be played out here, where the nation will be at home, not only to its own people but to all the world, in the City of Ottawa and the seat of government.

And for those who recalled her pet schemes of the 1950s, the following promise would have come as no surprise.

The housing of the people is a top priority. The hundreds of low rent houses built on substandards destroyed or brought up to standard, are the proudest records of my former term as Mayor. . . . And the further extension of low rental housing, which is what the city now needs, under and every provision, I shall press.

But these low rental housing projects I shall not place miles from people's work, nor concentrate, so that they become known as "relief housing." Nor shall I restrict them to single or row housing. They will provide apartment units as well.

She added that she would encourage the building of specialized single and double low-income units for "oldsters" and that low rental shelter of varying types would be built all across the city to avoid "herding the needy, the driven and the worried all together in designated areas or units."[8]

She challenged the other candidates to a debate which she won easily, leaving them fumbling through their notes. At one point in the campaign, Berger slipped and referred to her as "Mayor Whitton," much to his supporters' consternation! And it was about this time that she displayed her famed ashtray bearing the motto, "Ce que diable ne pas femme le fait"—roughly, "What the devil can't do a woman can." Although her faithful female vanguard rallied, including the campaign organizer, Lilian Courtney, as well as Jennie Armstrong, Whitton did not rely totally on woman-power. With a strong committee of lawyers and businessmen, she deliberately wooed male voters, promising them that she would pray, "Set a watch, O Lord Before my mouth; Keep the door of my lips."[9]

By the election day, 5 December, Whitton was clearly soft-pedalling her "Pankhurst feminism," especially since a previous supporter, Grattan O'Leary, publisher of the *Ottawa Journal*, had refused to back her. The enmity between them was unpleasant enough that guests at a public reception to which they were both invited were quite nervous should they confront each other. To dispell the tension Whitton called out to O'Leary, "Come here you old s.o.b. while I give you a kiss." It was, of course, after her victory. Having picked up Whitton's "kerchief ever so gallantly" in the fifties, the *Journal* never backed her again and the *Citizen* was now less forthcoming.[10]

Nevertheless, Whitton received 35,638 votes to Berger's 33,822. Controller Bob Jones came in with 9,317, and a fourth candidate, A.L. Dube, a former schoolteacher, had 2,673. Apparently many Ottawans were willing to overlook that moment in 1952 when she had challenged Paul Tardif to step out in the corridor "and slug it out" when they disagreed in Council; apparently they had forgotten that the snow piled up as the potholes got bigger and the sewage clogged the drains; apparently they had forgotten that she lectured the board "in marathon school marm style." None of these past events mattered. They wanted their star back; she did not "fit into a timid mould." She was refreshing—"a reincarnation of the fighting feminists of half a century ago." And it was not only Ottawa that clamoured for her comeback. The Saint John's *Telegraph-Journal* called her an "unquenchable obstacle mounter" and "an impudent woman full of ginger." *Time* quoted from her nomination speech: "they're trying to tree this old cat," but, the reporter announced, there was life in her yet. The article referred to her "troupe of militant ladies" and those "ever faithful feminists harping away from tearooms to tabernacles, from parlors to phone booths." She was a "keg shaped Tory dynamo who has made a political career out of needling men." However, *Time* missed the point—Whitton was *not* needling men and she was no longer depending solely on her "petticoat brigade."[11]

Within three months there were familiar complaints that the mayor kept city spending low by cutting back on garbage and snow removal. At the close of the year, the board was said to be in an "uproar," a place of "weird bombastics," violent wrangles, harsh words, and charges and countercharges. Her attacks on liquor outlets as "settings for concentrated vice" became vitriolic, and her criticisms of Diefenbaker's grants to the capital more pointed. Although most council time was spent in a "calm sea" of by-laws, transfer of funds, appointments, installation of water mains, and committee reports, "the volcanoes" that erupted were widely publicized and generally condemned. The press that had fawned around her in the previous decade now began to systematically undermine her credibility, and she gave them plenty of ammunition.

In November 1962, it was reported by the press as far away as Johannesburg that she had given "a thorough foot and fist drubbing" to a fellow Council member. The incident was not quite so dramatic. The *Journal's* summation seemed closer to the truth:

> Mayor Whitton lost her temper today at a closed meeting of Board of Control and flayed wildly with her fists at Controller Paul Tardif.
>
> 'She swung at me four or five times but didn't get in a good solid blow,' said the panting controller. 'She was absolutely berserk.'[12]

Apparently Tardif had contemptuously dismissed Whitton's comparisons of the burden of civic duties with the pressures of family life. He suggested that "she might have had children of her own if she hadn't been too busy with other things." Whitton's response to what she construed as a slur on her spinsterhood was spontaneous. Later she magnified a sexist remark into "filthy, obscene, personal remarks which would have got his face slapped by any respectable woman." Although Tardif must have felt foolish, judging by her conduct at the next board of control meeting, it seems that Whitton did not. On this occasion she pulled out "a toy cap gun from a civic ward chest," pointed it at an alderman, and for an instant it was seriously thought that she had actually gone quite mad!

On a CBOT telecast, the incumbent mayor passionately declaimed against James Groves and Sam Berger, her opponents in the 1962 campaign:

> My two opponents have become venomous in their attack—not on the promises made and trust fulfilled, not on the fair record of all but four or five of the Council I headed. *No, they attack* the Mayor herself, her personality, the woman who, for *eight years* has poured out all that God has given her, of strength, mind and spirit, in your service, as she swore she would.[13]

Though a disaffected press was no longer susceptible to her air of grievance, the viewers were still determined to support her.

Media events, such as her presentation of the keys to the city the British prime minister, Harold Macmillan or her being made Princess "Pretty Woman" of the Peigan Indian Band did not dissuade Whitton's detractors. Even when she was named woman of the year for the sixth time (with lawyer, Mme. Casgrain, the first woman cabinet minister in Quebec and women's rights crusader the runner-up), press criticism did not stop. Instead, commentators reminded the public of the arrogance which had caused alderman Jess Wentzell to resign in May of that year, and the Ottawa *Journal* spoke of "intemperate wrangles," "vanities," and "self righteous pomposity" at city hall. Such a "lamentable line of disorders" had "cheapened" Ottawa's civic life. But the very conduct that appalled some mesmerized others. Whitton had as always an uncanny sensitivity to mass psychology and used such exhibitions to her advantage. The people were not ready to abandon her. Her liveliness, zest, and sense of the absurd, fascinated and amused, and Ottawa wanted to revel in her colour. As far away as San Francisco, the *Chronicle* recorded it, and James K. Nesbitt of the *Vancouver Sun* reported that "Charlotte Revels in Male Agony."[14]

Accounting for her stewardship during the 1961-62 term, Whitton introduced her next re-election appeal with a request for "a three year term for the council elected in 1964" because "you can no longer carry on a $110 million dollar a year business"

with, really, less than 20 full business months in which to plan, develop and execute the terrific obligations of the city that is Canada's Capital, especially as we approach Confederation's 100th birthday.

Her stewardship was impressive: equitable assessments which had added $100 millions by the end of the year; limits to council borrowing; more equity between small home owners and large developers; a new sewage plan; increased (and controlled) building permits; agreements with neighbouring municipalities and the federal government; attention to housing needs; increased care facilities for the elderly, a training scheme for unemployed youth, and improved juvenile and family court facilities. She concluded:

> I solemnly promise you 'more of the same' with all I can offer, all my faults, all my failings, but never failing in my devotion to this City, heart of The Valley, and the land of my birth and love, and in whose hills, I trust, my tasks and days ended, I shall, in the end, find rest.[15]

The words "more of the same" rang ominously to her critics. Although *Time* wondered if her return would reduce "the civic administration to the unsatisfactory old ways of squabbling and dissention," Charlotte Whitton was elected mayor of Ottawa for the fourth time. James Groves, a civil servant, and Sam Berger were not able to defeat her despite their appeal to the strong male opposition. Whitton received 40,051 votes, Berger, 34,068, and Groves, 18,168. Although she had captured a plurality—and 43.5% of the vote—her popularity was declining. In this election another woman, Ellen Douglass Webber, won the seat vacated by Tardif.[16]

Post mortems of the election puzzled about Whitton's success. What were the sources of her plurality? Certainly it did not come from the female residents of "chic" Rockecliffe or Rideau, as *Canada Month* observed, while noting that on her return "many a man held his head and moaned 'Oh No!'" Since few voters acknowledged that they supported her, there must be a "Whitton Underground." The *Globe and Mail* speculated that "Somebody trying to analyse Miss Whitton's election success once said that every housewife in Ottawa sees in her antics the release of all their tension and frustrations and there are more women voters in Ottawa than there are men." Whitton received support in the working-class districts, which remembered her previous enthusiasms for low-cost rental housing and her sympathies for the problems of Ottawa's early morning female janitors. Yet even working class-men seemed divided on the question of their lady mayor. A cabbie was reported to have once said, "You're darn right I voted for Charlotte—that girl's got courage. That girl's got honesty," while another raised his eyebrows; "Yak," he said, "Yak. Yak. Yak."[17]

By the mid-1960's, it had become increasingly difficult to separate the private woman from the public image. Not having the usual family life or ordinary domestic commitments, Whitton's world had become entirely public. The press maintained this world, and she in turn provided all that it needed. A friend had commented to her in 1956 that she "who rides a tiger dare not dismount." This was even more true in 1964. She was, indeed, every "press agent's dream." When in late November 1964 Whitton noted, with some foreboding, that "the press makes the mayor fair game with open season for hunting," it was only half true. The dynamic between the press and Ottawa's controversial mayor was more complex, but Whitton dared not dismount her particular tiger.[18]

If her press image had not uniformly been negative, it had always been stereotyped. During her campaign for controller in 1951, Whitton was depicted as homey, even cheerfully cosy. But that was before her caustic tongue and quick temper asserted themselves once she was assured power as mayor. Such headlines as "Civic Minded Charlotte Can Cook Up More Than A Speech" had emphasized her ambidexterous talents and androgynous personality. Moreover, such comments as "manless though she may be she can sling a skillet as skilfully as a *bon mot*" established a positive view of her single status. In 1951, therefore, Whitton's image had been feminine and non-threateningly female. She had claimed, after all, that running the capital was like running a home—it merely required "good planning, good partnership and not spending above what you can make."

During her first years in public office, the press showed a conventional matron, and her photographs, where she sometimes resembled the Queen Mother, were not unattractive. Details described a "diminuitive mayor" who took size 16 in a dress and size two in a shoe and whose slim ankles had been admired by St. Laurent. Moreover, she worried about her waistline, wore a "low necked frock of black brocade" to official functions, sometimes donned "pastel pink," had a sensible hair do, and ironed her own lingerie. However, these insipid stereotypes of the woman-next-door, were transformed within a few years into cruel caricatures and cartoons, deliberately ugly photographs, and acerbic and contemptuous comments as she became more visible and more vocal.[19]

She was not conventionally attractive; and she did not age particularly well. Nevertheless, even in later years, sympathetic photographs show a not unhandsome woman. The numerous grotesque photographs are in marked contrast to the Karsh portrait that accompanied a *Chatelaine* article "What's the matter with us?" written in December 1944. His artist's lens drew out her ambiguities—strength and vulnerability, toughness and tenderness—a woman with a lovely and sensitive mouth and strikingly dark intelligent eyes. Generally, however, the press exploited crude and pitiless candid camera angles. They perpetuated the myth of Whitton the virago, the man-hater, just in case the extravagant reporting should be overlooked.[20]

A letter from a Vancouver woman in *The Province*, on 9 December 1964 shows that there were those who understood the implications of stereotyping before sexism became the subject of academic and feminist discourse. In "Why the Ugly Photos of Charlotte Whitton?" Evelyn Gown Murphy protested:

> As a mature Canadian woman, I am disgusted, vastly and completely, at your continually printing unpleasant candid pictures of ex-Mayor Charlotte Whitton. It is an insult to thinking Canadian women and to mayor Whitton who has five times been elected mayor of Ottawa. She is one of the outstanding women of Canada, yet you delight in depicting her in ugly photos and describing her as 'irascible' on each occasion you print a piece on her.

And a female reporter, May E. Logan, who wrote the Woman's World column in *Pembroke Observer*, noted, "Charlotte has enemies . . . and they are the press. . . . Don't try to make her a disgruntled woman battling against all males."[21] Of course, Whitton's public image was perpetuated largely by the ambivalent love/hate dynamic that emerged between the male-dominated press and Whitton herself.

Whitton desperately craved publicity: she submitted to it even as she dreaded and despised it. Publicity gave the mayor votes, and it gave the press good copy. As early as 1954 the editor of the Ottawa *Journal* had conceded that "the lady *was* news and entertainment" and that her "sense of drama, humour and timing" made her "newsworthy." She was not only a "press agent's dream," but also "the personification of everything the most zealous of public relations can wish for his subjects."[22]

In turn, headlines such as "Mayor Dares Council, "Mayor Jeered," and "Threats, Cries of Shame and Pandemonium" represented a carousel from which Whitton could not dismount. While the press parodied her, she pandered to it, terrified of anonymity. For Whitton, there was no prospect of life after celebrity. As long as people attended to her "alarums," they attended to her.

Thus, Whitton, whose strong claim to "character" was part of a nineteenth-century sensibility, had become a twentieth-century woman where character was replaced by personality and substance by celebrity. Second only to social uselessness, Charlotte Whitton feared loss of identity. As her private life retreated in the blaze of the public image, who was she now? Was she merely the image that the press fed to the public and that the public consumed voraciously? If her "record" failed, would the image sustain her?

The unkind photographs humiliated and wounded her, but she bitterly understood that this was the price she must pay for image making. She also had to maintain a fragile balance between the conservative views of the *Journal*, the more liberal views of the *Citizen*, and the fact that images confused substance with style.

The more attention she got, the more she wanted. What had before been politically expedient for re-election now became psychologically necessary. She was an obvious subject for caricature—a physical, aggressive, and public female figure. From the press Whitton could expect either praise or contempt and from the public, always fickle and easily bored, she could expect little more. Not surprisingly, during the late fifties and the sixties, Whitton herself began to assimilate to this stereotype, compulsively flaunting her "spinster" status. The press adopted the tag with relish.

In 1961 *Maclean's* commented on her collection of books on Queen Elizabeth I, "another waspish virgin who sometimes cut off the heads of troublesome gentlemen," and as far away as Johannesburg she was described as "Ottawa's 66 year old, 130 lb. spinster mayor," who also happened to be a "battleaxe." One unsigned letter from a group of workmen told her that

> the only thing that's bothering you is that so many soldiers were killed that not one was left for you . . . one of the fellows just remarked wouldn't it scare the hell out of a fellow to wake up and find that homely bitch in bed with you. One of the girls said if she found you in bed with her she'd figure she either shit the bed or had a miscarriage.

The insults that Whitton bore as a public figure were of a qualitatively different kind to those directed at married male politicians. They ranged from "senile sawn off old cunt" to recommendations that she visit a psychiatrist because her "mental outlook and frustration" being caused by the lack of a man, could be cured by a man, to the epithet "man hater" and the monotonous repetition of "frustrated old bitch" and "Ottawa's sexless wonder."[23] These vulgarities were part of the filtering down process of her press image into the public's psychic consciousness, and the same press that had assisted her into office in 1951 finally defeated her at the close of 1964.

10

ANGRY, ANXIOUS, AND AGING

*"A woman of contrasts, difficult to understand but
well worth understanding . . ."*

CITIZEN, 27/1/1975.

By November 1964, the "sixth Petticoat Brigade" was mobilized, but Whitton
must have found it ominous when only a dozen men attended the first campaign meeting. Immediately before election day, she claimed:

> I submit that La Tante Charlotte has not only been a good housekeeper but
> an A-1 business manager and banker for this city and that I am finishing out
> this fifth term of mine with money in the till, credit in the bank, and a
> $91,500,000 shopping list (of capital works) approved for 1964-1968.[1]

Although her figures were accurate, the electorate was no longer impressed by
the old housekeeping analogy she'd been using for fourteen years.

When Controller Don Reid won the mayoralty with 43,854 votes and became
Ottawa's mayor for 1965-66, the *Journal* parodied Porter's popular song, "It was
just one of those things" describing a love affair that was over. Coming in third
with 23,858 votes, Whitton reproached her brother-in-law, Frank Ryan, who
had also run against her. He finished second with 25,472 votes. At first, she
refused to acknowledge that the people of Ottawa had just "tired of the show,"
but on 7 December, Charlotte Whitton conceded, her days as mayor of Ottawa
over.[2]

Although her defeat was not entirely unexpected, Whitton saw it as placing
the seal of silence and invisibility on her. The years of public life had been
addictive, and now Whitton was scarcely able to distinguish the private woman

from the public image. Nevertheless, the petulant recriminations she directed at Ryan and her sister Kathleen reveal the extent of her distress. She had accused Kathleen Ryan of collusion in her 1958 federal election defeat. She now accused the couple of splitting the vote. Ignoring the fact that Don Reid had won "decisively," carrying nine of the ten wards and 43,854 of the 97,477 votes, she joked rather shamefacedly: "What's the use of having a family of Yorkshire and Irish descent if you can't have some murderous differences." Within three months Frank Ryan was dead, and on a CJOH telecast, she remembered the man who had attended Renfrew Collegiate and Queen's as "merry and generous of heart, keen of mind, inflexible of will, firm—indeed to a certain fierceness—in his convictions and loyalties." She generously concluded that "what he deemed right, he would pursue, despite all consequences."[3]

After the election, she bitterly attacked the line up of Liberal and Conservative party workers in the Reid camp, asserting that there was proof "that certain influences in my own party were as active against [me] in this election as in any Ottawa election before." Her exit was ungracious and ungenerous, and as a final gesture she set aside a fund for a civic funeral, insisting she wanted it whether she was in office or not. At the same time she promised to write a book that would make a lot of people "break out in a nervous rash." Fortunately for many, she did not follow through; she could have caused quite a stir.[4]

The national press mourned her departure; Ottawa would now settle down into relative dullness. Having created the same ambivalence that Whitton as a person provoked, the "Whitton Era" was either loved or loathed and the press reacted to its end with mixed regret and relief. A Hamilton paper noted

> She was the boss with a capital "B" and when she wasn't ruling by whim she was shouting at any him who got in her way. She was matriarch of all she surveyed and she preferred to do it herself rather than delegate responsibility. . . . The public that once applauded her act grew tired of the show.

However, the *North Bay Nugget* loyally defended her.

> She will have done more to encourage women into politics than almost any other member of her sex. "Charlotte" became a symbol of the militant female, and an example of what a woman can accomplish in a realm which is one of the most difficult for women to invade—politics.[5]

While other statements read like obituaries, Charlotte Whitton was determined not to be buried. Two years off seventy, excluded from national politics and defeated in the civic arena she had made her own, she was not about to be silenced. Early in 1965, she wrote an essay called, "I know what I want from my country but not where to find it." Temperamentally unable to wait for life to come looking for her or to risk it passing her by, she began searching for other avenues of service. Another woman in her late sixties might have resigned herself to anonymity, but Whitton's slogan for the next decade became "It's time to get off our rocking chairs!"[6] For those who assumed that there would be no further political activity for the ex-mayor, she provided a surprise. Between January and March 1965 she wrote articles for the "Dissent" series in the *Toronto Telegram* and went on spring tour lecturing on the Middle East, the USSR, politics, and "woman power." The *Albertan* gleefully announced that she was "ready and willing to be Prime Minister."[7]

"I am a Canadian," she wrote in the *Telegram* in January, "but I cling to the glorious triune crosses of the Old Jack." Thus she rejected the Canadian flag as "a poor thing but our own." Two months later, the *Telegram* published her views on "Selling Basic Freedoms for Vague New Civil Rights." Rejecting the Ontario Human Rights Code of 1961-62 that had replaced the freedoms of the British North America Act, she observed, "Moreover it does not seek to protect human dignity until you live in a housing unit of more than six suites, or work for an employer with more than 5 employees." The same month the *Telegram* published "Abolishing the Death Penalty for Those Who Deal in Death?" Her view that capital punishment should be retained never faltered. But some of her anti-separatist columns were not published. Apparently the *Telegram* was not about to endorse that particular dissenting view![8]

Fearing that a biography or memoirs would seal her fate, Whitton evaded several offers from publishing houses and rejected others by ghost writers, laughing that "being a High Church Anglican," she wanted to stay with "private confession." Nor did she co-operate with anyone who wanted to write general welfare histories. Despite her wealth of information on the subject, she declined collaborative suggestions. Asked about her memoirs, she regretfully replied that her book was "like a stuck zipper" and that she was "too busy to retire." Although she clearly understood that her obsession with activity and publicity left her no time for "contemplative writing" and regretted that she had "followed the will-o-the-wisp of the day," Whitton was unable to get off the whirligig. Even her ambitious plans for a two-volume history of the Ottawa Valley, started in 1966, were not fulfilled.[9]

No Anglican was more non-plussed, however, when Pierre Berton was commissioned by Reverend Ernest Harrison, the assistant secretary of the general board of education, to write a book on the Church in Canada. Instead of writing a book for Lenten meditation *for* Anglicans, he chose to write *to* Anglicans from the point of view of one who had left the Church. Not unexpectedly, his book, *The Comfortable Pew*, was an incisive attack on the Church, and in a review essay Whitton observed that because Berton was "an inimical agnostic" even if he was a "pre-eminent publicist," it was predictable that he would "decry the Church, denounce her dogma, deny its potency [and] generally downgrade all faith."

Outraged that he had received 20 per cent royalties for the 150,000 books that were sold at $2.50 and $4.50, she felt that he had done so at the expense of the Church's reputation. Arguing that *The Comfortable Pew* ignored all "uncomfortable" things such as sin, death, and the meaning of life and that it lacked a sense of history, since it was based on the limited, personal experiences of one individual's childhood and adolescence, Whitton blasted Berton's critique. Replying to a high school student, Jane Egan, who asked her to participate in a debate about the book at the Oakridge Secondary School in London, Whitton reaffirmed her religious convictions though she refused the invitation.

> You see, I am old-fashioned enough to believe in God; that God is; and that God is real; in fact, that God is the most dominant fact in all existence and, consequently I would be in a very peculiar position to endeavour to debate at all on this subject with a man whom I know as well as I do Mr. Pierre Berton, but who is a proudly professed agnostic, and even feels that he can define the type of Messiah whom we should have to save this world.[10]

Maintaining contact with the public and keeping herself in the public view were Whitton's way of keeping herself both socially productive and mentally alert. The local television station CJOH provided opportunities for her to maintain this dynamic. The "Dear Charlotte" program of 1965-66 was so popular that Whitton was overwhelmed by fan mail ranging from social commentary to personal requests for advice. She was part of a team on the 1967 program "Newsline," which addressed social and political issues, and during the same year she participated in "Crossfire," a forum debating social questions.

At times as "Dear Charlotte," she was transformed into a rather unlikely Ann Landers, with a doting female public seeking advice about children's behaviour, marital problems, and the role of women. The show ran for fifteen minutes five days a week and she appeared well over four hundred times. One can only speculate about what she thought of letters such as "Two Loves in a Mother's Heart" asking her opinion of Dr. Marie Robinson's *The Power of Sexual Surrender* in which a troubled wife questions her sexual fantasies. Whitton, always sexually prudish, would hardly have sympathized, let alone given practical advice or comfort. Likewise, what did she think of a letter from the battered wife of an alcoholic who was about to be evicted from her home and who desperately wrote to Whitton because she seemed so "sympathetic to women's problems"?[11] Such was the price of fame! In 1967, centennial year, she was overwhelmed by a deluge of requests from school children doing projects on "Famous Canadians," wanting her for lectures and interviews, asking for biographical information for school essays, or requesting that questionnaires be filled out. Whitton found this adulation intrusive and even a little ridiculous.

Her television appearances were not without problems; Whitton was no easier to work with just because she was older. For example, an irate Stuart W. Griffiths, the executive vice-president and managing director of CJOH, reprimanded her for refusing to appear three times on "Newsline" for trivial reasons. She had refused to comment on the situation at City Hall or to debate the problem of potholes with Charles Lynch merely because someone else with whom she disagreed was to appear *separately* on the same program! On another occasion, she refused to appear on a program with an advocate for the liberalization of contraceptives. She said that the speaker concerned was actually a champion of abortion—"a gad about tile cat" from Carleton University—and she refused to be subjected to the inevitable "ribald reference" to being a seventy-year-old spinster debating sexual matters with "that tartlett." Impatiently, she replied to Griffiths that she was perceived to be a "supernumerary" to the other panelists (Charles Lynch, Pauline Jewett, Douglas Fisher, George Bain, and Peter Stursberg) insinuating that they appeared more often than she did. Furious at what she thought to be an unreasonable admonition from Griffiths and believing that things were being "set down on a book" and "toted up" against her, she quit the program impulsively, saying that she had plenty of better offers.[12]

Psychologically addicted, Whitton did not easily abandon civic politics. After the initial withdrawal symptoms, she re-entered the 1966 aldermanic elections as a candidate for Capital ward, and for the next five years she again held political office. She had received 3,569 votes against a total of 1,252 for the other three candidates.

Caustically slamming the waste of women-power in public addresses, she pointed out that both Pearson and Diefenbaker had put men in Senate seats vacated by women. Bristling that she was not among the latter group, Whitton never failed to keep an accurate account of female representation in the provincial and federal legislatures.[13] During centennial year, Whitton denounced the distribution of the companions of the Order of Canada and the service medals in the first Canadian honours list, which was published in the summer of 1967. Humiliated at being overlooked, she saw the award of the more general "Centennial Medals" for achievement as a consolation prize. No person deserved the Order of Canada (whose insignia said, "Desiderantes Meliorem Patriam— They Desire a Better Country") more than Whitton. She was shocked not to receive such recognition. However, she received the Companion of Canada at the second investiture, in April 1968.

In 1967 Whitton left the apartment she and Grier had shared for twenty years to move into a charming little house on Renfrew Avenue. The Glebe area of Ottawa, which had always supported Whitton's political ambitions, and the pleasant green park and lawns behind her house were particularly attractive. Leaving Rideau Terrace once again distracted from her memoirs.

Even had she not settled into another home, she left no time for writing or sorting out her materials and papers because city council affairs took up most of her time. She was no more passive than she had been as mayor, and in the fall of 1967 she was summarily ousted from council because of her stand over a lease between the city and the Central Canadian Exhibition Association which she claimed had involved incorrect procedures.

Whitton had instigated court proceedings to quash the resolution on the Lansdowne Park lease, and she was dismissed from council on 23 October, when the Supreme Court upheld the resolution, on the grounds that she had forfeited her right to retain her seat because of implications of *personal* conflict. In "The Undoing of Charlotte," 25 November 1967, the *Citizen* stated that while it was not "enamoured" of the councillor concerned, nevertheless the lease had been "railroaded through council." Moreover, it questioned a law that summarily ejected a councillor because "a law that denies a councillor the right to take such matters to court is against the public interest."[14] Gambling once again on publicity and sympathy and relying on her reputation for honesty, Whitton could have retained her seat by challenging the lease's validity after it had been signed. This would have been the customary but more timid course of action. At seventy-one years of age, Whitton's political shrewdness proved intact; she received an overwhelming majority when a new election was called on 16 December 1967. She was re-elected again in 1969 for Ottawa City and as councillor, Ottawa-Carleton Regional for 1970-72, during which time she sat on the social welfare committee.[15]

Having advised senior citizens that it was time to get off their rocking chairs, Whitton showed how to go about it. The *Montreal Star* of 2 July 1968 noted that "peering round with her jaundiced eye Charlotte Whitton does not like what she sees these days." John Gray, the reporter, observed that "our hardhatted Whitton" still tilted at windmills such as the gross national product, leadership conventions, the new federalists, and medicare. She also deplored the tactics used by those in public relations. Having benefitted so greatly from public relations in her own political career, this last windmill is all the more remarkable. Before the Montreal Kiwanis, she called P-R promoters "the prostitutes of the people" accusing them of using "more cosmetics than cosmeticians;" they were the "putters-over" who made "rape seem like rapture." While never misunderstanding their function, neither had Whitton ever deceived herself that they were anything other than Professor Gordon's "spurious coin."[16]

With the "jaundiced" eye of an aging Jeremiah, she pessimistically told the congregation of St. Paul's Cathedral, London, Ontario, that "the evil and licentiousness" of the contemporary world could be compared with Rome before its decline, sentiments she repeated in the commencement exercises of Alberta College. Asserting that a rejuvenation of "character building" would counteract the disintegration that was threatening western civilization, she lamented the "decay of democracy."[17]

Nevertheless, she was not certain in the late 1960s that women were any more interested in political partnership than they had previously been. She criticized the stereotyping of women on television, saying it would effectively militate against improving their social role despite the changes over the last sixty years—where there had once been about ten categories of jobs for women, now there were 1,400 classifications. Before the 60th anniversary banquet of the Women's Canadian Club of Toronto, she summarized the "Happy Canadian Woman—Television Style": she is expected to be "a competent housewife with the cleanest wash in town, be sexy twenty-four hours a day, wear a mini frill and be able to make a good cup of coffee. All this in colour too!"[18]

There was, however, one final crusade awaiting Whitton. In keeping with a pattern in which social concerns emerged from the immediacy of her own life, it is not surprising that the topic was aging. She berated what she called "the youth binge." In speeches and articles with catchy titles—"Rear View Mirror"; "Changing Gears for Changing Routes in a Changing Past"; "What's Past is Prologue"; and "Gerontology, Geriatrics and the Golden Age," she was as arresting and as alert as ever. Such addresses were representative of Whitton's latest and last discharge.[19]

In arguing for "oldster power," Whitton anticipated much of the social concern expressed today in a manner not unlike the way she had anticipated "women power" in the forties. She kept press clippings that quoted Dr. Stanley Goldstein, Ottawa's first psychiatrist in geriatrics, who said that old age was commonly a period of loss and disengagement from life in contrast to the stability and productivity of middle age. He claimed a continuing sense of social usefulness was essential in order to prevent alienation and wastefulness among the aged. For some, retirement represented a new freedom, but for many others it represented "the end." These were Whitton's sentiments exactly. In short, Whitton became one of Canada's original "grey panthers."

Before the Toronto Gerontological Society, she argued that new ways of meeting the challenge of "senescence" must be studied now that more people were living longer and the birth rate was declining. Most spent a longer time in senescence than in earlier life stages, and the population was best represented by "an inverse triangle [with] millions of elderly people at the top and too few young people at the bottom."[20]

The *Chatelaine* article, "It's Time to Get Off the Youth Kick," in February 1970 is the best example of her interests in the last active years of her life. Quoting from 1966 figures of the Dominion Bureau of Statistics and from the findings of the Croll Senate Committee on Aging, she pointed out that of 21 million Canadians, 49 per cent were under 25.

> So with that, most of the general public at once envision a young, vigorous, vibrant Canada, just bursting with singing, running, laughing, dancing, jittering, swimming or snowmobiling youth and girls, young men and

maidens—the idol of the youth cult. The people and governments bow low in adulation before youth. And youth is heaven.

The antithesis to this cult was a contempt for maturity and age despite the fact that they were still a majority:

> The adult and mature (aged 25 to 64; 8,950,000) form the keystone in the arch of the structure of the nation, about 43 percent of the entire population. Overwhelmingly they are the producers and sustainers of the nation. Yet they "go youth" lest they themselves be considered to be slipping into middle age and older, both of which they are, or are destined to be.

> . . . The oldsters (65 years of age and up; 1,600,000) form the other 8 percent.

> Of them, I am one, and I dub us the AAA (Angry and Anxiously Aging). . . . The oldsters, the sixty-fives and up, have each racked up proof of *performance* for some forty years in this land, as against only the *promise* of youth for the forty years to come.

> . . . In this oldster power, a "woman's power" bloc is emerging, simply by survival. Canadian women are out distancing men in their life span by about nine years.

The article objected to stereotypes about the aged, age discrimination in the workplace, the ridiculing of old people in popular television comedies such as *The Carol Burnett Show* and *Laugh-In*, and the neglect of serious research on this age group compared to that devoted to children and youth, despite the predictions of increasing numbers of the aged.

With her usual acuity she pinpointed aging as a woman's problem rather than a man's. Single earning women accumulated less over a working lifetime because they had lower wages and fewer opportunities for advancement, because they took more family responsibilities for dependents than males (usually aged adults, who do not "grow out" of dependency as do offspring), and because the majority of single earning women never married or only married once whereas widowers proportionately remarried more. As astute as the article was, its omissions were significant. In keeping with her feminist concerns regarding the single woman, she failed to address the issue of poverty as a broader female issue in light of the numbers of widowed housewives who could barely make ends meet. If there was another more general problem common to both sexes, it was that they feared the great shadow of "not mattering any more." She observed, "The oldster wants to be regarded and respected as a *person*, to life's end, or at least, to the close of his or her own sane awareness of the living of that life."

The article concluded with recommendations: modern and humanized units for oldsters integrated into the local community at moderate rents; a central registry keeping in touch with their needs; a home-nursing service on a part-time hourly or daily basis as a social utility; meals-on-wheels; drop-in and social centres; family boarding homes, and *small* group homes on a foster care basis. (She insisted that old people no more wanted to live in congregate conditions than did any other age group, and nursing homes were anathema to her for they reminded her of "oldster farms" similar to the baby farms she had fought to eradicate decades before.)

Reminding her readers that this interest was not recent (as indeed her *Dawn of Ampler Life* testifies) or entirely self-centred, she concluded:

> Some thirty years ago, in the full lustihead of my own middle age, I was speaker at the tenth birthday of Bronson Memorial, a residence for older women, of which the Baroness (then Mrs. John A.) Macdonald had been one of the founders in the pre-Confederation year of 1864. What I said was as valid then and today as it was when "the Bronson" was founded more than a century ago.
>
> "There is no field of social work which so calls for understanding, for patience, for kindness, for imagination, as the humane care of the aged. The aged require consideration. They are often unreasoning, bewildered and confused. In many cases, they require much physical care and there is not the stimulating interest and appeal of the infant or small child. . . ."
>
> "The nation that ceases to care for its young as a definite community responsibility shortly loses its strength, but the nation which abandons consideration and care for its aged and broken loses its soul."

Meanwhile, Prime Minister Pierre Trudeau's deliberate appeal to youth continued to appall her; so much so that when actress Barbara Streisand visited him on Parliament Hill, she noted that she was "not accustomed to vaudeville on the hill." Deploring "Trudeau-trendiness," she said it favoured youth at the expense of older people and that nowhere was this prejudice more apparent than in government monies for seniors and youth. She spoke against the "free honorariums" granted to students and the Company of Young Canadians who received subsistence allowances between $200 to $225 a month "with an extra $100 for someone described as a wife." Before the Halifax Canadian Club, she insisted that "Youth Must Earn the Right to Do their Own Thing," that they must learn to dignify again a four letter word since vanished from the English language—"DUTY." When it was jokingly suggested that she might head the CYC, she responded by snorting contemptuously that she "wouldn't be a party to a fake." Those CYC paid workers who called themselves "volunteers" were a disgrace, and the CYC itself was a patent example of political patronage representing the "easiest hand-out if you [knew] the right people." As for American "draft dodgers" in Canada, Whitton's views were predictable. "Their consciences," she said, "disallow them to fight but not to enter another country illegally."[21]

Two years later, she was suggesting that society was heading for a "sexagenarian matriarchy." Because women generally outlived men, she appealed once again to "woman power." A keen observer of female political trends she never failed to point out the apathy of the political parties towards women, but neither did she fail to remind women of their reluctance to participate in the rough and tumble of the political arena. She was disgusted that in the 1972 federal elections only five women had gained seats. The *Ottawa Citizen*, 3 October 1972, agreed that "it was hardly a number to strike joy in the hearts of feminists." But her meritocratic views had not altered; she continued to rail against those women's liberationists who suggested a "quota system" or affirmative action. Convinced that privileges and compensatory programs on the grounds of gender were an admission of failure and a new form of injustice, she argued that women could achieve proportionately to men *if* they were prepared to work as hard at achieving, *if* they would cultivate similar ambitions, and *if* they would fight for social justice and equal rights for themselves.[22]

Still an alderwoman in October 1971, Whitton celebrated her twenty-year anniversary in civic politics with an "at Home for a Cup of Tea" held in the foyer of City Hall at 4:30 on the first of the month. She hosted many old friends—campaigners, voters, and admirers—including intimates such as Grace Towers, who had shared Margaret Grier's final hours, and her dear "Mo" from Queen's days.

There was no suggestion that Whitton would be retiring—or even tiring—until late 1972. As she got up from an afternoon nap, she caught her shoe on a rug and fell heavily. She lay helpless with a broken hip for nineteen hours before help came. In the next few years she spent periods in the Porter Island Lodge Home for the Aged struggling in vain to regain her strength and her former mobility. Unable to get around, unable to write even because her hands had become so muscle bound from the pressure and manipulation required for her crutches and canes, Whitton's last years were frustrating. For such an active, volubile, and visibile woman, her fate was intolerable. It is difficult to underestimate how much she suffered during these years—less physically than from a mounting and debilitating rage that such a stroke of bad luck had deprived her of that precious social meaning she had fought for all her life.

One important interruption to the now doleful course of her life was the official naming of the Council Chamber on Green Island "Whitton Hall," on 31 May 1973. After almost "300 days of navigation" on crutches and canes and with a remarkable, but typical, feat of will and determination, she managed to attend the ceremony. She was inspired by a flood of telegrams including those from the Queen Mother, Roland Michener, Pierre Trudeau, and Grace McInnis, and she was deeply moved by one that read, "and deep affection from three friends who have watched with pride and love the splendour of your career"—Mo, Gwen, and Jessie from her Queen's days. At seventy-seven, still "with a child's rebellious face and mischievous smile," she made her last public address, a sad speech in many ways, with a muted tenor of reproach mingled with a sardonic humour. She compared the aging faces around her with the "young Turks" now sitting on the board of control and headed by a mayor who was only thirty-four. She was now on "the wrong side of the generation gap." Within nineteen months, Charlotte Whitton passed over the final gap.

Her death was as quiet as her life had been noisy. In the darkest hours of the winter of 1975, at 3:30 A.M. on 25 January, after twenty-four days in Civic Hospital following a heart attack, she passed away. However, in keeping with her reputation as a woman "larger than life" the events that followed were not quite so unspectacular.

Whitton had set aside her own fund for a civic funeral, but probably she would have been the first mayor of Ottawa to be accorded this honour without such financial guarantees. Her body lay in state at Whitton Hall, her hands folded over her cherished and well-used Book of Common Prayer, opened at the pages of "The Order for the Burial of the Dead":

> My heart was hot within me, and while I was thus musing the fire kindled; and at last I spake with my tongue. . . . Behold, thou hast made my days as it were a span long; and mine age is even as nothing in respect of thee; and verily every man living is altogether vanity.

Buried at Renfrew in the space she had kept beside her friend Margaret, together in death after almost thirty years apart, the words she had kept close to her heart all these years were added to those already worn on the sombre grey celtic cross. The words memorializing Rose Margaret Grier, "beloved daughter of Robert and Rose Grier" were followed by:

> *and dear friend to*
> *Charlotte Whitton*
> *1896-1975.*

Epilogue

THE AMBIGUOUS FEMINIST

"There are two categories of women. Those who are women and those who are men's wives."

WHITTON, 1957.

The impressive body of feminist thought left by Whitton is by far her most important contribution to Canadian national life. While Whitton's views on abortion, marriage, sexuality, and female "deviance" do not fit well with today's feminist discourse, she had strong views on the single woman, female occupations, equal pay, and access to the political domain, and contemporary Canadian women identified her as a role model, so in her own mind there was no ambiguity in her criticism of a male-dominated ethos which placed severe strictures on women's full participation in Canada's social and political life. For example, could anyone *doubt* that the author of the following paraphrase of Marx was not a feminist?

> Women of the world unite; you have nothing to lose but your shackles, those of your own and your sister Woman's no less, no less than man's forging.[1]

And could anyone doubt that a woman who saw the telephone and automobile as technological innovations which advanced the cause of women's liberation was a feminist? She argued that the telephone allowed women at home to organize meetings, networks, and communications in a manner not previously possible and that the automobile "for the manless woman" permitted her to be mobile and not dependent on an escort for safe passage "in the strange ways at unearthly hours."[2]

There is, however, alongside Whitton's unambiguous public utterances a private ambivalence towards her own sex which at times coloured her feminist thought. To understand these ambiguities, even contradictions, is to grasp her commitment to two matters: the ascetic ideal which inspired her sense of public service; and those views of women's concerns which justified the objective conditions within which such public service would be realized. These two aspects of the feminism had emerged during the critical years when she chose the celibate life over marriage and motherhood.

Whitton and many of her contemporaries were committed to the "Cult of Blessed Singleness." She believed that chastity was also power; that the choice of celibacy invested women's lives with a unique vocational meaning which enabled them to express female virtues and attributes through womanly service. Celibacy provided women with personal power in their own lives, opened up choices and opportunities for mobility otherwise denied them, and fueled ambitions which would have been constrained by marriage. This celebration of celibacy was formulated in principles of self denial, sacrifice, and public responsibility. Beatrice Webb, the British Fabian socialist, had asserted, "It will be needful for women with strong natures to remain celibate; so that the special force of womanhood—motherly feeling—may be forced into public work."[3]

Two novels, *The Bostonians* (1886) by Henry James and *The Odd Women* (1893) by George Gissing, fictionalize this commitment to the ascetic ideal. Olive Chancellor in *The Bostonians*, demanding nothing less of her women friends than that they "renounce, refrain, abstain," observed,

> You know what I think—that there is something noble done when one makes a sacrifice for a great good—Priests—when they are real priests—never married, and what you and I dream of doing demands of us a kind of priesthood.[4]

Likewise, Rhoda Nunn, the Gissing heroine declared:

> There will have to be a widespread revolt against the sexual instinct. Christianity couldn't spread over the world without the help of the ascetic ideal, and this great movement for woman's emancipation must also have its ascetics.[5]

It is in the above context that we can place Whitton's thoughts. During the inaugural address in the Susan B. Anthony lectures delivered at the University of Rochester in 1947, she asserted:

> Woman's natural sphere is home and motherhood . . . and natural too is consecration to celibacy in the service of mankind . . . and upon all women, but upon the 'secular unmarried' especially, rests responsibility for leadership and education of women for public life.[6]

She also observed:

> How often the way of woman's escape and protestation of freedom, has
> been by cultivation of the one qualification which she alone can utilize or
> with-hold.[7]

The celibate life for women of Whitton's time and temperament was, as she
asserted, a potent means by which "women could most effectively protest where
they alarm men most." In choosing to withhold her sexuality from men, she
chose autonomy rather than dependence.

Recent feminist scholarship has analyzed female celibacy with acuity and
sympathy. In "Liberty, Sorority and Misogny" (1983), Jane Marcus interprets
Virginia Woolf's *A Room of One's Own* (a book Whitton admired) not only in
emancipatory and economic terms but also as a metaphor for chastity as
survival, a means of "producing female culture," or as observed elsewhere, "of
providing a creative space for women."[8] For Whitton, celibacy was not passive
and repressive; it was the source of creative energy that enabled her to be
productive and independent.

Believing that "by submitting, through the son of God, to incarnation, Christ
lifted womanhood and chastity to veneration," Whitton frequently confused
metaphysics with morality.[9] Connecting chastity with power in a personal sense,
she argued for the sublimation of Eros in the exercise of power over the
passions and thus the power to exercise free will intelligently. Celibacy could
produce the finest artifacts of society, the greatest achievements of humanity,
and the most inspired and potent female leadership. She had expressed this
belief as early as 1920 when she wrote that the "regulation and control of
instinct and emotion" was the basis for civilization and the "whole principle of
education" was to train individuals in this principle.[10]

Because she saw her own life as an exercise in the realization of such
strenuous principles, a demonstration that the sexual instinct could be channelled into socially useful and creative work, she advocated a moral matrix that
emphasized sacrifice and self-denial.

> for women know there is no strength without sacrifice, no purchase without
> price and that growth comes no less in the denials than in the satisfactions
> of life.[11]

And elsewhere she emphasized the "balance" that must be made between
freedom and social responsibility:

> This involves the complete rejection of the pagan concept of romantic love
> for its own satisfaction and implications of so-called sex freedom. The man

or woman who asks complete freedom of will and life in the most important of the race's relations cannot, in the next breath, ask to share in the protection of social responsibilities which he or she sets at naught. Such a disregard of Self-within-Society, reveals itself as springing from a complete unbalance, a concentration on the individual to the exclusion of any other responsibility, a denial of the fulfillment of the spiritual in a satisfaction of the material.[12]

Her emphasis on the relationship between creativity and morality increased during the 1940s. In "Intelligent Maternity: Responsible Paternity," an address given to the Cleveland Maternal Health Association in 1945, she observed:

The fulfillment of the relation of the sexes cannot be regarded as a spasmodic romantic incident that is the consummation of passion of a pagan philosophy, but a complete merging and dedication of strength and life in purpose and dedication to the creation, care, and nurture, of new life physically, in which the eternal ongoing spiritual life of the race will be embodied and transmitted.[13]

She agreed with the British Council of Churches on the use of birth control within the confines of martial fidelity, but Whitton regarded the modern emphasis of personality over character and psychology over sinfulness sceptically. She remained remarkably free of Freudian perceptions all her life, preferring to rely on "the power of the holy spirit to psychiatry."

Gland treatment or psychological analyses are by no means a sufficient answer to those situations in which our forebears would have gone to their confessor for striving and direction . . . but it is the sexual theatre, so to say, that personal life finds or loses its integrity.[14]

In her acceptance of the Montreal "Maker of Queen's" Medal, which recognized her work as a trustee of the university, she passionately declaimed that "surely we are not brute creatures of creature satisfactions solely?"[15] And she never ceased railing against what she perceived as return to "pagan materialism" evident in obsessive birth control measures, divorce rates, sexual indulgence, companionate marriage, and women leaving their "traditional tasks."[16] Abstinence and celibacy had become for Whitton the perfect prophylactics; and her tendency to punitive moralizing is best understood in light of her sense of vocation.

A comment made by Whitton in mid-life provides a clue to her decision to turn her back on marriage. She noted that women, withdrawn from gainful occupation in an industrialized society and increasingly confined to the domestic sphere, had become "an isolated reproductive organ," powerless and without identity, except through another.[17] A consistent part of Whitton's personality, which emerged in various forms throughout her life, was a deep-seated fear of anonymity.

Because women were sought and "feared, and revered by the male of the species," they had another source of power.

> She is sought because of her necessary complement to him if the race is to go on; she is feared because of the forces which passion can produce, of the power over a man's thought and life which a woman arousing it can exercise (and perhaps even maintain) and because of the unmanning and destruction of man and men, which her irresponsible or unprincipled exploitation of this power can bring.[18]

If female sexuality had power whether it was exploited or withheld, Whitton also attributed considerable power to evidences of independent female sexuality that suggested a superiority to men. One of her favourite biological metaphors was that of the Queen Bee, who "just soars beyond all experimentation and mates, on high, with any drone who has the strength and temerity to reach the same heights of her own rare life and soaring." Repeatedly, she used the analogy of the "Bonellia and the Barnacles," proferred as a warning about the masculinization of women and the psychological castration of men,

> which quite confuse man and science. The Bonellia swims about freely and has a bright life wandering all over the sea. She is large and comfortable and rotund and happy. She lives a free and easy life and scatters her eggs about in the ocean, where they float away. Those which remain free of life become females; the others, small, microscopic pigmy males are useless until they meet up with a female who promptly swallows them. Then they simply slide down as part of her food and are absorbed in the fertilizing tract; live and are fed only as long as they are necessary for the perpetuation of the species. Then they are sloughed off into nothingness. Darwin doesn't even call them males, just 'complemental males.'

No wonder there is consternation among men, and "marrying women"—who are not necessarily at all the same thing as married woman—at the twentieth century's dynamic explosion of the most prodigious myth of modern times, Rousseau's, 'We [men] could subsist better without them than they without us,' when science and fact now roll up their evidence that it is the other way around.[19]

This duality of male and female nature was, of course, profoundly conservative in nature. Elsewhere, Whitton noted that women, because of "biological fact," were more responsible and more sensitive than men; they had an innate sense of conscience and did not want "to duplicate, destroy or replace old structures." Were they to gain civic office, for which their fine sense of detail, planning ability, and "broader and deeper sense of moral values" eminently suited them, they would not revolutionize but "spring clean" in the "old household way." As mayor, she called her economies "good housekeeping" and claim that she was more successful than her male predecessors because she "never knew a man who could shop or handle leftovers."[20] After all, female realism and direct dealing were instinctive: women "faced facts as frankly as the preparation of a meal or the bearing of a child." Their talent for executive detail, however, helped perpetuate their subordination. Men were ready to exploit a skill that was "too easily purchased, like her virtue, for a pretty trinket, a passing courtesy, a temporary alliance during the election campaign, but without the entanglement and obligation of a continuing partnership." Because Whitton valued feminine qualities, she hastened to assert that women must not "act like a man, but a woman . . . and do a man's work as well," She found it deplorable, for instance, that middle-class, college-educated women who were "masculinized" failed to reproduce and "imitat[ed] the rooster because his life was so good." "She suddenly refused to sit on the nest; started to grow a comb, began to crow, developed all the characteristics of a rooster, and took over the barnyard." Contemptuous of "sexual indulgence," Whitton viewed the declining birth rate among educated woman as degeneration into "companionate marriage," a rather curious observation given her own choice not to marry or reproduce at all![21]

The ascetic ideal itself was founded on other premises which justified the choice of career over motherhood. They had also been articulated by Whitton when she was young, and her belief in them did not diminish over time. Between the Toronto years and the 1950s Whitton reaffirmed her commitment to assumptions which explained female interest in the "nurturing" professions as a non-conformist choice to express nurturant tendencies outside of marriage and motherhood. In short, she believed that women's greatest contribution lay in the fact that they were *different* from men. The "womanly women" of Levana had transformed into "the new power, the untried power," she wanted to see activated in the political forum. During her 1950 campaign for controller, Whitton made the well-publicized remark that

> The greatest single argument for women's participation in government is that we *are* different from men. The nation that fails to enlist the magnificent resources of its women is flying on one wing and bound for a crash landing.[22]

This ideal insists that women are qualitatively and positively different from men (which is not the same as arguing that women have had a qualitatively different experience from men) and that such highly valued characteristics must be maximized and politicized. In this instance, Whitton's feminism is remarkably similar to contemporary feminist thought. As an ideological position its intellectual roots can be traced, at least, to the nineteenth century; and it has been equally influential in its negative aspects in "the cult of true womanhood."

Whitton never relinquished the view that women are more nurturing, moral, humanistic, sensitive, peaceloving, and intuitive than men. Along with these innate characteristics, women also possess positive qualities commonly associated with the men such as ambition, rationality, assertiveness, and organizational skill. In short, that women are actually superior to men, and women's sensibilities made them more suited for vocational and service-oriented work. Moreover, they had a humanitarian role in public life should they elect a political route. Reporting in September 1951 that "Charlotte Whitton Urges Public Life Partnership" between the sexes, the Ottawa *Citizen* reaffirmed her views:

> Women have a finer sensitivity for ethical and moral values. Often then can draw to male attention something not previously expressed. No level of politics is unworthy of women, but the municipal field is one in which there are no interests foreign to them.[23]

The Dawn of Ampler Life had already described how a community could tap the wasted talents of home-bound women. It extends "woman's work" to include active involvement in the municipal government, volunteer associations, and "social utilities." It redefined a social organization that had failed to realize "the gathering momentum of these changes in occupational status, the economic power, the social setting, outlook and attitude of women."[24]

Believing strongly that motherhood had been sanctified by Christ's submission to the Incarnation, Whitton also accepted that woman's primary function was "the revivification through the family of the human race."[25] Although marriage and motherhood were the clear vocation of the majority of women, Whitton argued that the helping professions were equally important. "One will find it [vocation] in the merging of her life in another life; the other in the sense of vocational dedication to the ongoing life of society as a whole." Before the YWCA conference on postwar problems in October 1943, in an address on "Women and the Future of Family Life," she affirmed the women's special vocation for childrearing.

> The average woman finds satisfaction and fulfilment in home planning, family care and management, especially if educational and comparable

opportunity open the way to advancement, both for the income earning members of her family in their occupations, and the youngsters in their education and training.

And she related this to her commitment to family life as the linchpin of a stable society.

Therefore, I personally believe that the vista we should seek to travel should contemplate the continuance of the family home as its central factor, and, if need be, the recasting of the fiscal and legal structure of the state to assure that end.[26]

Because of this belief in motherhood (expressed in the baby bonus debate and elaborated in *The Dawn of Ampler Life*), she insisted that the state should guarantee mothers the means by which they could remain home and rear their young.

She firmly believed that if the special attributes of woman's nature—Beatrice Webb's "motherly feeling=were not expressed in marriage and motherhood, they could be equally well satisfied in vocational and service-oriented tasks. The mother principle inspired a yearning to "succour, comfort and create" so that women tended towards the "more humanistic needs" of society such as social welfare, hospitals, nursing, teaching, child care, and community and recreational programs.[27] Because increasing numbers of women were preferring to remain unmarried, Whitton argued that they "should be regarded as capable of finding a vocation in secular roles no less than religious life."

Accepting then the freedom of the woman's spirit and will to order her own life, in growth and social responsibility, there can be no question of the equality of her rights and treatment in all the spheres of social relations. This must imply her freedom of choice in the vocation and dedication of her life . . . generally, each soul, being an individual personality, will seek its fullest growth in its own realization. One will find it in the merging of her life in another life: the other in the sense of vocational dedication to the ongoing life of the society as a whole.[28]

In a 1943 address, Whitton affirmed her belief in the vocational aspects of woman's work at home and in the work place. Observing that since the Great War the unmarried career woman had been feared by men as a "horrid spectre of a warped and wanton womanhood," she insisted that it had been this generation especially whose "sense of usefulness and achievement that instinctively characterized the good mother" that was in all respects vocational. Again, during an address which commemorated the Hamilton child care worker and civic politician Nora Frances Henderson, she insisted that women like Henderson had "served not one family but thousands of families." One of her associates, herself a social worker, wrote to Whitton acknowledging that such women had "married into social work." Even the misogynist St. Paul, she said, had anticipated this purpose for women when he said "for the desolate hath many more children than she which hath a husband."[29]

Woman's role in the world was therefore enlarged by professional service that added to the traditional female vocations.[30] A single woman no longer had to be the "spinster of the parish," whose lack of independence represented a "hateful reliance upon tolerating relatives and friends."[31] This new status was in line with the ancient cults of goddesses such as Ishtar, Cybele, and Isis and a "natural projection of mediaeval monasticism"—a continuity of the living and the dead.

> All in all, the unmarried woman has adjusted herself to social change and found her footing in the shifting sands more successfully than most of her married sisters. But then the dislocation of her place in society came earlier, and, hers was a drab dependency through many long years of the self-contained home life which had no place for her. For the Reformation and the destruction of monasticism shattered the satisfying vocation of woman who had sought the purpose of life in spiritual seclusion. In the early and mediaeval Christian state, Europe had probably relatively quite as many able and responsible "unmarried women in gainful occupation" as any modern state for the great abbesses and their assistants were women of power who often attended on Parliament, and the Courts.[32]

Such ascetic ideals, which shaped her views of family life as well as her own jealously guarded sense of *vocation*, help explain Whitton's attitudes towards perceived sexual deviance and her condemnation of middle class married women who entered or remained in the work place after the Second World War.[33]

Her disapproval of working married women (to be understood as "mothers") unless they were acting under economic compulsion (widows, the deserted, and working class women) can be seen in comments made well after similar ones in *The Dawn of Ampler Life*, the baby bonus debates, and mothers' allowance briefs. The following opinions, which typify her concerns, were expressed between 1944 and 1967.[34] In a CBC broadcast from Vancouver, "The Remobilization of Our Woman Power," she noted

> 'Demobilize' and 'religion' are words carefully chosen because the shaken foundations of this nation's life cannot be repaired, its structure set upon

security, until and unless its women folk are remobilized to the primary responsibility of assuring that home life remains stable and strong. This is not to argue that women are to be either coerced or cajoled back into the home. It is to realize that this Canada cannot survive and reach full stature unless the home life of 2½ million households is set firm upon the rock of women's sense of devotion, sacrifice and responsibility.

And she made many other pithy remarks in the same vein:

'A woman has to choose. No woman's job and no woman's home can be balanced or subdivided. One or the other is short-changed.'

'The women who are enemies of women are those who marry, definitely planning to make wifehood and motherhood subordinate if not indeed incidental to their jobs or their jobs to their home and family life.'

'Yet the definite trend today is towards this type of woman whose career is the major motivating power of her life, who desires marriage as a satisfying attribute to her living, and accepts motherhood, incidental thereto, providing it occurs not too frequently nor too inconveniently.'

'No woman can hold a fulltime job without risking the home and husband, to another woman.'

The confrontational tenor suggests deep-seated anxiety. To a group of pre-dominantly single women of the Ottawa Dietetics Association in 1947, from whom she expected a sympathetic response, Whitton said:

Are the management of the household, the bearing and rearing of children to become incidental to the pursuit of gainful occupation outside of the family? If so, who are to staff the 'mothering' services, the clinics, the pre-school centres, the communal dining rooms, the play centres, the guidance centres? Will other women agree to do so for reward in service or in payment for other women's children or will they not rebel and refuse to be baby and child minders, home and husband 'tenders' and not demand that they too shall have both men and work.[35]

Calling home helpers "rescue squads for the Canadian home and family" who take over the country's work and children so that wives did not have "to stay therein," she continued that there had occurred a "crisis of distinction" among women themselves.

Shall we not have to face the fact that the woman who chooses wifehood and motherhood therewith assumes a status by her obligations, if accepted and discharged, that binds her in a different category from the man in gainful occupation or the woman who lives on her own? Will women not have to face the implications of their own choice of their own way of life? If a woman chooses to play her part in this most essential role of all a nation's building, the founding and nurturing of a home and a family, must she not stay with her bargain? And must society not make it possible for her to do so? And must not other women who believe their life will find its fullest happiness in service to the ongoing tide of the nation's life, as a whole, also have to play the game and pledge themselves decently and honestly to abide by their decision?

Surely it is not an impossible nor impractical challenge for women to answer for women know there is no strength without sacrifice, no purchase without price, and that growth comes no less in the denials than in the satisfactions of life? It is a time for cutting through to simple truths and honest facts in our day to day living; it is a time for each of us to serve well and truly at that post to which life and our choice have led.[36]

Whitton wanted to keep the dichotomy between marriage and the single vocation. She regarded married women who entered the nurturing professions as intruders. "You have to choose," she insisted when she spoke before the Wives of the Canadian Dental Association, "choose within your own capacity and with responsible regard to other citizens. God makes men and women free to make their choice and like it."[37] At times she cynically paraphrased Virginia Woolf's dictum that twentieth-century woman not only wanted "a room of her own" but now also wanted to "have her man and eat him too."[38]

Were there any objective reasons for Whitton—and presumably the single women she represented—to be anxious? To be fair, there were. The Second World War had seen a massive mobilization of women in agriculture, industry, and the armed forces, and Whitton found herself in the anomalous position of all pioneers, threatened by the second wave. Although she recognized that working wives were not merely a wartime phenomenon and that most women, particularly of the working class, were leaving the home "only to save it" because they had to purchase goods and services formerly produced at home, she nursed a deep suspicion of the middle-class contingent.[39] She also knew that many wives felt "walled off, idle and underworked" in the modern urban home "from which a mechanized age has taken nearly all the satisfying processes of homemaking and transferred them to assembly line settings. . . . The replacement of 'women's work' and interests by products and services purchased outside the home creates a dual problem."[40] Working women were not escaping marriage and home as much as they were "searching for satisfying use for the talents and training they possess, escaping the sense of waste, of frustration and futility that so breed unhappiness where there is idleness and underuse of endowment or skills."[41]

The role of women had changed considerably since Whitton left Queen's. Her world had become more threatening, divided now between female competitors in the workplace. The rivalry was between married aspirants to careers formerly monopolized by single women and single women who were losing ground in changing social and economic conditions. And single women's resentment was spurred by such observations as the following, made in a report of the Advisory Committee on Reconstruction on "Post War Problems of Women" in November 1943. The report, issued by a ten-woman subcommittee of whom eight were married, surveyed women in gainful occupation. It demonstrated a remarkable insensitivity to 876,000 single women in a comment that answered protestations about the married middle class woman's "right" to work.

> She is a better worker than the single woman in the sense that she has greater steadiness, resourcefulness and more sense of responsibility; this, in spite of the fact that the average married woman's absenteeism may be somewhat higher due to home emergencies.[42]

The report pointed out that the single woman's employment dropped rapidly after the age of forty and that she was more insecure about her future than men in general or married women. Those conclusions and the self-evident nature of the comments about comparative security must have been galling to Whitton, already resentful that she had not been asked to contribute to the committee by Dr. Leonard Marsh, who was the research adviser. They must have also annoyed all those other single women who had pioneered in the work force earlier in the century and proven themselves steady, resourceful, and responsible while opening careers for married women. While the report's tenor cast a stereotypical stigma on single women, available figures show that married women were becoming increasingly important in the work force.

Whitton's perception regarding the relative labour force participation of single and married women is borne out by census data for 1941, 1951, and 1961. In 1941, the female labour force was 79.9 per cent single, 12.8 per cent married, and 7.3 per cent widowed or divorced. The corresponding figures for 1951 were 62.1, 30, and 7.9; and for 1961, 42.3, 49.8, and 8. The married women's participation in "professional and technical occupations" is even more striking. In 1941, 92 per cent were single and only 5.4 per cent married and 2.5 per cent widowed or divorced. The corresponding figures for 1951 were 76.9, 19.1, and 4, and for 1961, 57.6, 37.4, and 5. In brief, in twenty years single female participation in the labour force had declined by 47 per cent and married participation had increased 3.9 times. The changes in professional and technical occupations for the same two decades show a decline of 37 per cent in single participation and a 6.9 times increase in married participation.[43]

Whitton believed that many a middle-class married woman wanted "her man, her family, her full-time holidays and her pay cheque too, while demanding services from other women."[44] This theme pervades much of her feminist critique. These "other women," who provided the substitutes for child care and other domestic duties, were presumed to be "of less essential value to the community which must not be deprived of her own intellectual, social or technical contribution." As Whitton pointed out, some women were shifting part of their jobs onto females of lesser social status. Visiting homemakers, child minders, pre-school caretakers, housekeepers, daily or weekly helps, mothers or mothers-in-law were contributing to a new gender-based subservient class. Impatient with middle-class complaints, endemic in new world societies, that satisfactory and plentiful domestic help was not to be found, she observed caustically, "In my own judgement, there isn't much hope of any widely effective answer for the simple reason that the woman who is seeking it is really looking for some other woman to do the household work which she does not wish to do herself."[45]

The most glaring inequity was that these "other women" were frequently the poorest, most disadvantaged, and the most burdened in society, often responsible for their own children, husbands, and homes. The "laden mothers" required to manage without such help or who could ill afford services were from low-income and rural groups, unable to compete with wealthier and more educated women who preferred "to be relieved of housework for congenial and profitable occupation." Apart from economic injustices, such arrangements perpetuated an odious socio-psychological environment of "the subservience of one woman worker constantly to another, if not to several others, males and females of all ages and temperaments, within the family group, and the absence of 'any right of appeal' from criticism or exploitation."[46] She offered as a solution an "order" of household helpers organized on lines similar to those of the Victorian Order of Nurses, with "a buffer element of impartial management as an equalizing agent." Uniforms and transportation would be useful so that helpers could take pride in being part of a professional service. With the organization and not the householder signing the paycheque, the householder would get a service, not a servant. Whitton would not oppose competition by private companies for those who could afford them, a circumstance that might erode the predominance of a gender-based labour pool.[47] There is a consistency between these views and those on "social utilities" in her *Dawn of Ampler Life* since such a service would function as a utility. Of course, Whitton's critique is just as applicable today.

What explains the churlish tone of some of these statements? Certainly Whitton perceived the entry of married women into the labour force as an incursion into her domain—one which threatened her sense of vocation. She had given up much for her career, and she resented those women whom she felt had not denied themselves. But she did not dare estrange them by public statements, for they would form her constituency if she entered politics. Given her strong identification with her own sex, hers was a painful predicament. Without vocational justification, the unmarried minority, who were already marginalized, were destined to become further so. How could she wear her celibacy proudly and proclaim that it had permitted her to make a *unique* contribution to national life if married women began to share in this contribution?

Whitton's generation was convinced that suppressing the sexual instincts and relinquishing marriage and motherhood were necessary in order to promote the greater cause of female emancipation. Career and vocation were one. But in Whitton's case, such sublimation had grave psychological and emotional costs, making her intolerant of those women of a later generation who saw the possibility of combining marriage with a career. The brilliant and perceptive 1950 essay "Women: A Necessary Evil" confronts her ambivalence about middle-class married women who worked.[48] These women were "enemies" of single women because they represented a marital hegemony in society which already favoured the married. They were "husbands' wives" or women "of the marrying mind," and they were now undermining the vocational leadership of the "secular unmarried."

Whitton insisted that it was the fear of other women which impeded women's progress and left the single woman isolated.

> Now men and women are working together again; they are rediscovering, re-aligning in a partnership with a profound change—the women who work with the men are not, ordinarily or widely, the women of their own families for work is indeed far, and all the time, getting farther from the home. To this, the greater number of women are adjusting, but a very large number are not; and they it is, even more than men, the husbands' wives and the women of "marrying mind" who are the most potent single force in maintaining discrimination against the new element of social stratum in organized society, to which the Pope gave the category "the secular unmarried" in his epochal announcement to the catholic Women's League of Italy in 1947. His Holiness, at that time, re-affirmed woman's natural spheres of consecration to the service of the home, and consecration to the service of mankind. But, in the evolution of social change and the casualties of recurrent wars, he recognized a third enlarging area of women's work and service "outside the family on one hand and the life of the religious on the other." The "secular unmarried" he described as fitted particularly for the

duties and leadership of women, and for "direct action indispensable in social and political activity" and "in the use of the electoral ballot."[49]

If the Pope could fully recognize the single woman, the matter was closed!

Convinced that "the modern married world on the whole, especially its women" resented those "who manage to live without men," Whitton never alluded personally to the contempt to which single women were subjected.[50] Instead, she said that the married resented the childlessness and the freedom of the single, penalizing them through differentials in taxation, inequalities in pay and promotion, and even the baby bonus. Unquestionably, Charlotte Whitton felt marginalized in her unmarried state. That she chiefly expressed such views before groups consisting largely of single women, such as professional and business women's associations, social workers, the Canadian Dietetics Association, and women's colleges, is telling. She was not only expressing her personal frustration; she was also articulating the anxieties that pervaded the ranks of similarly placed career women.

Whitton was like other early feminists who could not reconcile personal sexual liberation with broader female emancipation, and many other single women of her day were also suspicious of those who advocated the combination of marriage and career. Doing so suggested that her denial was insignificant or even irrelevant. She was both fearful and jealous of married women who were moving into careers without any sacrifice. She claimed it was imperative that a "distinction" be maintained between married and unmarried women in the workplace. Married women should not be compelled to work, and society should enable them "to stay with their bargain."

In all this, another paradox is striking. By alluding to the "vexing problem" of married women undercutting remuneration and openings "not only for the woman who must work, but for younger men," Whitton was in the strange position of reiterating typically male views. Although they were stigmatized socially, her generation of professionals identified more with working men, despite discrimination with regard to pay and promotion, than with married women. In the forties, the pool competing in the market was expanding so rapidly that she now found herself vying for both access and credibility with married women as well as all men.

An article on the "fiscal status" of earning women, published early in 1950 in *The Business and Professional Woman*, summarized Whitton's views about these inequities.[51] Before a sympathetic audience, she pointed out that there were 425,000 single female taxpayers and 125,000 married ones. She argued that dual incomes should lead automatically to dual taxation, with married couples considered as *personnes soles*, much as was the case with two men, two women, or an unmarried brother and sister cohabiting over time in "partnership families." If there was only one earner in what she called "dual households," whether a blood relative or not, they should be taxed singly, with the same provision for dependents as was made married couples. She had been struck by the immensity of the problem while considering the numbers of single people who cared for dependent parents, invalid or disabled relatives, or even non-earning friends. Pressure must erase the prejudice that favoured spouses and children as the only generally legitimate dependents. Here is a partial explanation for her protests during the 1940s about *universal* child allowances. She was not against them for low-income families, but she was opposed to them for those whose financial need was far from obvious. Had the allowance scheme been flexible enough to include a generalized "dependents" allowance, Whitton's campaign against "bonussing breeding" might never have been unleashed.

In the same article, Whitton pointed out that single people sometimes bore "heavier mutual financial obligations" than those of marriage or blood-family relationships. Here, she was clearly thinking of her own arrangement with Margaret Grier, with whom she held everything in common and for whom she was responsible, even to hiring household help during her intermittent collapses as well as providing for medical and hospital expenses. Because even insurance premiums were higher for two women than for husband and wife, Whitton found the "presumed heavier family obligations" of marriage offensive and discriminatory. Also discriminatory were the regulations governing inheritance in non-blood partnerships wherein members of partnership families were classed as "casuals," subject to the highest rates of tax. In 1970, Whitton confessed to a personal experience for which she had been totally unprepared when Margaret Grier died in late 1947. She had received a distressed letter from a sixty-eight-year-old woman, living with "a gentlewoman of 82" who had been like "a mother to [her] for over 40 years." This woman had learned about the exorbitant taxes that would become due if her friend's home and capital assets were left to her and not to a blood relative. Whitton replied,

> I have long been exasperated with the inequity of the situation you outline; indeed, I experienced it myself some 23 years ago when my close friend and housemate of thirty years died, and she and I held most things in common. We were each others' beneficiaries but her modest estate was shot to pieces in my inheritance because I was a completely 'outside stranger' downgraded worse than the most outside collateral!

The correspondent had observed glumly that "if one were married to a useless partner, no question would arise, but living with a superior Christian person, loyal, helpful and kind, is given no consideration."[52]

The discrimination went even farther, as, for example, in the distinction between householders and tenants when it came to municipal voting rights. Single professional women, who tended to be boarders or tenants, were thus disenfranchised. The situation affected "many more thousands of gainfully occupied women on their own than men," since, with their lower salaries, women were more likely to remain in the family home, often caring for elderly parents.[53] Since there is considerable evidence that single women did suffer economic and social discrimination, Whitton's increasing sense of marginality cannot entirely be attributed to "paranoia."

Many of these concerns regarding single and married women are found in the unlikely context of her criticisms of the Church of England in Canada. The Anglican Church, an institution which favoured its sons and to which Whitton remained a loyal, if less favoured daughter, she routinely subjected to aggressive commentary. In pointing out, at a time when it was uncommon to criticize the structures of organized religion, the general contribution being made by single women as well as the church's capricious neglect of the talents of its members, Whitton emerged as a Canadian pioneer in the feminist critique of organized religion. In a national survey of female members of the Anglican Church, Whitton encapsulates themes which recur frequently throughout her writings.[54] Moreover, her indignation and ambivalence towards the Church predates by forty years much of the conflict that Christian feminists feel today. It is, however, a criticism that predates Whitton's, as Florence Nightingale's comments in the previous century show. A celibate with a strong gynocentric view of the world and committed to the ascetic ideal, Nightingale observed:

> The C of E has for men bishoprics, archbishoprics, and a little work . . . For women she has—what? I had no taste for theological discoveries. I would have given her my head, my hand, my heart. She would not have them. She did not know what to do with them. She told me to go back and do crochet in my mother's drawing room; or, if I were tired of that, to marry.

She also wrote to Cardinal Manning, "You do know now, with all its faults, what a Home the Catholic Church is. . . . No one can tell, no man can tell what she is to women; . . . What training is there [in the C of E] compared to that of the Catholic Nun."[55]

In 1940, when the war had just got underway, Whitton prepared a preliminary draft study of "Women Not Affiliated" (WNA) to parishes despite their nominal Anglicanism.[56] The study, continued for the next five years, was commissioned by the church in a campaign of regeneration promoted by the Anglican Advance Appeal. Daisy Marshall of the IODE in Alberta, Dorothy King, formerly of the Montreal School of Social Work, and Nora Lea of the Toronto CAS were also involved in the project. Although they supported Whitton's conclusions, they would not have been quite as forthright in condemning the sexism in canon law, church policy, structures, and doctrine that discriminated against the female laity. In the preliminary study, Whitton accused the church of failing to "apprehend the great potentialities of a continuing partnership with its women," of harbouring a "niggling attitude" towards women in political life, and implying a form of "neopaganism" on the part of celibate, childless women, who had not fulfilled the primary destiny of motherhood.[57]

Whitton's later study, "Women of the Church," built on this work. She collected data in tours of the Maritimes, Ontario, and Montreal between March and June, and the West from September to early November, 1946.[58] Her grueling itinerary included centres as scattered as Fort St. John, Victoria, Brandon, and North Bay. After fifty communities, 115 meetings, and 13,000 miles, Whitton commented that she had "never struck anything as hard and worrying and wearying."[59] Speaking in Toronto in November 1946 on the question "Are the Churches Facing the Challenge of Women's Changed Status?" she said she was dispirited by the opposition of male vestries and clergy. By December, she collapsed from exhaustion.[60] Wryly, she quoted Dean Inge,

> All my forefathers were churchmen
> Fifteen hundred years or so
> And to every new proposal
> They always answered No

and added that he said nothing of the churchmen's wives, or the women in the church's appendages, who were no more progressive. She confessed astonishment at the personal antagonism she encountered, at how much mail was left unanswered or "lost," how many dioceses seemed to be falling apart, and how uninterested the church was in wages, hours, working conditions, housing, or anything that might distract it from its preoccupation with the "spiritual alone."[61]

Even those few clergymen who sympathized with Whitton's general position showed little interest in her specific concerns about women. The rural dean of Lethbridge, Reverend Leslie Grant, lauded her survey from the pulpit as the product of "one of the most brilliant minds in Canada," but Anne Meredith, who worked with her in that city, observed sardonically, "Working with men all my life, I know how seldom they give praise to women and how we have to fight for every inch of the way."[62]

The project included a national group co-ordinating the efforts of parish visiting committees to bring business, professional, and working women into the church. Whitton claimed these women were alienated from mainstream Anglicanism because it belittled them, even tending to reject them doctrinally. Canon law was not reassessing women's roles in the light of their present economic and political status; official thinking on this score was "inherited from a day when *ladies* embroidered the Church vestments." The church still saw "the preparation of our girls primarily for marriage, home and family life, though for a generation now only two out of three of them are likely to become homemakers," while large numbers would work before they married, and more and more were choosing to remain at work or re-enter the work force.[63] Whitton noted that Canada's population had risen by 120 per cent since 1900, with the numbers of women in paid work increasing by 350 per cent, from 237,000 to 1,100,000. This meant that one in every ten of the population, and one in four of the labour force, was a gainfully employed female. The phenomenon had significant implications for society in terms both of economics and of family life, and it was the major challenge to the church. Of the approximately 600,000 Anglican women over age fifteen, 250,000 were "not affiliated," and 200,000 were known but inactive. The majority of these women were engaged in gainful occupation.[64]

The alienation of women was made worse by their exclusion from higher church affairs. Whitton found the term "auxiliary" objectionable. Women wanted "autonomy," not "affiliation." Professional women in particular were disgruntled to find themselves forever "sitting on the bleachers" while men made decisions affecting their lives. Although the church had more women university graduates than it had clergy, only a few women could be delegates to deanery conferences or synods, and only one sat on General Synod.[65] Whitton repeated these same arguments to the Progressive Conservative party, calling women's auxiliaries political cheerleaders who served coffee and mailed out appeals for funds. Her essay "Women: A Necessary Evil" repeated these complaints.

> It would take the Twelve Apostles—and the assured absence of St. Paul from the meeting—to establish, in most of our dioceses in Canada to-day, that Anglican women have souls, equal in the sight of God, with the Anglican male. In some dioceses, boys at eighteen may be delegates to Synod, but women may not hold office of any but an advisory nature in even a parish vestry.[66]

She vented her anger again in "Our Need for Faith and Hope," a widely acclaimed and bold radio broadcast sponsored by the Ottawa *Citizen* on Trinity Sunday, 1959. The Ottawa Synod had recently denied its female laity equal voting power in the lay governance of the church, "decrying, deriding and denying status to Anglican women" and flying in the face of a majority lay vote at a time when nine Canadian dioceses admitted women to full voting equality. Under Ottawa's regulations, Whitton fumed, even the Queen, appointed head of the Church of England, could not enter Synod or vote, and even the "irascible St. Paul so recognized [women] and sent greetings to Aquila and Phoebe."[67] Her anger was the more poignant because she loved her church deeply.

Exhorting the church to create new support structures to accommodate working women and to challenge its women with responsibilities extending beyond their families, Whitton argued that without wider responsibility within church structures, there was "atrophy, not fulfillment, of personality." She pleaded passionately that the public concern and women's interests must coincide "in the demobilization and remobilization of our women for their fullest contribution to the national life."[68] Industrialization had marginalized women in the economy, deprived them of rights they had formerly enjoyed, and left them with what was beginning to be diagnosed as "housewives' frustration."

Whitton's indignation with the Anglican church can be understood on several levels. Obviously, she found it intolerable that a religion which professed there could be neither "bond nor free, rich nor poor, male nor female" would so readily perpetuate the opposite of such precepts. Secondly, the institutional church sanctified motherhood and saw family life as the foci of community. Whitton was committed equally to the solidarity of the family and to woman's full political and economic participation in the social order. But in the final analysis, while she did not deny mothers their right to "gainful employment" and economic independence, unconsciously she felt that they ought not to do it! The ambivalence of the church reflected her own. Just as the church denied women full participation on the grounds of their role in family life, Whitton's writings tended to deny married women and mothers full recognition in the workplace. Thus, Whitton *and* the church stood for equality, non-discrimination, individual justice, and freedom, and yet considered woman's first duty was to her home and children. She attacked contradictions she perceived within the church, but she projected her own.

Because married women no longer contributed to the household in direct remunerative ways, because there were more planned births and fewer children, and because more women were remaining single, Whitton argued that women would swell the workforce in ever greater numbers. Though she stressed that work satisfied emotional needs, she argued emphatically that most women sought employment for precisely the same reason men did, that is, *to live*.[69] She believed firmly that while a married middle class woman sought work for personal fulfilment rather than for economic reasons, whatever the status of the woman "in gainful occupation," she was entitled to demand equal pay for equal work and equal opportunities.

It is not democracy to permit the economically stronger—and more numerous—to exploit the economically weaker—and less potently organized. Yet in every walk of Canadian economic activity there runs the record of undoubted prejudice and economic exploitation of the woman who works . . . on the basis of inherited sex prejudice that we would not tolerate were it similarly applied on grounds of race, colour, nationality, or religion.[70]

Nevertheless, equal pay had to be honestly earned, and married women were not exempt from the demands of the workplace nor plead privileges:

> but women must earn this status, earn it by patient apprenticeship and long and careful training in those pursuits in which they have been granted short training and emergency entrance in Wartime. They must play the game with organized labour, to whom so many of the standards of living and of labour, they will enjoy, are due. They must not 'scab.'[71]

She was unsure, however, that many of the women to whom she was directing such admonitions were in fact willing to accept the proposition; among part-time and married workers she observed that

> the part-time wife, part-time worker . . . doesn't take the nightshift ever; she doesn't take the weekend shift ever; she takes holidays with her husband and children when schools are on holiday, so will take little or no 'vacation' work shift.[72]

These attitudes caused "grave discontent" among full-time workers and those who were committed to their work.

On the matter of equal pay, Whitton remained decidedly unambiguous as is demonstrated by her pithy essay "But He's a Man!" published as "The Exploited Sex" by *Maclean's* in April 1947. "It seems," she observed, "as if Adam and his sons have never forgiven Eve and her daughters their prior taste of knowledge."

> Most men seem bound by some silent compact that women must never again walk alone in the gardens of opportunity, or be suffered to enjoy equal access to the fruits of knowledge or power.[73]

She proceeded to cite the dismal figures of unequal employment opportunities and inequalities of pay, including the preserves usually seen as feminized occupations, nursing, teaching, and social welfare, now that the men were back from the war. Many women were released from employment in favour of men. "He's a drip," said a frank undergraduate, queried on the point. "But he's a man."

Deploring "males only" advertisements and instructions to women to use initials only in telephone listings and signatures so that they might not be recognized as female, she cited examples that pointed to the lack of promotional opportunities for women. Nor did she use examples only from the professions; she demonstrated also that discrimination existed in unskilled or semi-skilled jobs, for example, in rubber plants, in machine shops, in manufacturing, and in offices. "And why a man," she noted drolly, "draws 50 to

77 cents an hour for stuffing sausages beside a woman who draws 50 to 53 cents, only the sausages can tell!"

> The war did record some gains, of course. . . . But the war is over. The sudden gallant recognition of woman's equalness of worth seems to have been shortlived and fickle. In Canada, as a whole, and in each of the five economic areas of the country, the proportion of women in recorded employment in the nine leading industries has gone down definitely from the war peak of October 1944. The first survey of employment following the termination of hostilities in 1945 revealed a 7.5% overall reduction in employment, but this represented only a 5.3% recession among male workers as against 13.5% among women workers.[74]

And as a reflection of her own predicament, she wrote:

> Perhaps the worst discrimination is in social work, among the newest of organized professions, and one which calls for warmth, dedication and a sense of vocation. In the early twenties and on into the thirties it was overwhelmingly a woman's field. But 'the boys' have discovered it now, especially its enlarging administrative and executive opportunities, and they have come in, some transferring from arts or theology courses, more from other occupations, especially the 'good contact men.'[75]

Male social workers in Toronto averaged $1,392 and women, $1,119. In Winnipeg the rates were $1,567 to $1,289, and in Vancouver, $1,300 to $1,105.

Whitton may have been ambivalent about married women in the workplace, but in relation to equal pay and equal opportunity, she was as uncompromising as she was about women's participation in the nation's political life. Appearing as a speaker in the forties before scores of women's groups, she generally saw them as apolitical and innocuous. In fact, she quoted the British Labour M.P. Margaret Bondfield and Frances Perkins, the U.S. secretary of labor, in asserting that the proliferation of women's groups was actually a stumbling block to female participation in politics. She observed that they gave their members an illusion of prestige, power, and a sense of service "without the sordid realism of the party's politics and practices." In these complacent gatherings, they did not have "to face compromise and the bitter cleavings of the political arena . . . . So they afford the excitement of guerrilla clashes without the devastating slaughter of all-out political campaigns and warfare." Whitton had no patience with clubwomen who identified so completely with their husbands as to feel slighted if they were not included at business conventions and professional gatherings. She even suggested laughingly that husbands accompany their wives to IODE, NCW, or CWL conferences, just to "keep the girls in order a bit."[76]

In "Women the World Over" (1946) she appealed for greater female participation in politics.

> I think it stands with even greater force than one could claim two years ago, that in this new world, *the power that can be unleashed*, that has not been effective in the past, *is the power of women*, the active full citizenship of women that has not yet come into play in the world. The other day I said this in a small committee of one of the political parties, and the chairman of the Board of Strategy said to me afterwards, 'My Lord, and you say atomic energy is the worst force loosed on civilization. I would rather face a bomb than ten thousand women, if they ever got together and knew where they were going.'
>
> Now you can go to Babylon. You go to Syria. You can go to the Roman Empire. You can see that the fissures of the disintegrating elements begin with the carelessness of their women. That is the challenge today to the women here and everywhere, to save our civilization, and it is not a matter of claim. It is a matter of fact. We are moving rapidly to a matriarchy. Of the forty-three ranking powers of the world, in thirty-one nations, we outnumber the men, actually, in the population.
>
> Our destiny is upon us and are we going to make it effective?[77]

The under-use of female talent was not entirely the fault of men. In a 1947 article in *Saturday Night*, she exhorted her readers: "It's time for the woman voter to learn the facts of life. Then she'll be able to take care of herself. Until then—always a bridesmaid, never a bride; always a good party member never a member of the Legislature or Commons."[78] Her objections regarding the political parties' use of women as auxiliaries was based on the same protestations as the church's tendency to keep its women members "below stairs."

Musing ironically in private, Whitton wondered whether "it is because women are not mechanically minded that they have been content to remain back seat drivers on the party machine."[79] She did not believe this for a moment, being herself a capable carpenter and auto mechanic. She saw no reason whatever for women to continue to accept inferiority graciously, and even after nine years in civic office, she told the 1960 readers of the *Burlington Gazette*: "Ladies, if you had lived for the number of years that I have lived in Ottawa and seen some of the politicians that I have seen, you would realize that you *couldn't* have less than they have."[80] What made women so reluctant? Whitton never ceased to wonder about subordinate status and its relation with "the marrying mind," but she believed that "the fault dear Brutus, is not in our stars,/But in ourselves, that we are underlings."[81]

As auxiliaries, women chose to be "the butterers of bread, the cutters of cake, the brewers of tea, folders of letters, lickers of stamps—generally the handmaidens of the social trivialities." Writing in 1944 to the Honourable C.P. McTague of the Supreme Court of Canada, she advised that the Conservative Party recruit women without political convictions since the informed and competent ones were "now largely in the CCF" because it recognized women. The Conservatives must offer women real partnership and scrap the "pseudo Women's CP *Association of Canada*." Whitton was appalled that women had no decision-making power at conventions or provincial nomination meetings, and she failed to see why they were not as entitled as men to any office or consultant position within the party. A year later, she told Premier George Drew that, though she still believed in the party, she was giving up hope of "any possibility of a woman like me—and there are others—finding much real opportunity for worthwhile service in the Conservative party of the Dominion or even in the Province."[82]

Whitton's first foray into federal politics had been a bitter and humiliating experience. She had found herself betrayed personally and philosophically by a party that had proclaimed its opposition to the Family Allowances Act, encouraged her to write against the programme, and then did an about-face. Writing to another Conservative, Alderman Hilda Hesson of Winnipeg, she said:

> You could never have any hope of security or finality in any promise or policy after that, you know better than I that women (perhaps because of nature's penalties) are more bitter and unforgiving when double-crossed than men. It became quite unfeasible to think of lining up powerful women, getting a manifesto and promises and then having them left high and dry and deluded in the middle, perhaps, of a campaign when the firing got hot. So I signed off completely. If I come in, under the present nebulous picture at all, it will be as an independent. Meantime, I think there is still need for 40 or 50 women who believe in the respectability of self support, in the position and rights of women, in the decency and quality of family life, in the preservation of the only civilized structure modern society has—the British Empire—and in sharing the war's costs, if you are to share the benefits of peace, to get together and work out a statement for this bewildered and disintegrating land. The Council of Women is hopeless but the B & P, the IODE, the CWL, the FWI, YWCA, etc., all have good people. Surely we can foregather and light a light that need not go out?[83]

Because the major problem in mainstream party politics was the lack of female representation, a campaign to recruit women was necessary. Whitton realized that both Liberals and Conservatives, when they could be persuaded to support women candidates at all, sent them into "slaughter house ridings." A recent study by Janine Brodie, *Women and Politics in Canada* (1985) observes that even now "women candidates in Canada are excluded from winnable constituencies," that the roots of exclusion are found in a biased distribution of opportunities for election between men and women, and that winning the nomination is "a more formidable hurdle than winning the election." Whitton's observations were not exaggerated.[84]

Nora Frances Henderson, the only female member of the Hamilton Board of Control, believed Whitton's views were jaundiced, and she cautioned her against excess. Henderson thought it was exaggerated to see everything in terms of a masculine conspiracy: if women "stacked" the meetings, they could get the nominations. She warned Whitton about her diatribes on the apathy of the female electorate although she did not deny that they were, in fact, "hopelessly apathetic." As Whitton had observed, while there were no parties in municipal politics, neither were there many women. "It seems to me therefore very ill advised to begin this campaign for gathering the women into public office by attacking the men," Henderson wrote. "When women step out publicly to attack . . . the indifference of their sex they must remember they themselves are responsible."[85] Whitton followed her advice and "stacked" meetings when she ventured into federal politics again in 1958, winning the nomination by brilliantly orchestrated "women power." The bulk of her feminist writing in the fifties was more a rallying cry to women than an attack on men.

Whitton recognized that Canada had produced some politically militant and outstanding women, but she felt that they were far too often single-issue crusaders, with women's rights and the franchise secondary considerations. In this category she included Emily Murphy, Cora Hind, Louise McKinny, and Dr. Mary Crawford thought she described Isabella Scott, past secretary of the Montreal Suffrage Association, as a "real suffragette." Compared with British women like the Pankhursts, Mary Wolstonecroft, and Annie Kennedy, and Americans such as Susan B. Anthony, Elizabeth Cady Stanton, Lucretia Mott, Lucy Starr, Anne Howard Shaw, and Carrie Chapman Cott, "Canadian women got the vote as a gift rather than an award." She felt shame for her own sex as she recalled the courage and sacrifice of women who had fought for women's rights. "Would they not feel that we had let them down, though we have benefitted very fully—by all the privileges and opportunities they sought to make ours?" Women assumed few electoral responsibilities to justify their rights and "reported a sorry stewardship to the surviving of those who purchased their electoral freedom."[86]

Invited to give the first lecture in the Susan B. Anthony memorial series at the College of Women at the University of Rochester in February 1947, Whitton confessed sheepishly that Canadian political life was "distressingly sterile" for women. After thirty years of enfranchisement, women had yet to hold a portfolio at the dominion level or in any province, and of twenty thousand elected representatives at all levels in the country, not threescore were female. She compared these figures with the two dozen at Westminster and the one-third in the municipal chambers of Great Britain, with a woman chairing the biggest county council in the world, London.[87] Later she quipped that there had been but two women senators "for good behaviour in the past and to come," the "maximum capitulation of two gallant bachelor prime ministers to women's influence in the last quarter of a century."[88]

The "sorry stewardship" issue obsessed Whitton into the fifties, when she observed that 3.75 million female voters were represented by five women in legislative bodies and two in the Senate. By contrast, there were nine in the U.S. Congress, two hundred in state assemblies, seventeen in state senates, twelve times the Canadian proportion.[89] In 1951 she noted that Ontario women could still not be jurors, though British Columbia and Alberta had extended this right to women in 1922.[90]

In a 1952 *Maclean's* article headlined "Will Women Ever Run the Country?" she published a sadly unimpressive list: during the last three decades, five women elected in British Columbia, nine in Alberta, two in Saskatchewan, two in Manitoba, one in Ontario, and no more than five elected to the House of Commons after Agnes Macphail's initial victory in 1921. Of one hundred senators appointed since the second woman, Iva Fallis, was named to the upper house in 1935, none had been women, and "east of the Pre-Cambrian Shield no woman was elected to a provincial or federal house."[91]

Although 51 per cent of the electorate were women and they held 50 per cent of corporate stocks, 65 per cent of savings deposits, 70 per cent of private wealth through their longer lifespans, an increase in inheritance from war casualties, and alimony and divorce agreements, women entrusted all this to male-dominated trust companies, lawyers, and governing bodies. Whitton could ironically infer that women who earned or inherited income were handicapped by "a congenital deference to the male genus (probably instinctive from reliance, since creation, on an extracted male rib)" or "it may be, of course, just a wise and desirable supplementary of female intelligence and intuition by male experience." Whitton was convinced that "were one woman of substantial means to provide a moderate sum for a limited period to subsidize a Women's Federation for Political Action the whole face of Canadian public life would be 'lifted' in less than five years."[92]

Whitton would have been no more heartened by the recent record of Canadian women. In 1983 only 6 per cent of the total 1,172 provincial legislators were women and 5 per cent of provincial cabinets. Between 1921 and 1984 after Agnes MacPhail's debut in the House of Commons, only sixty-five members of parliament were women and 2.4 per cent of all candidates for federal office.[93]

Puzzling over the sorry stewardship of Canadian women, she wrote for *Chatelaine* in September 1946, "we remain the most inert in the consciousness or use of our power of women in nations the world over."[94] Since the eighteenth century, she argued, regard for women had declined as "men preached their theories so continuously, so vehemently, so unopposed that most women, too, came to accept them, even if some gallant souls, in the way of the sex, suffered them in silent, seething disbelief." Women accepted inferiority "too graciously" and failed to *market* their competence with enough insistence. "We're so fearful of the criticism, not so much of men, as of men's wives." The combination of half-submerged prejudices, led to "another and more terrible discrimination." Nevertheless, a major contributory factor was the prevalance of men-identified-women.

> There is an instinctive unease on the part of the male against the female sallying out from her customary settings and duties into the preserve he and his have long held undisputed and decisive sway. Most men are as unaware of this innate resistance to women leaving the compound as are many women of their deep and unconscious with-holding of their full enthusiasm and untrammeled generous support to other women who do take up spear and shield and offer to engage in mortal combat in the public square. And such men and women, just because they may not set out definitely to detract, are the hardest to engage in definite conflict.[95]

Women such as herself, who "from their cradles" had a "certain independence of mind," required the full support of other women if the male-dominated party machine was to be withstood. There could be no excuse for reluctance to oppose it actively or for failure to co-operate with women—unmarried women in the mold of "the powerful sisters of the Pharaohs, the intellectual hetaeras of the Greeks, the abbesses of the middle ages"—who were willing to do so.[96]

Whitton's suspicion of married women grew more pronounced as more and more of them entered the work force. She was not sure that the majority could overcome the handicap of being "husbands' wives." She upbraided women whom she recognized intuitively identified with the roles of the men in their lives. Since the married woman was so often economically dependent on her husband, either completely or through joint incomes of which hers was usually the lesser, she was "too concerned with her husband's position." Whitton maintained that this worked against women's responsible involvement in politics or employment. She was totally unsympathetic to the most common appeal of avoidance, "You know, my husband's financial and social interests must be considered—you understand, don't you, my dear?" A married woman was "*centred* in her husband and family," and this identification was one of the reasons for Canadian women being a "flop" in politics.

> The husband-wife, father-daughter technique is perhaps the most single potent force in strangling women's power and freedom within the organized parties. By this the women—and the women friends—of 'the family'

(the candidate, the prominent member etc.) become the discreet, moderately articulate and politically effective outward and visible sign of the party's inward and spiritual graciousness towards 'complete equality for women in all things' etc., etc., etc. Most of the women so deployed do not even know they are decoys; others are as aware as Judas of what they are doing but lack the virtue of remorse. . . . It is a sad memorial to the dream and aspiration of 1916.[97]

"Judas was a man," she noted caustically, "but he has many daughters." Was it, she wondered, entirely woman's passivity in the face of hostility, a form of negative resistance, or was there "too much friendly trading with the enemy?" Writing to a Windsor friend in 1946, she noted of party politics and women that

The mechanics . . . work beautifully as long as the car is standing in the show room. The boys will promise anything in the set-up but when you try to get the gears meshed down in the constituency behind a woman nominee, it is a very different matter. I am inclined to agree with you that a good deal of the trouble is the women who sell out either for their own or their husbands' or their sons' profit.[98]

In 1919, during the optimism of postwar reconstruction, she had written "it becomes the duty of every Canadian woman, on the eve of the extension of the franchise, to prepare herself for worthy citizenship."[99] She came to believe in this duty even more by the forties. Her ideas about the "After-the-War-Woman," who was called upon to develop the necessary attitude of mind and analytical power to "re-make" society, took on clearer shape. Yet never did she argue that male power structures alone explained women's powerlessness or excused their inertia. Well into her seventies, she would reject the Committee on the Status of Women as "an exercise in futility. . . . Changes won't be made by commissions but by women exercising their rights and entering into gainful employment."[100]

At the CWC, Whitton had felt no great need to argue the equality of the sexes. Working in and sustained by a feminized occupation, she was able to preserve the illusion that merit would generally be recognized: her own national prominence and economic security were proof. Once she was separated from this network, however, her comfortable meritocratic views required radical reassessment. Most particularly, in the forties, Whitton found herself contending with the dual problem of access to and credibility in politics.

The tensions in Whitton's feminism appear when she was no longer sustained by a support structure of like-minded women involved in a secular calling. It is also significant that her feminism does not emerge publicly and militantly until the forties, when she no longer participated in such a *vocational* calling. In her new situation, she became more aware of the constraints placed upon women in gainful occupation. In a precarious position herself, she began to sympathize more with women who were without the benefits of pension, secure income, opportunities for mobility, or claims of prestige. Consequently, her feminism became more coherent and the need to raise the consciousness of other women became more urgent.

It was, in short, Whitton's single status that primarily defined her feminism and its ambiguities. Even Virginia Woolf's *Orlando*, the archetype of androgyny in feminist literature, succumbed to the spirit of the age, crying "Life! A Husband! I am a woman, a real woman at last." Before marriage, Orlando saw that

> Wedding rings abounded . . . wedding rings were everywhere. . . . Gold, or pinchbeck, thin, thick, plain, smooth, they glowed dully on every hand. Couples trudged and plodded in the middle of the road indissolubly linked together . . . they were somehow stuck together, couple after couple. . . . Her ruminations, however, were accompanied by such a tingling and twangling of the afflicted finger that she could scarcely keep her ideas in order. Though the seat of her trouble seemed to be the left hand, she could feel herself poisoned through and through, and was forced at length to consider the most desperate of remedies, which was to yield completely and submissively to the spirit of the age, and take a husband. . . . 'Everyone is mated except myself,' she mused, 'I am single, am mateless, and alone.'[101]

Charlotte Whitton did not succumb, and in expressing the anger and insecurities of the single woman of her day she became their voice and their mirror. She refused to be coerced into silence or shamed into second class status by the norms of married society, and her frustrations reveal much about that generation of single women and their historical contribution. Her words remind us that the experience of the never-married is qualitatively different from that of the widowed, divorced, separated, or non-celibates who constitute so many of the single ranks today.

In the 1940s Whitton's prolific pen had contributed two score or so articles to *Saturday Night, Chatelaine, Maclean's Magazine, Queen's Quarterly*, and other magazines on social concerns.[102] However, none of Whitton's writings of that period were as incisive as her feminist critiques, and none of her other strictures were as original or as hard-hitting. The next two decades saw a re-iteration of those views discussed here.

In comparision to Whitton's feminist writings, which seem to erupt from her inmost being, the monthly articles she wrote for the "Offshore" series in the *Ottawa Citizen* from June to December 1949 when she visited Europe seem self-conscious. One example is her florid description of flying over London.

> Then the great corona of London was visible lighting all of the Thames.
> And we Canadians were someway a little prouder that we were British
> subjects too and could claim kinship with that land lying so tranquil there
> below.[103]

And her observations at the annual meeting of the Women's Institutes at Royal
Albert Hall sounded merely didactic, reminding her readers that Mrs. Alfred
Watt had introduced the "Canadian-born" women's institute into England thirty
years previously.[104]

And her description of a visit to the abbey at Tewkesbury is at once sincere,
trivial, and insipid:

> a past, so full and varied, would be vivid anywhere, but in this ancient abbey
> it pulses everywhere. By the fort, a huge bronze bowl was aflame with
> gladioli, glowing in bright, unusual colors. The black robed vicar was
> bending over them as we entered. We were happy in his guidance through
> this abbey, of his service and obvious deep affection.[105]

Historical pieces on King Arthur, the Britons and the Bretons, and her travel-
ogues of Norway and Sweden lacked fire and passion. The only piece that might
be compared favourably was the record of the trial of General Mannstein,
commander of the 11th German Army, for wartime atrocities. In Hamburg this
trial inspired her to write a paeon to British justice called "To No Man Will We
Delay or Deny Justice."[106]

Because her interest in history never waned, she contributed a great deal to
the local history of the Ottawa Valley. However, even these articles became more
alive, pithy, and provocative, when she deals with women as can be seen in "Two
Generations of Coeducation," written for *Saturday Night* early in 1949. In this
article she quoted Mary Wollstonecraft's "Vindication of the Rights of Women"
(1792).

> If women be not prepared by education to become the companion of men
> she will stop the progress of Knowledge for truth must be common to all or
> it will be inefficacious with respect to its influence or general practice.

And she also quoted Jean Paul Richter's 1806 essay on education, "Levana."
Looking at "the internecine jealousies by which women too often hold back
women from the fullest use of the ablest of our sex in public office," the German
writer said, "Oh! Mother, above all other things implant and cherish in your
daughter a love and reverence for her own sex."[107] Whitton's love and reverence

for her own sex was only put to the test when married women became competitors. Apart from the article's passionate ideological appeal, it is replete with anecdotes and historical facts which trace the difficult path of Canadian women entering university faculties, especially at Toronto and Queen's.

Even today, Whitton's feminist writings evoke strong responses; while they are cut deep to the core by her own ambiguities and reflect a darker side to the troubled existence she lived in the forties, they also expose contradictions with which women continue to struggle. She wrote her strictures with passion and with vigor, and they remain powerful indictments of female inertia, a poignant illustration of one woman's ambivalence towards her own sex, and a ruthless exposure of problems that remain. Finally, they are a vital and brilliant testimony to the emotional and professional deprivation that occurred in the lives of single pioneer career women after the Second World War.

NOTES

The major collections used for this study are the Whitton Papers (WP) and the papers of the Canadian Council on Social Development (CCSD) both in the Public Archives of Canada (PAC). Examples of the code denoting collection and volume numbers will be WP/14 or CCSD/23. Correspondence from Whitton will use the initials "CW."

CHAPTER ONE

Lottie

1. MS, "Marriage Out of the Faith," (circa, 1950), p. 10. Whitton Papers, Vol. 88, *Public Archives of Canada* (PAC). Hereafter cited as WP/88.
2. Ibid., p. 11.
3. Ibid., p. 1.
4. In "Royal Remembrances," (1957), WP/89.
5. See Robert M. Stamp, *Schools of Ontario 1876-1976* (Toronto: University of Toronto Press, 1982): 34-35; and Hilda Neatby, *Queen's University Vol. 1* (Montreal: McGill-Queen's University Press, 1978): 291-304.
6. "The Town on the Hills," *Renfrew Mercury*, Centennial Issue, 10-16/8/1958.
7. She passionately reaffirmed this belief in an article "The University Graduate as a Responsible Citizen," *The Queen's Review* Vol. 21, #1 (January 1947): 4-9. Also see "Character Building," *Edmonton Journal* 19/8/1967 and "Flunking the Finals," *Winnipeg Free Press*, 7/5/1952.
8. See Eighth Annual Commencement Renfrew Collegiate Institute 1914, O'Brien Opera House, 18/12/1914, WP/13.
9. Frederick W. Gibson, *Queen's University Volume 2, 1917-61* (McGill-Queen's University Press, 1983): 42, 161. Neatby makes

similar observations for the earlier period, p. 187.
10. Gibson, p. 62; and George Henderson, Queen's Archivist (1985).
11. Neil Guppy, "Access to Higher Education in Canada," *The Canadian Journal of Higher Education*, Vol. XIV-3 (1984): 79-83.
12. Whitton Collection 1106 Boxes 5, 7, 15, Queen's University Archives, (QU).
13. Myrtle to CW, 4/1/1923, quotes the poem, WP/3; and letter 28/7/1983 from Laura Gill, Assistant to the Dean of Women, Queen's University.
14. Neatby, pp. 209, 300-301.
15. "A Goodly Heritage," Address to Levana Society, 4/3/1955, WP/52.
16. Gibson, pp. 11, 12; and Neatby, p. 296.
17. Gibson mistakenly claims Whitton to be the first trustee, p. 434. For Rayside's appointment see D.D. Calvin, *Queen's University at Kingston* (Kingston: Trustees of University, 1941): 240.
18. Neatby, p. 207.
19. Op. cit., p. 207.
20. Op. cit., p. 299.
21. Annie C. Macgillivray, "History of the Residence Movement," *The Alumnae News* 10

(November 1925): 8-13; Queen's University Alumnae Association, coll. 3627, box 8, file E.16 Re: Women's Residence, 1901-1903; and "Queen's University Alumnae Association and Women's Residences at Queen's, 1900-1961," pp. 10-12.

22. Figures supplied by George Henderson, Queen's Archivist. Quote from Principal Bruce Taylor in Gibson, p. 12.

23. "A Goodly Heritage."

24. MacLachlan to CW, 28/11/1915, WP/3; and *Canadian Calvacade 1920-35* (CCW: 1935), p. 3.

25. Gibson quoting Neatby, pp. 5, 3.

26. Neatby, p. 300.

27. Wilhelmina Gordon to CW, 24/12/1916, WP/18.

28. Neatby, p. 299.

29. Information about Whitton's Levana friends is found in Correspondence, WP/3. Also see Frederick W. Gibson, "Women at Queen's: The First Century," *Queen's Alumni Review* (Sept.-Oct. 1984): 8-12.

30. Queen's Notes (1917-18), Box 4, QU.

31. *Queen's Journal*, 15/1/1918, p. 4.

32. Gibson, 105-107.

33. Marjorie—to CW, n.d., WP/3.

34. Gordon to CW, 20/3/1927, WP/3.

35. JB to CW, 23/4/1918, WP/1.

36. *QJ*, 20/11/1917.

37. *QJ*, Jan.-Feb. 1918.

38. See "O.D. Skelton," by W.A. MacKintosh in Robert L. McDougall (ed.), *Canada's Past and Present: A Dialogue* (University of Toronto Press, 1965), p. 60.

39. CW to Harry Hereford, n.d., WP/13.

CHAPTER TWO   *Initiation Into Public Life*

1. Richard Allen, *The Social Passion: Religion and Social Reform in Canada, 1914-28* (Toronto: University of Toronto Press, 1973): 13.

2. Allen, pp. 18-31 and 64-68.

3. Quoted in Ethel (Dodds) Cameron Parker Collection, MG 31 K6, PAC. Also see File: Social Service Council (1918-21), WP/18; Obituary for Shearer (1859-1925) in the Toronto *Globe*, 28/3/1925; SSCC Collection, MG 28 I327, PAC.; and Ethel Dodds Parker, "The Origins and Early History of the Presbyterian Settlement Houses," in papers of the Interdisciplinary Conference of the Social Gospel in Canada, March 21-24, University of Regina, edited by Richard Allen, pp. 86-121.

4. Evidence on Whitton's SSCC work comes from the SSCC papers which are part of the Canadian Council of Churches Records, MG 28 I327, PAC, and SSCC correspondence in the Hugh Dobson Papers, United Church Archives, Toronto and Vancouver. SSCC objectives are found in *Social Welfare* (*SW*) Vols. 1-111 (Oct. 1918—Sept. 1918), SSCC.

5. Legislation Committee minute, 19/2/1919, SSCC.

6. Report on Motion Pictures Committee, 21/10/1921, SSCC.

7. NCW Minute Book (June-December 1921), 9/8/1921, and Executive Minute, 5/11/1921, pp. 38, 130, MG 28 I25, PAC.

8. "Mental Deficiency as a Child Welfare Problem," (circa. 1921), WP/19.

9. "Unmarried Parenthood," p. 185; and "For Woman's Thought," *SW*, June 1919, p. 22.

10. See Carol Lee Bacchi, *Liberation Deferred? The Ideas of the English Canadian Suffragists 1877-1918.* (Toronto: University of Toronto Press, 1983), Chapter 7. Bacchi points to those suffragists who were "euthenists" rather than eugenicists. Although eugenics, racism, and science have been the subject of several notable American studies, comparable work has not been done in Canada. Among the more useful American studies are Mark H. Haller, *Eugenics: Hereditarian Attitudes in American Thought* (New Brunswick, N.J.: Rutgers University Press, 1963); Kenneth M. Ludmerer, *Genetics and American Society: A Historical Appraisal* (Baltimore: Johns Hopkins University Press, 1972); and Hamilton Cravens, *The Triumph of Evolution: American Scientists and Heredity—Environment Controversy, 1900-1941* (Philadelphia: University of Pennsylvania Press, 1978). For a British view see G.R. Searle, *Eugenics and Politics in Britain 1900-1914* (Leyden: Noordhoff International Publishing, 1976). Searle says:

Eugenists "were more worried by the existence of generous State and numerous ill-organized charities, which together (so they claimed) had created an environment in which a 'reversed selection' was taking place—in which diseased, parasitic, and incompetent persons of various kinds were assured of a comfortable existence at the expense of the 'efficient' who were being taxed to support them and their numerous offspring. pp. 45-46.

He points out that the eugenics movement was a response to the emergence of social welfare politics—it provided new arguments against the Radical Programme in a constructive alternative to Liberalism and socialism in defence of traditional economic theories. pp. 113-114.

11. Books on the juvenile immigration movement include, Joy Parr, *Labouring Children* (London: Croom Helm, 1980); Kenneth Bagnell, *The Little Immigrants* (Toronto: Macmillan of Canada, 1980); and Phyllis Harrison, *The Home Children* (Winnipeg: Watson and Dwyer, 1979).
12. "Child Labor," *SW* (January 1919): 142-144.
13. "Unmarried Parenthood and the Social Order," Parts 1 and 2, *SW* (April-May 1920): 184-187, 222-223, esp. p. 184.
14. P. 187.
15. P. 186.
16. "For Woman's Thought," *SW* (May 1919): 200-202, and (June 1919): 227-229, esp. p. 200.
17. P. 202.
18. P. 227.
19. Carolyn June Forsyth, "Whatever My Sex, I'm No Lady: Charlotte Whitton, Politican Welfare Pioneer," *MAKARA* 2(1977): 30.
20. In Harvey Cox, "The Whitton Story," *Ottawa Evening Citizen*, Nov. 18, Nov. 20, 1950.
21. Gordon to CW, 22/7/-, WP/3; and H.I.J. Coleman to CW, 16/9/1918, Whitton Papers, Queen's University.
22. Gordon to CW, 25/5/1919.
23. Mo to CW, 29/5/1919.
24. Mrs. J. Whitton to CW, 4/7/1920.
25. "Predictions from January 12, 1918 for Queen's 1928," Collection 1106, *Queen's University*.
26. Lillian Faderman, *Surpassing the Love of Men* (New York: William Morrow and Co., 1981) devotes several chapters to this historical phenomena.
27. See Ruth Hall, *Passionate Crusader: The Life of Marie Stopes* (New York: Harcourt Brace Yoranovich, 1977), for a clumsy treatment of this issue. Hall's description of the friendship between Stopes, British birth control crusader and Dr. Helen MacMurchy is not

understood in the terms of "romantic friendship." She seems unable to take same sex love seriously MacMurchy is dealt with in a vulgarised, ungenerous manner as an older woman who is "violently frustrated" and Stopes as a young "normal" woman who seeks reassurance in reaction to a failed love affair with a man.

28. Mo to CW, n.d., WP/3.
29. Grace S.—to CW, 1/12/1918.
30. Grace S.—to CW, 20/5/1919.
31. MacCallum to CW, 4/10/1919; 4/12/1920; 10/1/1922. Of all Whitton's friends, MacCallum was the most successful. For an overview of her remarkable career see Jean Bannerman, *Leading Ladies: Canada 1977* (Belleville: Mika Publishing Co., 1977). MacCallum deserves a biography of her own.
32. CW to Esther L.—28/2/1918.
33. Esther to CW, (circa 1918).
34. Nell to CW, 4/2/1919.
35. Nell to CW, 6/3/1919.
36. Nell to CW, 4/2/1919.
37. Dorothy—to CW, 11/5/1919.
38. Mo to CW, 6/4/1919.
39. Esther to CW, n.d.
40. Esther to CW, 27/2/1918.
41. Mo to CW, 3/6/1920.
42. Margaret Grier to CW, 5/6/1920.
43. Mo to CW, 10/10/1921.
44. Mo to CW, 22/1/1922.
45. Virginia Woolf, *Mrs Dalloway* (London: Granada, Atriad Panther Books, 1976): 30-33.
46. Rosalind Rosenberg, *Beyond Separate Spheres: Intellectual Roots to Modern Feminism* (New Haven: Yale University Press, 1982): 36-43.
47. Although Emily (Ferguson) Murphy wrote articles and book reviews for money when her husband was in financial straits, Murphy's father was a wealthy landowner and businessman. The Ferguson connections were more than helpful. Sir John A. MacDonald had been a visitor to the Ferguson home in her childhood and her grandfather was a conservative politician and newspaper owner. An uncle was Sir James Gowan of the Supreme Court and a Senator while another uncle was Mr. Justice Thomas Ferguson, Judge of the Ontario Supreme Court. Her lawyer brother was a member of the Supreme Court also. Murphy had attended Bishop Strachan, the exclusive grammar school, and her brothers attended Upper Canada College. By his forties Arthur Murphy was wealthy once

more—his wife had servants— having sold his timber interests and invested in Alberta mining.

48. For biographical information on Murphy see Una MacLean, "The Famous Five," *Alberta Historical Review* (Spring 1962): 1-4; Catherine L. Cleverdon, *The Woman Suffrage Movement in Canada* (University of Toronto Press, 1950); and Byrne Hope Sanders, *Emily Murphy: Crusader* (MacMillan Co., 1945).

49. Murphy to CW, 26/7/1928, 28/5/1923, 10/4/1922, 6/2/1923, 30/5/1923, WP/3 and 31/1/1925, WP/114.

50. Helen R.Y. Reid papers, McCord Museum, Montreal. Margaret Gillett discusses the first McGill women students in "*We Walked Very Warily*": *A History of Women at Montreal* (Montreal, Eden Press, 1981).

51. Quoted in Margaret Gillett, p. 260.

52. Helen R.Y. Reid papers.

53. Reid to Currie, 27/7/1932, 23/6/1927; Currie to Reid, 27/6/1932, 28/7/1923, RG 2C 73, McGill University Archives. An example is the exchange between Reid and John W. Ross, Secretary of the Canadian Patriotic Fund, 7/2/1918, McCord Museum.

54. Reid to CW, received 27/6/1934, File 17 (1934), CCSD/4.

55. Reid to CW, 19/6/1925, and correspondence (1924-25), CCSD/6.

56. "Infant Mortality Rate Higher in Renfrew Than In New York," *Renfrew Mercury*, 31/3/1922.

57. Allen, pp. 243-244.

58. Allen, pp. 244-247.

59. *Report of the Executive of the Social Service Council of Canada, 1922*, pp. 12-13, Canadian Council of Churches, MG 28 I327, PAC.

CHAPTER THREE   *An Ottawa Marriage*

1. "A Children's Bureau for Canada," *Social Welfare* (1 January 1919): 84-86; and "The Chief of the Children's Bureau of Canada," *Social Welfare* (March 1920): 150. The American campaign to establish a Federal Children's Bureau prompted similar interest in Great Britain where the Home Office convened a conference on the need for a "Central Council on Child-Welfare, 31 April 1909. HO45/20115/455959, Public Record Office. The establishment in 1912 occasioned the Dominion Government to appoint Robert H. Murray and Ernest H. Blois to report on the feasibility of a Canadian bureau. E.L. Newcombe, Deputy Minister of Justice, Circular Letter, 10/10/1913, Minnie Julia Beatrice Campbell Papers, MG14, C4, file: Child Welfare, Provincial Archives of Manitoba; and R.H. Murray and Ernest H. Blois, *Report and Recommendation regarding the Establishment of a Children's Department or Bureau, at Ottawa* (Halifax, 1913). Women's organizations and their leaders provided strong support for a Children's Bureau for Canada. See for example, Emily F. Murphy to Sir George Foster, Acting Prime Minister, 17 February 1920, Robert L. Borden Papers, MG26, H1(C), Microfilm C-4384, p. 101834A, PAC.

2. Holland Cox, "A Fighter For Any Cause She Believes In," *Ottawa Citizen*, 18/11/1950,

pp. 1 and 3; O. Mary Hill, *Canada's Salesman to the World* (Montreal: McGill-Queen's University Press, 1977): 242-43; and RG32, C-2, vol. 479, file—Whitton, PAC.

3. Emily Murphy to CW, 10/4/1922, WP/8.

4. "On Taking Leave," by CW and sub-editorial comment, *SW* (July 1922).

5. Hill, pp. 302 and 275-76.

6. Mo to CW, 5/5/1917, WP/3.

7. In File: Correspondence, Family (1923-29), WP/1; and J.B. Whitton to CW, 24/2/1924.

8. CW to JB, 12/2/1924.

9. Stephen Whitton to CW, 7/9/1929.

10. F.R. Clarke to CW, 15/6/1936.

11. Max Boe to CW, 27/12/1923, WP/3.

12. Telegram and Reply, 21/1/1924.

13. CW to Executive, 9/4/1924.

14. CW to Nickle, 9/4/1924.

15. CCCW to Attorney-Generals, 12/6/1924; and CW to Nickle, 12/10/1924.

16. Journal Entry, 12/7/1924, WP/13.

17. Journal, 14/7/1924; and "Twenty Five Years Ago," Offshore column, *Ottawa Citizen*, 23/6/1949.

18. Journal, 22/7/1924.

19. Journal, 22/7/1924.

20. E.T. William and Helen M. Palmer (Eds.), *Dictionary of National Biography, 1951-1960*, (Oxford: Oxford University Press, 1971): 122-123; Charlotte Whitton, "The Right Honorable Margaret," *Chatelaine* (August,

1929); and Margaret Bondfield, *A Life's Work* (London: Hutchinson & Co., 1949).

21. The speech is reported in "The Social Background in Canada," *Social Welfare* (January 1925): 70-74.
22. Journal, 22/7/1924.
23. Journal, 22/7/1924; and Florence Fisher to CW, 30/4/1924, CCSD/20. Mary Allen's flamboyant behaviour included wearing jackboots and uniform even to official dinners. These actions were ominous in that she became a fascist in the 1930's having met Hitler and Goering. She was forced to retire in disgrace, humiliating for a woman who had been imprisoned several times as a suffragette and imprisoned in 1920 again for her stands about the women's police force.
24. Journal, 24/7/1924.
25. See Lee Virginia Chambers-Schiller, *Liberty, A Better Husband: Single Women in America, The Generations of 1780-1840* (New Haven: Yale University Press, 1984): 24; and George Gissing, *The Odd Women* (New York: New American Library, 1983), and Introduction by Elaine Showalter, p. xxi.
26. Journal, 17/8/1924, 27/8/1924, 28/8/1924.
27. "The Holy Year of Jubilee," Offshore column, *Ottawa Citizen*, 31/12/1949.
28. Will and Testament, 24/2/1926, WP/14. Whitton's will, 8/4/1964, WP/12, attests to her devotion to Grier also even after Margaret's death. Carolyn June Forsyth suggests Grier and Whitton lost lovers in the war in "Whatever My Sex, I'm no Lady: Charlotte Whitton, Politician, Welfare Pioneer," *Makara* Vol. 2 (1977): 27-31. The theme of tragic love was popular in antebellam America also when spinsters were frequently seen "to be single through the tragic end of a love affair or the death of a loved one to whom they remained eternally faithful." See *Liberty, A Better Husband*, p. 24.
29. See Lillian Faderman, *Surpassing the Love of Men* (New York: William Morrow & Co., 1981): 190; Robert Brain, *Friends and Lovers* (New York: Basic Books, 1976); and Carrol

Smith-Rosenberg, "The Female World of Love and Ritual," *Signs* 1 (Autumn 1975): 1-29. For a discussion of romantic love which assists in understanding past sensibilities see Denis de Rougemont, *Love in the Western World* (rev. ed.; New York: Harper Colophon Books, 1974).
30. She referred to herself in these words in her journal, 13/7/1924, WP/14.
31. Poetry (circa 1920's), WP/13.
32. For a description of their living arrangements see the third part, "The Whitton Story," by Holland Cox, *Ottawa Citizen*, 21/9/1950, WP/38.
33. Gordon to CW, 20/3/1927; and Murphy to CW, n.d., WP/3.
34. Woereshoffer to CW, 2/8/1922, CCSD/18.
35. Proceedings, CCCW (1925-26), p. 12.
36. See Donald S. Birn, *The League of Nations 1918-1945* (Great Britain: Clarendon Press, 1981); *The Aims, Methods and Activity of the League of Nations* (Geneva: Secretariat of League of Nations, 1935): 164-174; and Richard Veatch, *Canada and the League of Nations* (Toronto: University of Toronto Press, 1975).
37. See CW to Skelton, 5/10/1925, 15/10/1925; Skelton to CW, 13/10/1925; CW to Abbott, Telegram, 3/10/1925, 5/10/1925; Abbott to CW, 6/10/1925; CW to Riddell, 10/10/1925, CCSD/2; Riddell to Austen Chamberlain, June 1925, RG 29, vol. 32, PAC.
38. CW to Skelton, 15/10/1925, CW to Riddell, 10/10/1925, CCSD/2.
39. Riddell to Thorburn, 10/10/1925, RG 25, DI, vol. 815, file 635, 1925-1927.
40. Executive Minute, 20/11/1925, SSCC (1926-27), MG 28 I327, PAC.
41. CW to Riddell, 10/10/1925, CCSD/2.
42. Riley to CW, 14/11/1925.
43. MacLachlan to CW, 16/11/1925, 24/11/1925; CW to MacLachlan, 6/11/1925, 19/11/1925; Riley to CW, 14/11/1925, and CW to Abbott, 8/12/1925.
44. Minutes of 37th Session, 14/12/1925, report Whitton and Lathrop's appointments, Item W/105, FO 371/161/75, *Public Record Office*, London.

CHAPTER FOUR   *The Empire Builder*

1. In Pt. 3, "The Whitton Story," by Holland Cox, *Ottawa Citizen*, 21/9/1950.
2. "Why I Holiday Where," by CW, WP/7;

and "Charlotte Whitton," by KMH, *Winnipeg Free Press*, 12/12/1941.
3. Minutes of Montreal School of Social Work,

History Applications (1920-26) and School for Graduate Nurses papers, *McGill University Archives*. Professor E.J. Urwick to H. Cassidy, 24/01/1929 and 16/04/1929, Vol. 65, Cassidy Papers, *University of Toronto Archives*.

4. W.L. Scott papers, MG 30 C27, vol. 13, PAC.

5. Manitoba Royal Commission correspondence, MG 28 I 10, Vol. 29 and "Report of the Royal Commission of Child Welfare Division, Manitoba (1928)", RG5/G2, Box 2, *Provincial Archives of Manitoba* (hereafter PAM) and CCSD/29; New Brunswick Survey Correspondence, CCSD/36-39, and 19. The juvenile immigration survey has been fully discussed and documented by the authors in Chapter 7, *Discarding the Asylum: From Child Rescue to the Welfare State 1800-1950* (Lanham, MD.: University Press of America, 1983): 186-223.

6. CW to Nicholson, 25/2/1926, IODE (1926-27), CCSD/3. See similar views in Report in "Immigration and Travelers Aid Survey 1928-29," YWCA, MG 28 I198, PAC.

7. CW to Blair, 24/5/1926, League of Nations, CCSD/2.

8. In *Echoes* (October, 1929): 34.

9. CW to Blair, 16/1/1929, CCSD/12.

10. Kenneth M. Ludmerer, *Genetics and American Society: A Historical Appraisal* (Baltimore: Johns Hopkins University Press, 1972), makes an interesting, if unconvincing, case for evaluating scientists and others as products of their times, pp. 5-6 and 25-33.

11. Irving Abella and Harold Troper, *None is Too Many* (Toronto: Lester and Orpen Dennys, 1982.)

12. CW to King, 3/11/1928, CCSD/37.

13. "Report of the Royal Commission of Child Welfare Division, Manitoba," RG5/G2, Box 2, PAM and correspondence, CCSD/29.

14. Murphy to CW, 26/7/1928, WP/3.

15. Mutchmor to CASW, 20/2/1931, RG5/G2, file 10, PAM. In 1940, of 816 social work graduates Toronto had graduated 545, McGill 154, and UBC, 117. Also see J.R. Mutchmor, *The Memoirs of James Ralph Mutchmor* (Toronto: Ryerson Press, 1965).

16. In F. Ivor Jackson, "Profiles 4: J. Howard Falk," *Canadian Welfare* (Nov.-Dec. 1965): 266-273. Details of Falk's Montreal career are found in Office of Principal, RG2, C66, file 1920-22, Department of Social Service; and Montreal Council of Social Agencies 1921-76, MG2076, McGill University Archives.

17. Mutchmor, *Memoirs*, p. 78.

18. Sr. M. du Coeur to CW, 3/5/1929, CCSD/29, *PAM*.

19. Madame J.E. Vajkai, Hungarian Junior Red Cross, to CW, 29/3/1937, CCSD/129.

20. Lela B. Costin, *Two Sisters for Social Justice: A Biography of Grace and Edith Abbott* (Chicago: University of Illinois Press, 1983): 91-92.

21. Pp. 94, 95. Also Sir William Joynson-Hicks, Under Secretary of State, made it known that he wanted *one* assessor from North America and one from South America on the child welfare committee and this was the position of S.W. Harris, the British representative who in turn would have impressed such views on Crowdy. FO 371/11071 (1925) W/161, *Public Record Office*, London; and Lathrop to CW, 16/8/1926, CCSD/129.

22. Costin, p. 96.

23. Lathrop to CW, 29/12/1926, CCSD/2.

24. "Changing Concepts in Social Welfare" (1939), by CW, WP/19.

25. "The Holy Year of Jubilee," Offshore column, *Ottawa Citizen*, 31/12/1949.

26. Ibid.

27. CW to Sir Eric Drummond, n.d., CCSD/2. The British correspondence felt that the committee was disorganized and did not discriminate between appropriate problems of child welfare. See S.W. Harris (Home Office) to C. Howard Smith, 6/5/1932, FO 371/16452; A.G. Maxwell and J.I. Wall, Home Office Report (1932) W/377 and W/383; Harris to A.M. Cadogan, 7/5/1930, W/5575/9/98, W/218; and Sir Austen Chamberlain to Lord Cecil, 31/5/1927, FO 371/570, W/5250, *Public Record Office*, London.

28. Lathrop to CW, 24/11/1926, 3/7/1926 and 2/2/1928, CCSD/2.

29. The Reports and Committees Whitton was involved with are: Child Welfare Report of the Final Committee, 13/9/1928, A.54. 1928.iv; Report of the Work of the Second Session (March 1926) of the Advisory Committee for the Protection of Children and Young People, C.224.M.80 (1926) iv; Report of the Fifth Session (April 12-19) C.169. 1929.iv; and Report, CEP 141. She contributed to the later discussions on Studying the Position of the Illegitimate Child, C.805.1925.iv. Also, Report on the Work of the Tenth Session of the Child Welfare Committee, CPE476(1), 12-17 April, 1934, "The Effects of Economic Depression and Unemployment Upon Children and Young

People"; Enquiry into the Question of Children in Moral and Social Danger, C.185. M.123.1934, 2/4/1934; Report Submitted by Fifth Committee, A.52. 1934.iv, 25/9/1934; "The Placing of Children in Families," C.260.M.155.1938, 21/ 10/1938; and Re-Organization of the Advisory Commission, Paris, April 17, 1936, C.192.M. 121.1936.iv.

30. See Veronica Strong-Boag, "Wages For Housework: Mothers' Allowances and the Beginnings of Social Security in Canada," *Journal of Canadian Studies*, vol. 14, #1 (Spring 1979): 24-34, for a discussion of Whitton's views. Also see, "Aid to Dependent Mothers and Children in Canada: Social Policy Behind Our Legislation" (circa. 1929), WP/3; and "Report of a Committee appointed by the Government to Investigate the Finances of B.C.," 12/7/1932, *Health and Welfare Supervision Board*, RG5 G2, Box 1, file 9, PAM. In

Whitton's report on Mothers' Aid in Manitoba, she says, "the means whereby the funds for the service are provided are direct—there is no alchemy whereby generous impulses become financial resources."

31. "Child Welfare Workers Oppose Family Allowances," (circa. 1929), CCSD/2.

32. Memorandum re Child and Family Welfare in the Province of Quebec, The Quebec Commission on Social Insurance, March 1931, CCSD/43.

33. Pp. 1-2.

34. P. 2.

35. P. 14.

36. P. 8 of section "Mothers' Allowances."

37. CW to H. Usher Miller, New Brunswick Protestant Orphans' Home, 20/3/1930, CCSD/38.

38. Quoted in Russell Kirk, *The Conservative Mind* (Chicago: Henry Regnery Co., 1950): 15.

CHAPTER FIVE   *A Larger Stage*

1. Memorandum from the President and Secretary, CCCW, Ottawa, 26/02/1929, CCSD/4.

2. Tamara Haraven, "An Ambiguous Alliance: Some Aspects of American Influences in Canadian Social Welfare," *Social History* (April 1969): 82-98; and P.T. Rooke and R.L. Schnell, *Discarding the Asylum*, pp. 347-387. Also see *Retrospects and Prospects* (CCFW, 1922-35), p. 4 and CCSD/21 for evidence of such growth.

3. Riley to CW, 6/6/1931, CCSD/21 and Executive Minutes, CCSD/25. Also see Dobson Papers, Microfilm 766, Section B (1926-33) which express similar views. United Church Archives, Toronto.

4. "Better Provision For the Protection of Girl Life," in Bulletin of the Council for Social Service of the Church of England in Canada (May 1933).

5. Ibid., p. 33.

6. CW to Skelton, 22/12/1931, CCSD/28.

7. CW to Skelton, 2/3/1932, CCSD/28; and A.B. Butler, L.L.D. to CW, 28/5/1932, CW to Butler, 13/6/1932, CCSD/2.

8. R.B. Bennett Papers, MG 26 K (M-1398), PAC; WP/19, vols. 26-27; and CCSD/28, and 99, PAC. James Struthers, *No Fault of Their Own: Unemployed and the Canadian*

Welfare State, 1914-1941 (Toronto: University of Toronto Press, 1983).

9. James Struthers, p. 75.

10. Extracts of CW's Report to the League of Nations, "Some Relationships Between Unemployment and Child and Family Welfare in Canada 1933," CCSD/33.

11. CW to Winslow, 30/1/1932, CCSD/28. Similarly conservative views are found in, "Canada's Problems in Welfare and Assistance," an address before the Empire Club, Toronto, 20/3/1936, WP/19; "Suggestions Re: Federal-Provincial Systems Re Direct Relief (1932)," CCSD/13, "Organization of Aid to Persons in Distress: Report for NEC" (1937), WP/26; "Toward National Wellbeing," (CWC: 1936); "Problems in the Social Administration of General and Unemployment Relief-Canada 1933," CCCFW Conference May 1-4, 1933; "The Relief Outlook, Autumn and Winter 1933-34," (CCCFW, 1934), MG 26 K (M1398); and "The Alleviation of Distress in Canada," (n.d.), WP/27.

12. Struthers, p. 77.

13. CW to Bennett, 23/1/1935; CW to Hon. W.A. Gordon, Minister of Labour, 15/11/1933, M-1445, BP; and *The Challenge for Relief Control*, p. 4, (CCCFW: 1934).

14. "Suggestions Re Federal-Provincial Systems . . . 1932," p. 43.

15. Address before Canadian Conference on Social Work, Ottawa, *Globe and Mail*, 8/6/1937 and "Now is the Time to Solve Relief Problems," *Halifax Chronicle*, 1/11/1937.
16. Struthers, p. 215 and Stephen Peitchinis, *The Canadian Labour Market* (Toronto: Oxford University Press, 1975): 15 and 176.
17. "More Effective Co-Operation and Co-Ordination of Voluntary Resources," p. 102, in *Organization of Aid to Persons in Distress: Report for NEC* (1937); and "Two Meals and a Bed," *Financial Post*, 26/9/1936.
18. "Report: Unemployment and Relief in Western Canada (Summer 1932)," p. 9, CCSD/13.
19. Working Copy of *Unemployment and Relief*, pp. 12-13, BP.
20. "Report: Unemployment and Relief in Western Canada," p. 27.
21. Struthers, p. 78.
22. Ibid., pp. 78-79.
23. Ibid, p. 105.
24. Ibid., pp. 106-108.
25. Ibid., pp. 108-109.
26. CW to Miller, 14/12/1933, BP.
27. Bennett to CW, 22/12/1934, BP.
28. CW to Bennett, 14/8/1946.
29. CW to Reid, 8/6/1933, CCSD/30.
30. Falk to CW, 28/2/1929, WP/18.
31. CW to Moore, 22/6/1933, CW to Kennethe Haig, 5/6/1933, and CW to Mrs. S. Gandier, 8/11/1933, CCSD/6 and CCSD/10.
32. CW to MacLaren, 18/9/1933, MG 26 K, Vol. 955, pp. 0604968-0604971, and CW to Bennett, 18/1/1933, M-3179, CW to Mac-Laren, 26/9/1933, M-1398, BP. This has been fully developed by R.L. Schnell, "A Children's Bureau for Canada? The Origins of the CWC 1913-35," unpublished manuscript. The merger with the Child Welfare Division is documented under the years and subject in the Department of National Health and Welfare, RG29, PAC.
33. Letter of Introduction, 4/6/1932, WP/24.
34. CW to Bennett, 10/2/1934, M-1069, Bennett Papers, PAC.
35. Price to Bennett (n.d.), M-1069, BP; and McLeod to CW, 3/01/1934, WP/4.
36. CW to Bennett, 30/4/1934, M-3178, BP.
37. Struthers, pp. 140-141 and 143.
38. Harry Baldwin, Superintendent of Relief Division, NEC, to CW, 20/7/1936, 6/8/1938, 10/8/1936, RG 27 3356, File 8.
39. See Richard Veitch (quoting James Eayres) *Canada and the League of Nations*, p. 21; and Struthers (1983), pp. 154, 181.
40. CW to Arthur B. Purvis, Chairman, NEC, 29/3/1937. See WP/25-26 for NEC information; "Confidential Services of NEC," 26/11/1936, WP/26; and "Non-Residence and Migrancy as a Factor in Social Need (Nov. 1937), RG 27 3370, File 1.
41. Struthers, pp. 153-154. See also the discussion by Struthers, "A Profession in Crisis: Charlotte Whitton and Canadian Social Work in the 1930s," *Canadian Historical Review*, LXII, 2(1981): 169-85.
42. Struthers, p. 170.
43. "Canada's Problems in Welfare Administration," 20/3/1936, p. 10, WP/19.
44. *Financial Post* (Sept. 5-Oct. 31, 1936).
45. In "The Relief Outlook . . . 1934"; and *Financial Post*, 26/9/1936.
46. Struthers, pp. 175-180; and Mackenzie King diary, 26/1/1938 as quoted in *No Fault of Their Own*, p. 181. Also see Denis Guest, *The Emergence of Social Security in Canada* (Vancouver: University of British Columbia Press, 1980) for a discussion of the depression decade and H. Blair Neatby, *The Politics of Chaos* (Toronto: MacMillan of Canada, 1972).
47. Details in File 25-3-2 Pt. 2. RG29, Vol. 32, PAC.
48. BBC, 1/5/1936, WP/94.
49. Memo submitted by Canadian delegate Re: Re-Organization of Future Programmes (Jan. 1937): Advisory Committee on Social Questions (Notices and Agenda, 1936-39); and Advisory Committee on Social Questions Future Work: Report of the Sub-Committee on Plans for Future Work, 15/4/1937, CCSD/131.
50. "K. Lenroot, US Delegate to Committee on Social Questions, Geneva 1936-41," CCSD/131.
51. Social Questions Report by the Fifth Committee, A.62.1938.iv, 26/9/1938, p. 3. Details of the compilation of the report (officially C.260.M.155.1938.iv, Oct. 21, 1938) are found in WP/32.
52. Foreign Office, 9/12/1938 to CW, "Re: The Placing of Children in Families," Ln.doc. C.260.M.155.1938.iv, Vols. 1 & 2," B-4968, DO 35/561/F334/39, CCSD/129.
53. "The Social Worker Pleads For Faith" (1935), p. 13, WP/19 and "Notes on Social Work," Toronto, 6/3/1934, CCSD/1.
54. CW to Parker, 12/3/1936, Box 6, CASW, University of Calgary.
55. CW to Heise, 30/3/1937, CCSD/30.

56. "The Social Worker Pleads For Faith" (1935), p. 13, WP/19.
57. "Notes on Social Work," 6/3/1934, CCSD/1.
58. CW to Blois, 19/1/1932, CCSD/30.
59. "Notes on Social Work."

60. "Changing Concepts in Social Welfare," WP/19.
61. "Comment Re Proposals for Legislation in Quebec, submitted by the CWC," 6/12/1939, CCSD/49.

CHAPTER SIX   *Career in Crisis*

1. Bennett to CW, 15/2/1939, WP/4.
2. CW to Davidson, 26/4/1929; and Lawson to CW, 16/5/1939. Distressed letters to Stapleford, 28/4/1939, and Bessie Touzel, 3/5/1939, substantiate this opinion. Unless otherwise indicated correspondence on Whitton's resignation is found in WP/8.
3. CW to Stapleford, 8/3/1940.
4. CW to Davidson, 26/4/1939.
5. Lawson to CW, n.d.
6. Lea to CW, 16/11/1939.
7. CW to Stapleford, 8/3/1940.
8. Stapleford to CW, 12/3/1940.
9. For examples see, Montgomery to CW, 25/2/1929, 10/10/1930; CW to Montgomery, 6/10/1930 and 13/10/1930, CCSD/29, Public Archives of Manitoba (PAM); Bradford to CW, 17/5/1938, WP/18. Bradford had also been promoted by Emily Murphy, and had followed Whitton and Elizabeth MacCallum at the SSCC. See Judge E. Murphy, "The New Assistant Secretary," *Social Welfare* (June 1924): 166. Also Marion Royce, *Eunice Dyke: Health Care Pioneer* (Toronto and Charlottetown: Dundurn Press, 1983): 158, 177, 184, 200, 201; and Davidson to CW, 19/4/1939, CW to Davidson, 26/4/1939. Davidson also became director of the CBC, President of the Treasury Board, and Undersecretary for Administration at the United Nations within the next 25 years. Correspondence between Cassidy and Whitton or about Whitton in CCSD/99, WP/4, and Vol. 39, 62, 58, Cassidy Papers, University of Toronto Archives.
10. "The Time Has Come," 31/12/1941, WP/21; and "Signing Off" (December 1941).
11. CW to Gordon, 15/1/1942, RG 64, vol. 433, File 10-29-1, PAC.
12. CW to Sanders, 5/2/1942, RG 64, vol. 433, File 10-29-1, PAC.
13. *Memberscript*, #26, vol. 4 (May 1942), Oklahoma City, YWCA; and *Los Angeles Times*, 28/9/1942. Whitton did not have "fiery red hair" as James Struthers claims in *No Fault*

of Their Own, p. 75. Although her voice tended to be high pitched during *emotional* situations in later life it was described as deep "contralto" in her younger days.
14. The lectures and the details surrounding them are in WP/80.
15. "Canterbury and Social Armament," WP/24.
16. *A Hundred Years A 'Fellin—Some Passages from the Timber Saga of the Ottawa in the Century in which the Gillies have been cutting in the Valley, 1842-1942* (Printed for Gillies Brothers, Braeside, Ontario. Ottawa: Runge Press, 1943). The historian D.C. Masters stated that it contained "a great deal of material of interest to general readers who would not be reached by works of more formal scholarship, and much personal reminiscence which will be of concern to those actually associated with the trade." *Canadian Historical Review* 25 (June 1944): 209.
17. *Chicago Sun*, 14/2/1943.
18. *Ottawa Citizen*, 4/5/1943.
19. CW to Viscount Bennett, 14/8/1946.
20. CW to Mrs. James A. Richardson, Grain Exchange, Winnipeg, 29/1/1944, WP/95.
21. Virginia Woolf, *A Room of One's Own* (London: Hogarth Press, 1959), p. 139. Whitton had been impressed by Woolf's book.
22. Sources and drafts of manuscripts related to *Dawn* are found in WP/28.
23. Williamson to Smith, 11/10/1945, WP/5; and CW to Bracken, 2/4/1943, WP/81.
24. "Citizenship," *The Torch*, Vol. II, #3 (Jan.-Feb. 1926): 38-41.
25. MS, undated and untitled, WP/97.
26. One weighty work which discusses subsidiarity is Joseph N. Moody, (ed.), *Church and Society: Catholic Social and Political Thought and Movements 1789-1950* (N.Y.: Arts Inc., 1953), pp. 331-340, 508-533, 542-548. Also see its practical and political implications in the papal encyclicals of Leo XIII and Pius XI, especially *Quadragesino Anno: On*

Reconstructing Social Order (1931) by which Whitton was obviously influenced.

27. Hiram McCann, "Now It's the Whitton Plan," *Saturday Night* (October 16, 1943). Also see Arthur McArthur, "Canada's Road to Social Security," *Canadian Business* (March 1944).

28. Allan Irving, "Canadian Fabians: The Work and Thought of Harry Cassidy and Leonard Marsh 1930-45," *Canadian Journal of Social Work Education*, Vol. 7 (1981): 10.

29. Dick Davis, Secretary, Canadian Institute on Public Affairs, to CW, 29/7/1943, WP/4.

30. Manning to CW, 10/3/1945, WP/4.

31. Cassidy to CW, 15/2/1944, WP/4.

32. CW to V.R. Smith, President, Confederation Life Association, Toronto, 13/6/1945, WP/5.

33. CW to Waterman, 28/7/1945, WP/22; and to Bennett, 14/8/1946, WP/4.

34. One example of this was the open disagreement between Whitton and Miss Elisabeth Wallace of the CASW. See "The Fight For Family Allowances," *Moose Jaw Times Herald*, 28/7/1944.

35. CW to Cassidy, 11/12/1943, WP/4.

36. CW to Edith Abbott, School of Social Service, Chicago, 20/6/1945, WP/5.

37. *Canadian Historical Review* 25 (March 1944): 63-66.

38. *Queen's Quarterly* 50 (1943): 423-26. A descriptive overview of the reports by Marsh, Cassidy and Whitton is in "Letters in Canada: 1943," *University of Toronto Quarterly* 13 (April 1944): 348-350.

39. Cassidy to Mackenzie King, 10/12/1943; and General correspondence (Sept.-Dec. 1943), n.d., WP/4.

40. CW to Abbott, 20/6/1945 and to V. Smith, 13/6/1945, WP/5; and R.A. Bell to CW, 1/8/1944; CW to Harry Willis, Dominion Organizer, Progressive Conservative Party, 29/7/1944; WP/81.

41. CW to Hesson, 11/8/1944 and to Macphail, 7/4/1945, WP/81; and Macphail to CW, 24/2/1945, WP/4.

42. Henderson to CW, 19/7/1944, WP/81.

43. CW to G.P. McTague, 1/8/1944, WP/81.

44. CW to Hardy, 29/6/1945, WP/5.

45. CW to Bracken, 29/7/1944, WP/81.

46. CW to Hesson, 11/8/1944, WP/81.

47. CW to Bennett, 14/8/1946, WP/4.

48. CW to Canon W.W. Judd, Secretary, Social Service Council of the Church of England, 4/4/1942, WP/22; and address before the Ontario Public School Trustees and Ratepayers Association, Toronto, 10/4/1944, p. 10, WP/83.

49. "Child Welfare Workers Oppose Family Allowances," n.d., CCSD/2. Also see "Dependency and Organized Relief Work: The Case of the Dependent Mother and Children," (circa 1919-22), WP/19, for similar views.

50. Memo from CW to Bracken, n.d., MG 27 III, c/6, Vol. 136, Bracken Papers, PAC.

51. Address before Ontario Public Schools Trustees, 10/4/1944.

52. Report of a Committee appointed by the Government to Investigate the Finances of B.C., 12/7/1932, pp. 36-39, RG5/G2, Box 1, File 9, *Provincial Archives of Manitoba*.

53. CW to McTague, 11/8/1944, WP/81.

54. Telegram, 19/2/1945, WP/4.

55. CW to Manning, 30/1/1945, Manning to CW, 10/3/1945, WP/4.

56. *Baby Bonuses*, pp. 18 and 20.

57. *Renfrew Mercury*, 7/12/1944, *Ottawa Citizen*, 13/11/1944 and the *Boston Globe*, 18/1/1945.

58. CW to Drew, 28/3/1945, WP/4.

59. CW to Lorne Pierce, 20/11/1945; and Pierce to CW, 26/11/1945, WP/5.

60. CW to Smith, 15/6/1946 and 4/6/1946; and CW to George Drew, 20/8/1945 and Drew to CW, 11/6/1946, WP/5.

61. Letters to the Editor, *Ottawa Citizen*, 18/10/1945.

CHAPTER SEVEN   *Mid Life Resolution*

1. A.E. Rose, Chicago to CW, 28/5/1946, WP/5; and Box 7, File 23 (Corresp. 1949), *Queen's University Archives*.

2. Marjorie Bradford to CW, 13/3/1946, WP/5.

3. Address given, 20/11/1946, Toronto, and published in *The Queen's Review*, Vol. 27 (Jan. 1947): 4-10.

4. Details leading up to the 1947 Alberta survey comes from the following: R.C. Marshall to CW, 16/4/1945, 2/6/1945, 11/12/1945, 29/6/1945; CW to Marshall, 11/12/1945; Mrs. R. Schroter, Secretary, Provincial Survey Committee, IODE, to CW, 29/6/1945; Holland to CW, 29/6/1945,

WP/31; CW to Premier Manning, Premiers Papers 69.289, *Provincial Archives of Alberta* (PAA); and *Toronto Daily Star*, 9/12/1944, 11/12/1944, 18/9/1945, WP/32.

5. In "Request of S. Bruce Smith, Council of the Commission for the Government of Alberta, to reproduce extracts of Correspondence" in File: 1945-46, WP/31.

6. CW to Bilora P. Cutler, n.d., WP/4; CW to Manning, thanking him for his courtesy in their recent interview, 19/10/1946, and to Cross, 19/10/1946, 69.²89, PAA.

7. Neatby to CW, 1/1/1947, WP/5.

8. Correspondence, reports, clippings, briefs, releases etc., are found in WP/31, 32, 34.

9. *The Albertan*, 29/1/1947, described her as social work's "First Lady."

10. O'Byrne to CW, 28/7/1947, WP/31.

11. CW to State Department of Welfare, Montana, 13/1/1947, and "The Cross Border Export of Alberta Babies," IODE report, pp. 24-26, WP/31.

12. In "The Cross Border Export of Alberta Babies," pp. 24-26, WP/31.

13. File: House of Commons Debates, WP/34.

14. CW to Hoehler, 9/1/1948 and to Sheane, 26/1/1948, WP/31. Correspondence from her close friend Marjorie Crowther indicates that Whitton was well aware of the probable conclusion of Grier's illness. Crowther to CW, 20/10/1947, 6/11/1947, and 12/12/1947, WP/2.

15. CW to Fr. MacDonald, 4/1/1948, WP/31.

16. CW to Hoehler, 9/10/1948 and to Sheane, 26/1/1948, WP/31.

17. CW to Castendyck, 18/02/1948, WP/32.

18. Towers to CW, 13/8/1948, WP/4.

19. Holland to CW, n.d., WP/3.

20. CW to Parker, 23/11/1949, MG 31, K6, PAC.

21. Laird to CW, 17/7/1951, WP/6.

22. Margaret and Dora Grier were the nieces of the founder of the order and were related to Miss Rose J. Grier, the former principal of Bishop Strachan school who had signed the charter of St. Hilda's College.

23. Sister Dora Correspondence is found in WP/1-3, and Memorial Information in WP/14.

24. CW to Reverend Mr. Aquila, 2/1/1948 and to C. Beatrice Smith, 13/10/1948, WP/14.

25. CW to Aquila.

26. CW to Smith, 25/10/1948 and 30/10/1948, WP/14.

27. In WP/14.

28. In *Courier Advocate*, (Trenton), 30/4/1957, WP/14.

29. CW to Helen Franks, Trinity College, 23/2/1950, WP/14.

30. CW to Rev. Frank S. Morley, Grace Church, Calgary, 14/2/1948 and to Gwynneth Howell, Montana Council of Social Agencies, 17/3/1948, WP/31.

31. "Special Notes to Council Re Article," WP/32.

32. Harold Dingman, "Babies for Export: Alberta's Tragic Traffic in Babies," *New Liberty* (27 December 1947): 5-7 and 33-34.

33. "Welfare in Alberta," Pamphlet #17, *Winnipeg Free Press* (August 1947), p. 3. This pamphlet came from editorials on the topic.

34. Calgary *Herald*, 23/2/1947.

35. Manning to Johnston, 3/12/1947; Manning to Kennedy, 29/1/1948, 69.289.1378, PAA. Emphasis added.

36. *Edmonton Bulletin*, 5/4/1948.

37. In "Epistle to the Socians," by CW, 24/6/1948, WP/34.

38. R.E.G. Davis, CWC, to Manning, 27/2/1948; Manning to Davis, 4/8/1948, File 1716, PAA.

39. *Time*, 29/12/1947 and 16/2/1948; *The Albertan*, 7/1/1948; *Globe and Mail*, 7/1/1948; and Calgary *Herald*, 12/1/1948.

40. *The Albertan*, 26/1/1948.

41. "Epistle to the Socians."

42. Cassidy to CW, 30/1/1948; and CW to Steer, 25/2/1948, WP/31.

43. Hilliarde to CW, 3/2/1948, WP/31. A similar point of view was expressed in the Montreal *Daily Sun*, 6/4/1948. The editorial in the Regina *Leader Post*, 6/6/1947, titled "Secrecy in Alberta," had referred to Social Credit's "high minded authoritarianism."

44. "Provisions on Guardianship and Other Measures For Children in Pre-Nazi and Nazi Germany," (Feb. 1948) and "Legislation on Unmarried Parenthood, Marriage, Divorce, Guardianship, Adoption and Other Measures Relative to Children in the USSR," (Feb. 1948); and Elsie Castendyck to CW, 23/03/1948, WP/32.

45. CW to Steer, 13/3/1948, WP/31.

46. A. MacNamara to CW, 1/4/1948, WP/32.

47. CW to Rev. Canon W.W. Judd, Church of England Social Service Council, 14/2/1948, WP/31.

48. Adams to Manning, 23/1/1948. Also Annie A. Kennedy, R.N., wrote on 22/1/1948, that the charges were calamitous and should be withdrawn, 69.289.1716, PAA.

49. From *Hamilton Spectator* to CW, 25/2/1948, and Calgary Women's Club to CW, 30/1/1948, WP/31.

50. See C.B. MacPherson, *Democracy in Alberta* (University of Toronto Press, 1953) for an account of Social Credit in Alberta. Whitton speaks of the News Information Act in a letter to Katharine Lenroot, U.S. Children's Bureau, 11/3/1948, WP/31. Also see *Edmonton Journal*, 4/3/1948; J.R. Mallory, *Social Credit and the Federal Power in Canada* (University of Toronto Press, 1954), pp. 77-78; and John J. Barr, *The Dynasty: The Rise and Fall of Social Credit in Alberta* (Toronto: McClelland and Stewart, 1974), p. 109. *The Times* referred to this decision of the Privy Council and explained that this, with two other bills, was virtually a "muzzling of the press," 7/7/1938, File 701, PAA. Moreover, the Social Credit government itself had been on the receiving end of a "criminal charge of publishing a defamatory libel" in 1937 when J.H. Unwin, government Whip in the legislature and George Frederick Powell, a member of the staff of the Social Credit Board, were sentenced respectively to six and three months of hard labour at Fort Saskatchewan. Mallory, pp. 81-83, and Barr, pp. 109-110. The amendment to the Criminal Code is found in the *Revised Statutes*, Canadian Criminal Code (1927), Section 888, Chap. 39.

51. "Report on the Child Welfare Branch, Department of Welfare, Province of Alberta," 3/12/1948, WP/34.

CHAPTER EIGHT   *A Woman Not a Lady*

1. "Between You and Me," by Margaret Aitken, *The Telegram*, 15/2/1956; and James Finar and Lawrence Elliott, "The Ringmistress is No Lady Clown," *Canada Month* (June 1963).
2. "Charlotte Sounds Off—On Almost Everything," *Ottawa Citizen* (*OC*), 4/9/1965; and Phyllis Harrison, "In the Beginning was Charlotte," *Canadian Welfare*, 2 (April 1975).
3. File: Campaign Finances (1950), 6/11/1950, WP/38; and "The Beginning of It All," *Ottawa Journal* (*OJ*), 1/12/1950.
4. Campaign Clippings (1950) and Campaign Finances (1950), WP/38.
5. CFRA, 8/11/1950, WP/38.
6. *OJ*, 21/11/1950.
7. *OJ*, 21/11/1950; *OJ*, 22/11/1950; Evening *OC*, 22/11/1950.
8. *OC*, 27/11/1950; *OJ*, 1/12/1950 and Campaign Clippings (1950).
9. "The Case for More Day Nurseries," *OC*, 10/2/1951; Letter to the Editor, *OC*, 13/4/1951; and "Day Care in Toronto," *OC*, 31/7/1951.
10. "Now It's Baby Sitting," *OC*, 5/7/1951.
11. "Provincial-Municipal Integration of Welfare Services," 12/6/1951, WP/50.
12. Southam to CW, 6/7/1951, WP/6; and "My Mother," *OC*, 5/7/1951.
13. "The Ringmistress," p. 17; "To The World Outside of City Council Charlotte Whitton is Ottawa's Mayor," *OJ*, 3/9/1951.
14. "The Mayor Restores Historic Chair," *OJ*, 3/10/1951. For later discussions see, "Ottawa Council Disrobes," *OJ*, 19/10/1954; and "Council Robes and Mayor's Chair," Minutes of Council, 2/3/1953, WP/43.
15. See Correspondence (1953) WP/116; also *OC*, 10/10/1951.
16. "Flunking the Finals," *Winnipeg Free Press*, 7/5/1952.
17. Address on Inauguration as Mayor of Ottawa, 15/10/1952, MG 12-1-12, *Ottawa City Archives* (*OCA*).
18. Nomination Speech, 21/11/1952, MG 12-1-4, and Campaign Rally, 31/10/1952, MG 12-1-3, OCA.
19. Inaugural Address, 15/10/1951, WP/38.
20. Circular Letter (n.d.), WP/3.
21. In Clippings (circa 1952), WP/51.
22. *Globe and Mail*, 10/1/1984.
23. See Correspondence (1953), WP/116; and *OC*, 10/10/1951.
24. "Memory of the Coronation," *OJ*, 11/5/1953.
25. "Our Sovereign Lady," *OC*, 26/8/1957.
26. "Freedom Wears A Crown," *OC*, 25/9/1957.
27. Marguerite S. Nasmith to CW, 7/12/1954, WP/39.
28. "Ottawa Council Disrobes," *OJ*, 19/10/1954.
29. "Charlotte's Strategy Awaits Her Memoirs," *OJ*, 11/12/1954.
30. *OJ*, 3/11/1954 and 11/12/1954; *Press Clippings*, (Nov. 15-Nov. 19, 1954), WP/132; Nomination Address, 26/11/1954; and Radio Broadcast (1954), WP/39.
31. In "The Decay of Democracy," The Samuel Robinson Memorial Lecture, Prince of Wales College, Charlottetown, 22/4/1945, MG 12-1-5, published in *The Dalhousie Review*, Vol. 35, #2 (Summer 1955): 100-119; and "Slams Waste of Woman Power," *Windsor Star*, 16/5/1966.
32. "Huge City Works Program," *OJ*, 5/1/1955.

33. "CWC Study of Social Service Department, City of Ottawa, reported 3/10/1955," WP/40.

34. "Not By Grants Alone—Can Municipal Government Be Served and Saved in Canada Today?" 29/2/1956, WP/50.

35. Stanley Westall, "Charlotte I of Ottawa," *The Globe Magazine*, 28/11/1964.

36. "Whitton Committee Won't Lead Draft Move," *OJ*, 31/10/1955; OC, Editorial, 31/10/1956; "Whitton Won't Be Running," *OJ*, 19/10/1956; *Toledo Blade*, 22/2/1954; "Experiment in Housing: Ottawa's Method," *Saturday Night*, 14/8/1954; *OJ*, 27/11/1954; and "Exciting Ottawa Mayoralty Fight," *OC*, 27/11/1954.

37. "Whitton Stays in Office to Direct Works Project: May Later Join Cabinet," *OC*, 23/6/1955.

38. *OJ*, 19/10/1956; Editorial, *OC*, 31/10/1956; and "See Whitton Facing Three Political Targets," *OJ*, 1/12/1956.

39. See Correspondence and Cuttings in WP/94.

40. See *Chatham News*, 23/5/1957 and correspondence in WP/116 for details of May election.

41. Gordon K. Fraser, Peterborough, to CW, 11/5/1957, WP/81.

42. CW to H. Nellist, VP Creamery Package Co., Toronto, 30/5/1957, WP/81.

43. WPCA of Ottawa West to Allister Grossart, National HQs, PCA of Canada, 6/1/1958, WP/81; and "It's War Between the Past and the Present," *OC*, 24/12/1957.

44. *OJ*, 25/2/1958, WP/81; Nomination Speech for Ottawa West, 24/2/1958, WP/81.

45. *The Telegram*, 25/12/1958.

46. "Tory Flood Engulfs Opposition Parties," *OC*, 1/4/1958; and *Herald Tribune*, 26/2/1958.

47. *OC*, 1/4/1958; and "She's 62 Today, In Fightin' Trim," *OC*, 8/3/1958; and Election Expense Act, 1974.

48. "We'll All Miss Charlotte," by Margaret Aitken, *Telegram*, 8/4/1958.

49. "Charlotte Blames Family," *OJ*, 8/12/1964.

50. See Private and Confidential Memo for Rt. Honorable Prime Minister (August-December 1958), WP/6.

51. CW to Diefenbaker, 3/8/1959, WP/6.

52. *Clippings* (1943), WP/115. The *OC*, 23/4/1963, claimed that she had been named Ambassador to Eire in 1962 but Diefenbaker retracted because of her conduct with Paul Tardif in City Hall. There is no evidence in Whitton's files such an offer had been made unless it was over the telephone. Given Whitton's vanity, it would be surprising that she did not keep a record of the offer in some form or other.

53. "Where Do You Go, Fair Lady?" *OC*, 23/8/1957.

54. "The Power of Woman," *OC*, 17/9/1958.

55. "How Could You Hamilton?" *OC*, 10/10/1958.

56. "Salvation By Sex," 3/6/1959; and Venerable W.D. McL Christie to CW, 10/6/1959, WP/6.

57. "Welcome Women of the Press," *OC*, 9/9/1959.

58. "Prophets, Priests and Puritans," *OC*, 22/5/1959.

59. "Report on the State of the City," 3/1/1956, WP/39.

CHAPTER NINE   *No Angel But a Good Mayor*

1. "Through the Motions," *OC*, 13/5/1960.

2. Correspondence on "The Other Woman" is in WP/94.

3. CW to Frost, 20/4/1960, 26/4/1960 and CW to Diefenbaker, 20/5/1960, WP/6; and "CBC Denounced by Whitton," *OC*, 27/5/1960.

4. "Featuring—Lies For Sale," *OC*, 18/5/1960 and "The Discussion of Divorce," *OC*, 27/5/1960.

5. Susie H. McRae to CW, 30/5/1960.

6. "In Search of Oneself" (circa. 1960s), WP/94.

7. "Charlotte In; Bids to Block Spending," *OJ*, 14/11/1960; and "The Unsinkable Charlotte Whitton," *Maclean's*, 22/4/1961.

8. Nomination Speech, 25/11/1960, pp. 1, 12, 14-15 WP/53.

9. Mayoralty Campaign Clippings (1960), WP/78; *Star Weekly Magazine*, 1/4/1961; "The Unsinkable Charlotte Whitton"; and "The Door of My Lips," *Newsweek*, 16/1/1961.

10. *Star Weekly Magazine*, 1/4/1961; and "Our Fair Lady," *Ottawa Journal* (*OJ*), 21/11/1964.

11. *Toronto Daily Star*, 27/6/1960; "Whitton In Front All the Way," *OC*, 6/12/1960; "Ottawa's Amazing Charlotte Whitton," Saint John's *Telegraph-Journal*, 10/12/1960; and "Charlotte at the Barricades," *Time Magazine*, 19/12/1960.

12. *The Star*, Johannesburg, 26/11/1962; and

OJ, 13/11/1962 and 15/11/1962.
13. CBOT Broadcast, 30/11/1962, WP/53.
14. "Princess Pretty Woman," *Lethbridge Herald*, 3/7/1961; *OJ*, 28/2/1962; "Miss Whitton and the Men," *Globe and Mail* (*G & M*), 15/11/1962; "The Housing Delays," *OJ*, 18/4/1962; "Alderman Jess Wentzell Resigns," *OJ*, 2/5/1962; *San Francisco Chronicle*, 25/11/1962 and *Vancouver Sun*, 30/8/1962.
15. Appeal for Re-Election (Fall 1962), WP/53.
16. *Time*, 14/12/1962, p. 2; "Miss Whitton and the Men," *G & M*, 15/11/1962; and "Whitton is Back," *OJ*, 4/12/1962.
17. "The Ringmistress is No Lady Clown," *Canada Month* (June 1963); "Miss Whitton and the Men"; and "The Unsinkable Charlotte Whitton."
18. *OJ*, 20/11/1964.
19. See *Cuttings* (1950-54), WP/51; and "The Ringmistress."
20. See especially "Canada's Dynamic Heartland," *National Geographic* (July 1963); "The

Mayor's No Angel," *Reader's Digest* (July 1963); "Her Worship, Charlotte," *Woman's Day* (November 1955); and "Canada's Capital," *Holiday* (December 1955).
21. "Reporters Keep off the Grass," *The Pembroke Observer*, 22/11/1960; and *The Province*, 9/12/1964. These views are supported by recent letters to the authors in reply to a letter to the editor by them "Welcome Picture," *G & M*, 21/8/1984 which discussed the press's sexist photographs of Whitton. Ms. E. Cunningham, Puslinch, Ontario, 25/1/1984; R. Alison Ghent, Kingston, 28/1/1983; G. Campbell McDonald, Ontario Ministry of Tourism and Recreation, 25/1/1984; and M. Smythe, Middle Musquodoboit; N.S., 27/1/1974.
22. "Who Will Be the Next Mayor?" *OJ*, 9/7/1964 and *OJ* editorial, 4/11/1964.
23. E.P. Gray to CW, 22/3/1972 and "The Gang From Studio TR2" (n.d.), WP/62.

CHAPTER TEN   *Angry, Anxious, and Aging*

1. "Candidates Make Final Vote Pitch," *Ottawa Journal* (*OJ*), 5/12/1964.
2. "Mayor Mobilizes Troops," *OJ*, 2/11/1964; "Our Fair Lady," *OJ*, 21/11/1964; "The Last Suffragette," *Toronto Daily Star*, 9/12/1964; "Ottawa Will Vote Tomorrow," *New York Times*, 6/12/1964; and Stanley Westall, "The Last Suffragette," *The Globe Magazine*, 28/11/1964.
3. "Reid in a Walk" and "Charlotte Blames Family," *OJ*, 8/12/1964; and Tribute to Frank Ryan, CJOH, 2/3/1965, WP/94.
4. *OJ*, 8/12/1964.
5. "A Hamilton View of the Whitton Era in Ottawa," and "Miss Whitton—An Example of What Women Can Do," in Campaign Clippings (1964), WP/53.
6. MS. (1965) in WP/79.
7. *The Albertan*, 6/4/1965.
8. "The Armorial Saints Go Marching into Obscurity," 20/1/1965; "Selling Basic Freedoms for Vague New Human Rights," 20/3/1965; and CW to Editor, "Leave the English Alone," 31/7/1967, WP/93.
9. CW to Goldwin Smith, Wayne State University, 29/3/1965, WP/7; *Hamilton Spectator*, 16/10/1967; *The Province*, 11/3/1967; F. Ivor Jackson to CW and CW to Jackson, 6/2/1965; WP/7; Correspondence (March

1965), dated 29/3/1965, WP/7; and Edwin McCormick, President, Publishers of the North American Relations Foundation, to CW, 21/6/1966, WP/7.
10. An Essay in Review by CW of "Review of Just Think Mr. Berton (A Little Harder)," by Ted Byfield (Winnipeg, Company of the Cross), 1965; and CW to Miss Jan Egan, Secretary, Senior Debating Club, Oakridge Secondary School, London, Ontario, 12/4/1965, WP/7.
11. Mrs. A. L-, Hull, to CW, 3/2/1965 and Mrs. Joan May B-, to CW, 10/1/1967, WP/7.
12. Griffiths to CW, 27/4/1967 and CW to Griffiths, 2/5/1967, WP/94.
13. "Slams Waste of Woman Power," *The Windsor Star*, 16/5/1966.
14. "Whitton Bounced From City Council," *OJ*, 24/10/1967.
15. Minutes, 14/1/1970, WP/76.
16. "Hard Hatted Charlotte Hammers at Windmills," *Montreal Star*, 7/2/1968; and miscellaneous correspondence, WP/129.
17. "Today's World Compared to Rome Before the Fall," *London Free Press*, 13/11/1967; "Character Building: Disintegration Cure," *Edmonton Journal*, 19/5/1967; and *Clippings*, 21/4/1968, WP/129
18. MS., notes and address in WP/85.

19. Notes in WP/86-87.
20. *OC*, 31/12/1970; Address at 23rd annual banquet of the Toronto Gerontological Society, 21-24 October 1970; "Gerontology, Geriatrics and the Golden Age," (n.d.), WP/89; "Now's the Time to Get Off Our Rocking Chairs," *The Daily Colonist*, 21/10/1969; and "Always One More Crusade," *The Tribune*, 31/10/1971.

21. "It's Time To Get Off The Youth Kick," *Chatelaine* (February 1970); notes in WP/89; "Youth Must Earn Right To Do Their Own Thing," *Halifax Chronicle*, 8/10/1969; *OC*, 21/10/1969; *The Spectator*, 20/2/1970; *The Enterprise* (Yorkton, Sask.), 12/11/1969; and "Charlotte's Off On a New Crusade," *The Edmonton Journal*, 28/10/1969.
22. *OJ*, 29/6/1972; *OC*, 3/10/1972, and 31/10/1972.

EPILOGUE   *The Ambiguous Feminist*

1. "Women: A Necessary Evil" (1950), p. 8, WP/84.
2. Address to Hamilton's Women's Club, 29/3/1952, WP/52.
3. See Introduction by Elaine Showalter, in George Gissing, *The Odd Women* (Newport: New American Library, 1983), p. xxi.
4. Henry James, *The Bostonians* (Middlesex, Harmondsworth: Penguin Books, 1966): 119.
5. Showalter, p. xxi.
6. "Society and the Revolution in the Status of Women," first lecture of the Susan B. Anthony Lectures, The College for Women, University of Rochester, 15/2/1947, p. 21, WP/84.
7. "Society and the Revolution," p. 18.
8. Jane Marcus, "Liberty, Sorority and Misogny," in *The Representation of Women in Fiction* edited by Carolyn G. Heilbrun, Margaret R. Higonnet (Chicago: Johns Hopkins Press, 1983): 60-65; and "Sapphistry: Narration as Lesbian Seduction in 'A Room of One's Own,'" paper presented to the *NWSA*, 1983. Also see "Letters to the Editor" from Jane Marcus, *Women's Review of Books*, Vol. 11, #3 (December 1984): 18-19 and from Sue Fawcett, Vol. 11, #7 (April 1985): 18.
9. "Society and the Revolution," p. 15.
10. "Unmarried Parenthood and the Social Order," *Social Welfare* (April-May 1920): 186.
11. Address "Rebuilding Canadian Home and Family Life," *Canadian Dietetic Association*, 11/6/1947, WP/84, PAC.
12. "The Church Woman in the Nation's Life," 26/2/1945, pp. 6, 13, WP/24, PAC.
13. "Intelligent Maternity: Responsible Paternity" (1945), p. 5, WP/85.
14. "In 'Notes on Women,'" (n.d.), WP/96; and "Intelligent Maternity . . . ," p. 12.
15. "Flunking the Finals," 1/5/1952, p. 7, WP/52.

16. "Towards a New Era of Family Life," (circa 1943), pp. 19-20, WP/82.
17. "Women: A Necessary Evil," p. 12.
18. "Society and the Revolution," pp. 7-8.
19. "Women: A Necessary Evil," p. 12. A shorter version was given to the Montreal Business and Professional Women, 19/10/1950. Also see "Society and the Revolution," p. 28.
20. "Women and the Future of Family Life," (1943), WP/83; "Where Do We Go From Here?" (1943), WP/88; "Government of the People . . . "; "Women In a Man's World," *The Burlington Gazette*, 1/10/1959; and "Can a Woman Behave Like a Man?" address to Alumnae Society of McGill (1963).
21. "Can a Woman Behave Like a Man?"; "The Hen of Conrich," *A Woman on the Line*, 3/11/1950, WP/91; and "Canada Looks Forward: Place of Women," (1944), WP/88.
22. "Women the World Over," *The Quotarian*, Vol. 24, #7 (October 1946), p. 4, WP/24; "The Place of Women," Queen's University lecture, *Kingston Whig-Standard*, 18/1/1944; and James Finar and Lawrence Elliott, "The Ringmistress is No Lady Clown," *Canada Month* (June 1963). For similar views see also: "The Matriots," *A Woman on the Line*, 27/3/1951, WP/51; "Government of the People, By the People—Including Women," *The Quotarian* (October 1954): 8-10, an address to the Chicago Gyro Club, 12/6/1954; and "Women in Public Affairs Prove Fallacy of a 'Man's World,'" Sudbury Star, 16/11/1962.
23. *Ottawa Citizen*, 15/9/1951.
24. "Women and the Budget," *Ottawa Citizen*, 8/7/1946; "Who Governs?" 31/5/1951, WP/91; and "Offshore," the *Ottawa Evening Citizen*, 3/1/1950.
25. "The Churchwomen and the Nation's Life," *The Bulletin* (October 1945), p. 4.

26. "Towards a New Era of Family Life," Health Education Group, Board of Health, Vancouver, Vol. 9, #8 (circa. 1943), p. 21, WP/28. This was probably a lecture given to the UBC School of Social Work.

27. "Charlotte Whitton Urges Public Life Partnership," *Ottawa Citizen*, 15/10/1951. Also see "The Matriots," 27/3/1951, WP/91; "Government of the People, By the People— Including Women," *The Quotarian* (Oct. 1954): 8-10.

28. "Women in the Post War Period," *The Bulletin*, 10/10/1945, p. 8, WP/22.

29. "Towards a New Era of Family Life," p. 19; Address to the Hamilton Women's Club, 29/3/1952, WP/52; Martha Moscro to CW, 24/5/1955, WP/6; and Memo: Problems Re Women and the Working Women in the Church of England in Canada, 31/12/1948, p. 8, WP/22.

30. "Women: A Necessary Evil," p. 19; and "Society and the Revolution," p. 21.

31. "Women in the Post War World," p. 8.

32. "Society and the Revolution," pp. 8, 12, 24.

33. Histories of earlier American and British single women are found in Lee Virginia Chambers-Schiller, *Liberty A Better Husband: Single Women in America: The Generations of 1780-1840* (New Haven: Yale University Press, 1984); and Martha Vicinus, *Independent Women: Work and Community for Single Women 1850-1920* (Chicago: University of Chicago Press, 1984). Showalter, p. xxii. Also see Shiela Jeffreys, *The Spinster and Her Enemies: Feminism and Sexuality, 1880-1930* (London: Pandora Press/Routledge and Kegan Paul, 1985). Much has been made of the ideological components of sexual liberation of the 1960s and its relationship to chemical control of female reproduction. The same amount of attention has not been given to what must be judged as an equally impressive revolution by the late 1940s. For women to enter the workforce in such numbers two things had occurred: there was ready access to effective birth control measures, but more importantly, this reaffirms what birth control historians have thoroughly demonstrated, that there were moral and attitudinal shifts other than economic causes for such entrance to be legitimated. The war alone cannot explain the shift since it was followed by a concomittant phenomena, that is, the flight into domesticity of the post-war years.

34. Quotes taken from CBC Broadcast, 9/10/1944, WP/93; "Women and the Budget," *Ottawa Citizen*, 8/7/1946, WP/88; "Women: A Necessary Evil," (1950), pp. 20-21; "A Woman on the Line," *Ottawa Citizen*, 22/3/1951; and "Where Are You Going To My Pretty Maid?" address to Brescia College, 13/1/1967, p. 9, WP/85.

35. "Rebuilding Canadian Home and Family Life," p. 10.

36. Pp. 10-11.

37. Acting Mayor Whitton to wives of the Canadian Dental Association (1951), WP/52.

38. For example see "Notes on Women" (n.d.), WP/96.

39. This economic argument is found in "Canadian Women and the War Effort (MacMillan of Canada: 1943); "A New Home Guard," 10/11/1950, WP/91; MS. notes "On Women and the Party Conventions," n.d., WP/96; and "Women and the Future of Family Life."

40. "Women: A Necessary Evil," p. 8.

41. "Society and the Revolution," p. 25. Similar views are found in "Rebuilding Canadian Home and Family Life."

42. "Advisory Committee on Reconstruction: XI Post War Problems of Women," Final Report of Sub-committee, 30/11/1943, (Ottawa: 1944), pp. 19, 33, WP/104; and Gail Cuthbert Brandt, "'Pigion-Holed and Forgotten': The Work of the Subcommittee on the Post-war Problems of Women, 1943," *Histoire sociale/Social History* 16 (May 1982): 239-59.

43. Canada, Dominion Bureau of Statistics, *1961 Census of Canada*, Bulletin SL-1, *Labour Force: Occupation and Industry Trends* (Ottawa: Ministry of Trade and Commerce, 1966), Table 11.

44. "Where Are You Going to my Pretty Maid?"

45. See "Domestic Help," 12/7/1951, WP/91; and "Notes on Women," WP/96.

46. "Cook General and Live-Out" (1946), WP/89. See also, "Domestic Helpers Need New Deal in Household Work," *Saturday Night* (July 6, 1946); and "Shortage of Home Helpers Relieved By New Order," *SN* (July 13, 1946).

47. "Cook General and Live Out."

48. "Women: A Necessary Evil" (1950) traces the economic vitiation of women historically but relates this to the "degradation of regard" generally:
    Yet woman is, deep in the heart of

many males, deemed a necessary evil, tolerated but kept under discount economically, socially, politically, ecclesiastically. . . ." (p. 14).

49. "Women: A Necessary Evil," p. 19.

50. "Prejudice Against Women in Municipal Life in Ottawa," address to St. Lambert's Women's Club, 6/4/1960, WP/74.

51. "The Fiscal Status of the Earning Woman in Partnership Families," MS. WP/88, published in *The Business and Professional Woman* (Jan.-Feb. 1950). Also see CW to Mrs. Elizabeth Hammond, *Family Herald and Weekly Star*, 30/7/1946, WP/5.

52. R.B. Adams to CW, 16/3/1970 and CW to Adams, 23/3/1970, WP/7.

53. "Five Planks in Search of a Platform," address to Business and Professional Clubs, 8/5/1951, WP/52.

54. Anglican Advance Appeal Correspondence is found in WP/22-24.

55. Quoted in Cecil Woodham-Smith, *Florence Nightingale* (London: Constable and Company, 1950): 98.

56. See draft of "The Church and the Changing Status of Women," (1946), WP/24, for her views of "Women Not Affiliated."

57. The Women of the Church," 31/12/1948, p. 14; and "The Church and the Changing Status of Women," (1946), WP/24.

58. An earlier study was "Better Provision for Protection of Girl Life," *The Bulletin* (May 1930) and "Community Study For Community Service" (1940), CCSD/132.

59. CW to Mrs. W.P.M. Kennedy, 30/12/1946, and to Miss Margaret Wherry, 11/10/1946, WP/23.

60. "Are the Churches Facing the Challenge of Women's Changed Status?" 24/11/1946, WP/23.

61. CW to Kennedy, 30/12/1946.

62. Meredith to CW, 21/10/1946, WP/23.

63. "The Women of the Church," (1947), pp. 4-6, WP/22.

64. Op. cit., and Progress Report to WNA Committee Re WNA, 23/5/1946, WP/24.

65. CW to Dean Luxton, London, 8/11/1946; to Rev. Derwyn T. Owen, Archbishop of Toronto, 5/4/1946, WP/23.

66. "Women: A Necessary Evil," pp. 17-18.

67. "On Thinking It Over," 24/5/1959, Transcript of Broadcast, WP/94.

68. "Women in the Post War World," p. 8.

69. "Society and the Revolution," p. 22; "Women and the Future of Family Life," p. 5; and "A

New Home Guard," *Ottawa Citizen*, 10/11/1950.

70. The original manuscript for "The Exploited Sex," *Maclean's Magazine*, 15/4/1947, p. 40, was called "But He's a Man!" (1946), WP/88.

71. In "Canada Looks Forward: The Place of Women" (1944), WP/88.

72. In "Notes on Women," WP/96.

73. "The Exploited Sex," p. 9.

74. P. 38.

75. P. 9.

76. "What's the Matter With Us?" *Chatelaine* (December 1944); "Husband's Wives," 26/6/1951, "Women's Groups," 8/3/1950, and "Do Clubs Hold Women Back?" 27/6/1951, WP/91.

77. "Women the World Over," p. 14.

78. "It's Time For Women to Learn the Facts of Life," *Saturday Night*, 12/4/1947.

79. "Women and the Party Conventions."

80. "Women in a Man's World."

81. "Women Hold the Balance of Power." (1945), WP/88.

82. CW to McTague, 3/5/1944, WP/81; and CW to Drew, 26/6/1945, WP/5.

83. CW to Hesson, 11/8/1944, WP/4.

84. Janine Brodie, *Women and Politics in Canada* (Toronto: McGraw-Hill Ryerson Ltd., 1985), pp. 58, 99, 106-107, 113, 115.

85. Henderson to CW, 22/5/1945, Box 16, Ontario Association of CASs, UM 5087, *Provincial Archives of Ontario*. Whitton admired Henderson very much and in 1952 she described her as "gay and gallant, a creature of charm, courage, honour and faith." In "Nora Frances," an address to the Hamilton Women's Club, 29/3/1952, WP/52.

86. "Will We Ever Tackle Politics Seriously?"; "Will Women Ever Run the Country?"; "Is the Canadian Woman a Flop in Politics?" *Saturday Night*, 26/1/1946, MS. in WP/89. These sentiments were repeated into the late sixties, e.g., "What Would They Say?" address to Soropomist Club, Windsor, 5/7/1966.

87. "Society and the Revolution"; and "Will Women Ever Run the Country?"

88. "Is the Canadian Woman a Flop in Politics?"

89. "Women in Canada 1900-1950," *Ottawa Citizen*, 3/1/1950.

90. "A Woman On the Line," 22/3/1951, WP/91.

91. "Will Women Ever Run the Country?"

92. "The Fiscal Status . . . "; and "What's the Matter With Us?"; "Canada Looks Forward," and "Women Hold the Balance of Power."

93. Janine Brodie, *Women and Politics in Canada*, pp. 2-5.

94. Quoted from "Women the World Over," in Catherine L. Cleverdon, *The Women Suffrage Movement in Canada* (Toronto: University of Toronto Press, 1950), p. 268.

95. "Will Women Ever Run the Country?" *Maclean's* (August 1952).

96. Ibid.

97. "Women: A Necessary Evil"; "What's the Matter With Us?"; and "Is the Canadian Woman a Flop in Politics?"

98. "The Ringmistress . . . "; "Women Speaking," *Seminar in Rome*, 2-15 October 1966, WP/97; and CW to Mrs. Cameron Montrose, Windsor, 8/2/1946, WP/4.

99. "For Woman's Thought," *Social Welfare* (May 1919): 200.

100. "Charlotte Whitton: Always One More Crusade," *The Tribune*, 31/10/1969.

101. Virginia Woolf, *Orlando* (London: Hogarth Press, 1928): 228, 218-224.

102. " 'O Canada' Could Not Take the Place of 'God Save the King,' " *Saturday Night* (October 20, 1945), is one example.

103. "Life Aloft and Grounded," *Ottawa Citizen*, 2/7/1949.

104. "A Gift from Canada," *OC*, 7/7/1949.

105. "At Tewkesbury Too One Thinks of the Valley," *OC*, 3/12/1949.

106. *OC*, 10/12/1949, 24/10/1949, and 17/9/1949.

107. *Saturday Night*, 2/2/1949.

INDEX

Macdonnell, Dr. May L., 13, 16
MacGill, Helen, 39
McIllraith, George, 160-62
Mackintosh, W.A., 96, 97
MacLachlan, Judge Ethel, 65
MacLachlan, Margaret, 13
MacLaren, Dr. Murray, 93
McLeod, Ella Percival, 95
MacMurchy, Dr. Helen, 22, 46, 65, 93
Macphail, Agnes, 95, 120, 214
MacPhail, Mary, 31
MacPhedran, Mary, 38
McQuaig, Stanley, 138
McTague, C.P., 122, 212

Manitoba Child Welfare Act, 73
Manning, Ernest, premier of Alberta, 115,
    123, 128-29, 130, 138, 140
Margaret, Princess, 156, 158
Marsh, Dr. Leonard, 111-12, 115, 116, 117,
    118, 119, 200
Marshall, Mrs. R.C. ("Daisy"), 129, 205
Massey, Vincent, 30
Mead, George Herbert, 42
Meredith, Anne, 206
Miller, A.H., 138
Mills, Robert E., 42, 79, 99, 124, 129, 132, 140
Moberley, Vera, 42, 99
Monk, Elizabeth C., 99
Montgomery, Dr. E.W., 107
Montreal Council of Social Agencies, 42
Montreal *Gazette*, 52
Montreal Woman's Canadian Club, 48, 69
Moore, Edna, 93
Moore, Marjorie, 38, 73, 129
Moore, Thomas A., 19, 54, 64, 88
Moral and Social Reform Council of Canada,
    19
Mowat, Lillian, 12
Murphy, Emily (Janey Canuck), 2, 38, 39, 41,
    42, 47, 55, 61, 73, 75, 100
Mutchmor, Reverend James, 73-74

Nairn, Margaret K., 42
National Conference on Social Work (U.S.),
    64-65
National Council of Women, 21, 27, 39, 72,
    84, 210
National Employment Commission, 95, 96,
    99, 101, 111, 140
National Health Service Plan, 1948, 149
Neatby, Hilda, 11, 12, 13, 129
Nicholson, Bertha F., 69
Nickle, W.F., 51-52

O'Brien, M.J., 5

O'Byrne, Patrick, 130
On-to-Ottawa Trek, 1935, 97
Ottawa Citizen, 52, 124, 175, 182, 186
    publisher Harry Stevenson Southam,
        149-150
Ottawa Council of Women, 144-45
Ottawa Journal, 170-71, 172, 175, 177
    publisher Grattan O'Leary, 170
Overseas Settlement Board, 53, 56, 99

Paget, A. Percy, 42, 74
Parker, Ethel Dodds, 86, 95, 100, 129, 134
Parslow, Henry, 155
Pearson, Lester, 167, 181
Perkins, Frances, 2, 210
Pierce, Lorne, 124
Plumptre, Adelaide, 42
Price, Elizabeth Barley, 95
Pritchard, Ada, 165

Quebec Commission on Social Insurance, 80
Queen's University, 1, 8-17, 28-31, 49-50, 100,
    103-4, 127, 178, 219
    Alma Mater Society, 11, 12
    Alumni Review, 16
    Journal, 11, 12, 15, 16, 20
    Levana Society, 10, 11, 13, 14, 15, 16, 36,
        38, 194
    Whitton's friends from Queen's, 14-16,
        28-32, 34-40
        Dorothy, 35
        Esther, 34, 35, 36
        Grace, 32
        Gwen, 187
        Hilda, 32
        Jessie, 187
        Mo, 31, 32, 35, 36, 37, 49, 186, 187
        Nell, (Mrs. S. Gandier), 31, 34, 93
    Women's Residence Association, 12-13

Raney, Reverend Mr., 43
Rayside, Edith, 12
Red Cross, 15, 40
Regina Manifesto, 1933, 97
Regina Riot, 1935, 97
Reid, Don, mayor of Ottawa, 1965-66, 177
Reid, Helen R.Y., 2, 38, 39, 40, 41, 42, 55, 63,
    65, 75, 92
Renfrew, Ontario, 5-6, 8-9, 120, 134, 187
Renfrew Collegiate Institute, 8-9, 46, 57, 178
Riddell, Dr. W.A., 63-64, 75
Riley, Maude, 42, 65-66, 84, 100, 128
Ritchie, A.H., 157
Rogers, Norman, 97
Rowell, N.W., 53
Rowell-Sirois Commission, 111